J. D. Atlas
School of Historical Studies
The Institute For Advanced Study
Princeton, New Jersey 08540
U. S. A.

Philosophy in Question

# PHILOSOPHY IN QUESTION

## ESSAYS ON A PYRRHONIAN THEME

DAVID R. HILEY

THE UNIVERSITY OF CHICAGO PRESS
CHICAGO AND LONDON

David R. Hiley is professor of philosophy and director of the Center for the Humanities at Memphis State University.

The University of Chicago Press, Chicago 60637
The University of Chicago Press, Ltd., London


Printed in the United States of America

98 97 96 95 94 93 92 91 90 89    54321

Library of Congress Cataloging-in-Publication Data

Hiley, David R.
Philosophy in question: essays on a Pyrrhonian theme / David R. Hiley.
p.    cm.
Bibliography: p.
Includes index.
ISBN 0-226-33433-3
1. Skepticism. 2. Life. 3. Philosophy. I. Title.
B837.H55    1987    87-19986
149'.73—dc 19    CIP

For Angela, Patrick, and Erin

# Contents

# Acknowledgments

The ideas that are explored in these essays began to direct my study and writing long before they began to take the shape of a book. In 1976–77, I was able to participate in Richard Rorty's year-long seminar, "Empiricism, Pragmatism, and Historicism," while I was a National Endowment for the Humanities Residential Fellow, and the paper that was to become chapter 5 was written during that period. More than that, however, Rorty's seminar, his elegant and provocative writing, and his generous comments on my work have continued to stimulate, influence, and trouble me, and the significance of his work and the brilliance of his teaching form the background motivation for my book. I was especially fortunate to participate in Hubert Dreyfus's 1983 NEH summer seminar on "Heidegger and Foucault," and chapter 4 grew out of work that he stimulated. Although my interpretation of Foucault is not one that he would share, it has benefited from his work and his comments on my own work. Chapter 2 was written with the support of an NEH summer stipend, and I am also grateful to Memphis State University for a one-semester research leave to complete the final chapter. Finally, this work has benefited from the many useful recommendations of an anonymous reader for the University of Chicago Press and from Charles Guignon, who supplied the perfect balance of sympathetic reading and tough-minded criticism.

Portions of this work have appeared as articles in various journals. Chapter 1 is a revised version of a paper under the same title in *The Journal of the History of Philosophy* (1987). Chapter 4 incorporates two articles, "Foucault's Analysis of Power: Political Engagement without Liberal Hope or Comfort," in *Praxis International* (1984), and "Foucault and the Question of Enlightenment," *Philosophy and Social Criticism* (1985). Chapter 5 is a substantially revised and expanded version of an article under the same title in *International Philosophical Quarterly* (1978).

# Introduction

In the most powerful and persuasive image in Western philosophical literature, Plato had Socrates compare our condition to that of prisoners fettered in a cave. "Picture men dwelling in a sort of subterranean cavern with a long entrance open to the light on its entire width. Conceive them as having their legs and necks fettered from childhood, so that they remain in the same spot, able to look forward only. . . . A strange image you speak of, [Glaucon] said, and strange prisoners. Like to us, [Socrates] said."[1] The allegory is well known. Through it, Plato identified ignorance with enslavement and cast philosophy in the role of liberator—as that which provided the possibility of a way out of our ignorance, of an escape from shadows into reality, from falsehood to truth, from the contingent and changing to the necessary and eternal. By linking the virtuous life with the life of reason, he established the place of philosophy in culture and the importance of philosophy for practical affairs.

The idea that philosophy provides an escape from the contingencies of our condition, the idea that knowledge is a matter of clarity of vision that increases in proportion as its objects are more fundamental, foundational, and changeless, and the idea that the criticism and justification of our beliefs and values is possible only by vindicating the autonomy and authority of reason are strands of a single, central thread running through the history of philosophy, strands that, together, support the place of philosophy in the link between reason and virtue. We, in the twentieth century, are heir to the way these strands are woven together with Enlightenment hope—the Enlightenment identification of virtue with freedom and the confidence that the growth of science and the spread of reason would necessarily produce our autonomy and bring about social equality.

There is another thread, however, that runs on the bias, pulling in the opposite direction. Philosophy's quest for clarity, certainty, and security, its pursuit of ahistorical foundations, and its claim for the necessity of its own place in the goal of freedom are opposed by those who would sever the connection between reason and virtue by doubting both the possibility and desirability of knowledge.

The oldest form of this opposition to philosophy is Pyrrhonian skepticism. Though doubts about the possibility of knowledge were to eclipse the more fundamental Pyrrhonian doubts about the value of knowledge for common life, Pyrrhonism constituted a coherent *moral* stance against philosophy. The latest form of this opposition is various "postmodernist" attacks on the traditional image of philosophy—the image from Plato through Descartes and Kant that has taken knowledge to be accurate representation of reality, philosophy to be the task of grounding knowledge on ahistorical foundations, and reason as the tribunal before which all practices, beliefs, and values are to be judged. The postmodernist attempt to overcome philosophy or bring it to an end aims at releasing us from the Platonic illusion that our autonomy or our happiness is to be found in the philosophical escape from the finitude of our beliefs, the fallibility of our practices, and the contingency of our condition. Just as the Pyrrhonian skeptics had claimed that philosophy was destructive of mental health and Rousseau had claimed that progress in the sciences and arts and "taste for philosophy" corrupted our morals, recent critics of the philosophical tradition call it into question out of essentially moral concerns. In his later writings Martin Heidegger diagnosed technology and nihilism as inevitable outcomes of the Platonic tradition, and he criticized philosophy in order to discover a more original mode of relation to Being, a sense of belonging to tradition and freedom in relation to technology. Michel Foucault criticized modern philosophical conceptions of human beings for contributing to the emergence of modern forms of power, coercion, and control. Richard Rorty has referred to the Platonic demand to escape our condition as "the impossible attempt to step outside our skins—the traditions, linguistic and other, within which we do our thinking and self-criticism—and compare ourselves with something absolute."[2] I shall claim that this recent opposition to the traditional image of philosophy shares the Pyrrhonian aim of opposing philosophy in order to return us to the traditions and values of ordinary life. Since the very beginning, Western philosophy has been acutely self-conscious about the nature of its activity and its subject matter, and the history of philosophy can plausibly be read as a history of identity crises about the enterprise. But like the Pyrrhonians, Montaigne, and Rousseau, however, the postmoderns are not merely attacking the current manifestation of the traditional enterprise. They oppose the enterprise itself and its claims for its place in social life, not only because the Platonic-Cartesian-Kantian view of philosophy is problematic on its own terms, but primarily because they believe that the end of philosophy, not the practice of philosophy, will return us to ourselves.

I intend to recover the moral significance of the Pyrrhonian stand against philosophy, and I will recast contemporary concerns about power, rationality, and legitimacy—concerns which come in the wake of the call for postphilosophical culture—in terms of Pyrrhonian themes. I am not so much concerned to structure a single argument that runs from Pyrrho to postmodernism as I am to present case studies against which philosophy must assert itself if it is to reclaim a place for its traditional role and nature. I also want to suggest the serious dilemma the Pyrrhonian challenge poses not only for philosophy but for our understanding of our relation to the traditions and values of common life.

I will set out in a variety of ways what is so deeply problematic about the opposition to the Platonic notion of philosophy. The rejection of the philosophic aim to free us from our condition results in an accommodation of ourselves to our finitude, fallibility, and contingency which presents a double threat. On the one hand, when we reject the emancipatory and foundational role of philosophical inquiry and when we reject the autonomy and universality of reason as a tribunal, the result appears to be an uncritical, unreflective acquiescence in the traditional and customary. If the legitimacy of our beliefs, values, and institutions rests merely on the authority conveyed to them by tradition and custom, or simply by the fact that they are *ours,* the threat of dogmatism and a wooden conservatism seems unavoidable. On the other hand—or perhaps what is merely the reverse of the coin—if our beliefs and values are not grounded or admit of no independent rational legitimization, then, from the perspective of alternative beliefs and values, any one of them appears to be as good as any other. The fact that certain beliefs are ours is merely a contingency of history, and if their legitimacy rests on that contingency then they are in some sense optional and arbitrary, and relativism seems the unavoidable result.

Cast in the dialectical space between dogmatism and relativism, the urge to reassert the Platonic notion of philosophy seems all the more tempting. Yet those who have opposed philosophy for essentially Pyrrhonian reasons—Montaigne, for example, or Hume, or Rousseau, or Rorty—are also motivated by the attempt to avoid dogmatism without lapsing into a pernicious relativism. They locate dogmatism, however, in the philosophical tradition itself. The dogmatism of philosophy is opposed by their various skeptical strategies, at the same time that they hope to avoid relativism by reasserting the authority of nature, or tradition, or the customs of common life, or our normal practices of inquiry.

The Pyrrhonian theme that runs through the opposition to philosophy is that the philosophical desire to escape has led only to estrangement from ourselves and our tradition. However, if our autonomy is not realized through philosophical inquiry traditionally conceived, if we are to appreciate the authority of tradition as the source and transmitter of values, if we are to be at home in our culture and our age, and if we are to make loyalty to ourselves foundation enough for morals and social action, we cannot do so unreflectively. The question of whether at the end of philosophy there is the possibility of nonarbitrary and undogmatic criticism of our beliefs, values, and institutions must be satisfactorily answered if we are to believe that the philosophical desire to escape from the contingencies of common life to the transcendental or ahistorical is not only unfulfilled but ill conceived.

Because I intend to discuss the force of recent attempts to overcome philosophy by returning to more remote opposition, I must anticipate some possible interpretative misunderstandings about the sort of story I wish to tell. In moving from Sextus Empiricus and the Pyrrhonians through Montaigne, Hume, and Rousseau to Foucault, recent philosophy of science, and Rorty, I will not be trying to establish lines of influence nor will I make claims that remote figures anticipated the more recent. I am not intending to suggest that the postmodern opposition to philosophy is less radical, less original, or less problematic because "it has all been done before," even though I do want to show that what appears to many as marginal and merely iconoclastic about postmodernism is part of an important theme running through Western thought. While the book must necessarily unfold in linear fashion, the interpretive development does not. The reason for this is partly personal, partly because the themes I am interested in will not admit of an obvious, neat delineation, and partly because I hope these studies will show relations of mutual illumination between more recent and older views.

On this last point, I think, for example, that interpreting the Pyrrhonian tropes along the lines of what Derrida would think of as deconstructive strategies or what Rorty calls abnormal discourse serves to blunt one sort of argument against the Pyrrhonians—an argument to the effect that even though they propose that we live without beliefs, their tropes must nevertheless entail beliefs if they are to succeed. In the same way, I think that understanding how Foucault's genealogy of modern forms of power is connected with the Enlightenment project of autonomy allows us to rethink the significance of Rousseau's neglected *Discourse on the Sciences and Arts*—a discourse credited with creating his celebrity but never taken seriously for its arguments. I shall suggest that it is a serious critique of modernity that supports and is supported by his notion of true freedom and genuine social relations, and that the way Rousseau worked out the connections between his opposition to the demands of culture and notions of the self and society can illuminate more recent postmodernist notions of self and society.

On the point about the neatness of the line being drawn from Sextus to postmodernism, the reader will have to judge. In a study of this kind it is inevitable that the detailed working out of certain views and connections will be glossed to suggest thematic relations, and it is inevitable that different readers will differ on where I can get away with applying the gloss. My hope is not so much that the glosses will be excused but that they will be tolerated to the extent that they allow me to focus the Pyrrhonian theme I wish to illuminate.

While the connections will not always be neat, it may be useful to say something about their relations in my own thinking that has motivated this work. I was a well brought up analytic philosopher. My early concerns came to focus at the intersection of the controversy over the mind-body identity theory, foundationalist epistemology, and postpositivist philosophy of science. In retrospect, I can see that there were two contributions to the then current debate over the identity theory that led to the eventual shape of this project, moving me in one direction toward the history of early modern philosophy and in another to Heidegger and recent Continental philosophers such as Foucault and Derrida. The first was Richard Rorty's "disappearance theory" of mind and the connected antifoundationalist consequences of his work on the incorrigibility of the mental.[3] As I came to see that his was not merely one among alternative attempts to defend a materialist conception of the mental but implied a more fundamental indictment of the Cartesian framework as a whole,[4] I became interested in understanding how and to what extent Descartes' foundationalist project and his conception of the mental was motivated by the skeptical tradition of Montaigne—and of course in how Montaigne was motivated by Sextus Empiricus. The second contribution was Thomas Nagel's fascinating piece on what it is like to be a bat.[5] Whereas most opponents of the mind-body identity theory had argued against it for reasons having to do with epistemological issues and with doubts about the explanatory or descriptive adequacy of materialism, Nagel's argument made explicit the more serious background worry about the relationship between materialism and our uniqueness as conscious subjects.[6] That led me to concerns about the connection between notions of autonomy, the self as moral agent, and the Cartesian notion of the self as subjective consciousness, and it eventually led me to Heidegger and the recent French tradition in which the critique of the Cartesian subject had become a rallying cry. I need not complete the autobiography to indicate how the eventual development of a work that moves from Sextus and Montaigne and Hume, through Rousseau and Foucault to Rorty, is perhaps better thought of less as points on a line than as overlapping circles, and it is for that reason that I have subtitled this work "Essays on a Pyrrhonian Theme."

That having been said, I need to add, however, that there is a developmental strategy at work. The first half of the book is historical. It aims to recover what I call "the Pyrrhonian challenge" and to oppose to that challenge Enlightenment views about the relation between the progress of knowledge and freedom. The second half of the book treats various recent controversies in the context of opposition to Enlightenment values and how that opposition reinstates the Pyrrhonian challenge in Enlightenment terms. Chapter 1 examines the moral thrust of Pyrrhonian skepticism by returning to Sextus Empiricus and Montaigne, and presents it as a coherent view despite Hume's argument that one could not live one's skepticism. I argue that Hume's criticism of Pyrrhonism fails and that Hume's own view is more at home with the consequences of the Pyrrhonian tradition for common life. My thesis in chapter 2 is that the Enlightenment defense of the connection between freedom and the progress of reason, not post-seventeenth-century opposition to epistemological skepticism, is the significant response to the Pyrrhonian challenge. I will consider this response in terms of Enlightenment themes about the connection between knowledge and power, scientific rationality and public reality, and universal history and autonomy. I will argue that the coherence of the Enlightenment response to Pyrrhonian skepticism depends on the way these connections are made in terms of a metaphysical backdrop and philosophy of history without which the response cannot succeed. In chapter 3, I take up Rousseau's opposition to the Enlightenment connection of freedom and knowledge and I develop the implications for philosophy of a "post-Pyrrhonian" stance by considering Rousseau's *First Discourse,* setting it in the broad context of the place of intellect in culture. The last three chapters focus the issues of power, rationality, and legitimacy in the work of Foucault; the "new philosophy of science," following Kuhn; and Rorty's attack on epistemology-centered philosophy. These issues are not meant to exhaust the implication of the Pyrrhonian challenge for current discussion but to illustrate it. However, selection of these particular themes in contemporary thought is motivated by the fact that we are heir to the Enlightenment response to Pyrrhonism at the same time that we have rejected the metaphysical backdrop, philosophy of history, and view of scientific rationality that made that response coherent. The failure of the Enlightenment attempt to reconnect reason and virtue through the idea that the progress of reason would produce our freedom, reinstates the Pyrrhonian challenge to us in Enlightenment terms: can we retain the Enlightenment commitment to autonomy, the possibility of reasoned criticism of society, and a genuine role for the intellectual in culture without retaining the Enlightenment separation of power and knowledge, its view of the universality and autonomy of reason, or the foundational project of philosophy?

Chapter 4 takes up this question in terms of Foucault's argument, based on his analysis of modern forms of power, that knowledge cannot exist in the absence of power. I consider Foucault's analysis of modernity in light of the charge made by Jürgen Habermas and Charles Taylor that his analysis provides no possibility of liberation from relations of power, and results in a conservative accommodation to current power regimes. In chapter 5, I consider the implications of recent philosophy of the natural and social sciences for conceptions of the universality of reason, casting the debate over the nature of rationality in the dialectical space between the dual threats of dogmatism and relativism. The question that recent debate over the rationality of science, the rationality of alien systems of beliefs, and the plausibility of conceptual relativism opens up is whether a pluralistic conception of rationality is compatible with the idea that incommensurable systems of beliefs and values could, nevertheless, be subject to meaningful criticism and comparative evaluation. I interpret various answers to this question as ways of responding to the Pyrrhonian dilemma of whether, in the absence of some conception of the universality of reason, it is possible both to accept the philosophically ungrounded beliefs and values of common life and to engage in criticism of those beliefs and values. Finally, in chapter 6, I consider Richard Rorty's attack on epistemology-centered philosophy as an attempt to oppose the Platonic conception of philosophy without eliminating the possibility of social criticism, and I recast the challenge of Pyrrhonism in his terms. Though I do not take his view to be the solution to the challenge, I think that reading his position in terms of the challenge provides a way of bringing coherence to otherwise incompatible strands of his thought, and I think that it situates his views as an attempt to retain Enlightenment social hope without the philosophical conceit that tries to ground that hope in human nature, the nature of reason, or universal history. My aim in discussing each of these contemporary issues is more interpretive and diagnostic than conclusive, since I want to suggest both the nature of the challenge to philosophy and the nature of the tension at the heart of that challenge.

# 1 The Deep Challenge of Pyrrhonian Skepticism

Ancient Greek skepticism and early modern skepticism were directed as much against the desirability of knowledge as against its possibility. The Pyrrhonian skeptics' epistemological arguments had a fundamentally moral purpose; in their opposition to the dogmatism of philosophical theory, what was at issue was whether knowledge could bring happiness. In order to suspend belief and achieve quietude the Pyrrhonists opposed the philosophers' claims to know. Contemporary epistemology has lost this moral point of skepticism. In the epistemological tradition since Locke and Hume, skepticism has been identified with a rather narrow set of technical issues arising from the theory of ideas and the representational theory of knowledge which emerged in the seventeenth century. For post-seventeenth-century skepticism the fundamental problem was the impossibility of penetrating the "veil of ideas"—that is, the impossibility of bridging the gap between foundational ideas in the mind of the knower and the world independent of thought. This identification of skepticism with "the problem of the external world"—for all the subsequent interest it has held for philosophy—ignores the deeper challenge of Pyrrhonian skepticism.

The last two decades have seen a renewal of interest in skepticism from two directions. Among epistemologists, skepticism has become problematic again because of vigorous defenses and close examinations, beginning with Peter Unger's *Ignorance: A Case for Universal Scepticism* [1] and extending through Barry Stroud's recent book, *The Significance of Philosophical Scepticism.* [2] Among classicists, there has been a revival of scholarship on the Greek skeptics, partly because of their intrinsic interest and partly because of their relation to the Stoa, which also has seen a revival of scholarly interest. This renewed interest is evident in two important recent collections of essays, *Doubt and Dogmatism: Studies in Hellenistic Epistemology* [3] and *The Skeptical Tradition.* [4]

With the recent epistemological interest in skepticism, there has been practically no attention given to Pyrrhonism as a moral stance except in passing. There are exceptions worth noting, however. Oliver Johnson, in his *Skepticism and Cognitivism,* devotes a chapter to Arne Naess's defense of Pyrrhonism.[5] Benson Mates, in his 1984 presidential address to the American Philosophical Association, distinguishes and discusses in turn three forms of skepticism—Pyrrhonism, Berkeleyan skepticism, and Humean skepticism.[6] Both accounts share a common feature. They realize that the epistemological arguments of Pyrrhonism are distinct from its moral goal and they find the primary interest of Pyrrhonism to be epistemological. Johnson finds the moral goal of Pyrrhonism more plausible than the epistemological arguments but claims that an examination of Pyrrhonism as a moral movement is out of place in a study of skepticism as an epistemological theory. Mates emphasizes the fact that the aim of Pyrrhonism is to achieve inner quietude by suspending judgment; however, he considers the moral thrust of Pyrrhonism only insofar as doing so allows him to conclude that the skeptic's tropes apply not only to knowledge proper but to the rationality of belief as well. Neither takes Pyrrhonian skepticism seriously as a practical challenge relevant for the conduct of life. In Stroud's recent book, he is concerned with the consequences of skepticism for everyday life, but the form of skepticism that he claims is deeply rooted in the human condition is external-world skepticism and he dismisses Pyrrhonism in the preface as a "historical question." I suspect that epistemologists have considered Pyrrhonism of merely historical interest because we have too readily accepted Hume's claim that one could not live one's life without belief; that Nature defeated Pyrrhonism.

My purpose in this chapter is to consider the practical significance of Pyrrhonism on its own terms. I hope to show that Pyrrhonism constitutes a challenge both to the possibility and the desirability of philosophy. It did not seek to call into question the appearances and customs of daily life but instead opposed the philosophical attempt to get behind those appearances and ground them in something foundational or ahistorical. Its goal in opposing philosophy was to live tranquilly in accordance with instinct, custom, and tradition; in that sense, its attack on philosophy aimed to restore the appearances of common life as guides for conduct. In much the way that Berkeley had claimed that his rejection of the independent reality of material things was an attempt to restore common sense, and just as paradoxically, I shall argue that the moral thrust of the Pyrrhonian opposition to philosophy was to restore the reliability of the appearances and values of common life as a guide to action. In the course of my examination, I will consider Hume's opposition to Pyrrhonism and I will argue that he failed in his direct argument that one could not live one's skepticism. Hume's own view, however, turns out to be much closer to the tradition of Pyrrhonian skepticism. Ultimately I will suggest that the antiphilosophical and conservative consequences of Pyrrhonism constitute its deepest challenge, and that it remains problematic for contemporary thought.

## I

In its original form post-Aristotelian skepticism arose as a moral philosophy. There had been doubt about the possibility of sense knowledge long before Pyrrho, but it was Pyrrho and his followers who transformed doubts about the possibility of knowledge into a way of life.[7] Like the contemporary followers of Epicureanism and Stoicism, the Pyrrhonians took the aim of philosophy to be happiness; thus the attack on the possibility of knowledge was coupled with the charge that the pursuit of knowledge had failed to bring happiness or to produce virtue. Sextus Empiricus, our most complete source of knowledge about Pyrrhonism, stressed the point early in the *Outlines of Pyrrhonism* that

> the Sceptic's end is quietude in respect of matters of opinion and moderate feeling in respect of things unavoidable. For the sceptic, having set out to philosophize . . . . so as to attain quietude thereby, found himself involved in contradictions of equal weight, and being unable to decide between them suspended judgement; as he was thus in suspense there followed, as it happened, the state of quietude in respect of matters of opinion.[8]

Whereas philosophy had promised that our happiness would be achieved through our release from ignorance—from our escape from appearances to reality—Pyrrhonism was motivated by the realization that it was the promise of escape, not our ignorance, that was the real source of our unhappiness. With the subsequent development of skepticism, the purely epistemological aspects of Pyrrhonism increasingly overshadowed the moral ones and took on a life of their own. However, the original and fundamental point of skepticism was to call into question the possibility of knowledge and the reasonableness of belief in order to undermine their desirability. In opposing philosophy, the purpose of the Pyrrhonian strategies was to return us to the authority of nature, custom, and tradition.

By doubting the possibility of knowledge and the reasonableness of belief, the thrust of Pyrrhonism was to sever the Socratic connection between knowledge and the virtuous or happy life. The conviction that there is an important connection between knowledge and virtue has been one of the dominant themes in Western philosophy. For Plato—and for Aristotle later—two ideas came together in the claim that knowledge was necessary for virtue. First, knowing was considered a unique and fundamental human activity. Second, the virtue of a thing—its excellence—was considered to be the realization of its essential nature. Since it was claimed that human beings are essentially knowers, virtue was to be found in the pursuit of knowledge. In addition to its opposition to the dogmatism of philosophical theory, what Pyrrhonism rejected was the claim for knowledge as that which enables us to reach our true aim. Thus the Pyrrhonians were not merely acquiescing in the skeptical attitude because inquiry had failed, nor were they merely reconciling themselves to the demands of intellectual honesty. As David Sedley has put it, "what above all characterizes Hellenistic skepticism is . . . its abandonment of [the desire for knowledge]—its radical conviction that to suspend assent and to resign oneself to ignorance is not a bleak expedient but, on the contrary, a highly desirable intellectual achievement."[9] In opposing philosophy the Pyrrhonians praised ignorance as a positive mental condition. Skepticism was practiced as the *activity* for perpetuating mental health.

Sextus had characterized the activity this way: "Scepticism is an ability, or mental attitude, which opposes appearances to judgments in any way whatsoever, with the result that, owing to the equipollence of the objects and reasons thus opposed, we are brought firstly to a state of mental suspense and next to a state of 'unperturbedness' or quietude" (*Outlines,* p. 7). In this activity, then, there were three distinct phases: (1) the practice of doubt that continually deployed tropes or counterarguments to oppose the dogmatists' claims to know; (2) *epochē,* or the mental attitude of suspense of assent or belief achieved through the practice of doubt; and (3) *ataraxia,* or the unperturbed and tranquil mind achieved through the perpetuation of suspension of belief or through indifference. There was, in addition, an essential consequence of *ataraxia* for action: though the skeptical practice could produce a suspension of belief, it could not produce a suspension of action, thus skeptics "follow a line of reasoning which, in accordance with appearances, points us to a life conformable to the customs of our country and its laws and institutions, and to our own instinctive feelings" (*Outlines,* p. 13). It is important to be clear, then, about what is being opposed and how that opposition is related to conduct. The knowledge called into question is philosophical knowledge—claims about truth beyond the appearances of common life—and it is opposed so that we can live a tranquil life in accordance with appearances. Furthermore, and in anticipation of a point I will argue for, the Pyrrhonians understood the term "appearances" more broadly than the meaning it gets from phenomenalist epistemology, including not only sense impressions we act on involuntarily but also the guidance of nature, the laws of one's country, traditional values, instruction in the arts, and so on, and I shall use the term in their broad sense.

Since there could be no philosophical conclusion on which to base one's life, the practical consequence of moral quietude was to ground action on appearances, instinct, tradition, and custom. It follows from this that Pyrrhonian scepticism as a moral stance was inherently conservative since, in eliminating the possibility of standing outside the appearances of ordinary life and of rationally evaluating alternative beliefs, practices, and institutions in terms of truth, it resulted in the accommodation of ourselves to the customary and the traditional. It was this conservative consequence of Pyrrhonism that contributed in part to its revival in the sixteenth century as a weapon in the Counter-Reformation. Pyrrhonism was to become an apology for the existing order. I will return to this point shortly.

## II

In developing the practical significance of Pyrrhonism, we will need to consider why, according to Sextus, philosophical theorizing was dogmatic, how dogmatism contributed to mental unrest, and how the practice of skepticism contributed to mental health.

Sextus began the *Outlines of Pyrrhonism* in the following way: "The natural result of any investigation is that the investigators either discover the object of search or deny that it is discoverable and confess it to be inapprehensible or persist in their search" (*Outlines,* p. 3). From this brief beginning, Sextus reduced philosophers to three main types: the dogmatists, who claim to have discovered the object of their search; the academics, who claim that knowledge of the object is impossible; and the skeptics, who continue to search. The identification of skeptics with inquirers—with the ones who continue to search—is surprising since we would think that inquiry implies and is motivated by the possibility of achieving one's goal. If this is what is implied by Pyrrhonism, then it is not as radical as it first appears, since its opposition to current knowledge-claims leaves open the *possibility* of knowledge.[10] To preserve the force of Pyrrhonism, we must understand in a different way Sextus's identification of the skeptic as the inquirer.

David Sedley has suggested that what Sextus meant by the inquirer must be understood in terms of its antithesis, the dogmatist, and that it carries the sense of "open-mindedness." I think, however, there is another, more plausible interpretation that can be given. Sextus had cautioned that in opposing the dogmatists the skeptics should not be understood to be using the term "dogma" simply in the sense of someone who approves of something, because skeptics also approve of feelings and appearances that are involuntary. Instead, the skeptic "uses 'dogma' in the sense . . . . of 'assent to one of the non-evident objects of scientific inquiry'; for the Pyrrhonian philosopher assents to nothing that is non-evident" (*Outlines,* p. 11). Sedley notes that what Sextus meant by dogmatism should not be confused with our sense of dogmatism. The dogmatist is not the one who holds a belief with unusually intense conviction or accepts a belief from insufficient or unwarranted evidence. Sedley suggests that it means "someone who holds *dogmata*—not merely beliefs but theoretical doctrines, tenets, or principles."[11] The dogmatist is the *philosopher*—the one who holds beliefs or constructs theories about reality.

To this understanding, it is useful to add an insight of Michael Frede's. In an especially illuminating discussion of the relation between Pyrrhonism and Stoicism, Frede notes that they were rival schools of thought and that one must understand the skeptical arguments against the background of the Stoa. He suggests that one can see the Stoics and Pyrrhonian skeptics as each coming down on a different interpretation of Socrates' profession of ignorance.[12]

On one interpretation, the Socratic style of questioning merely revealed that those under cross-examination did not know what they claimed to know. So construed, Socratic questioning and Socratic ignorance hold open the possibility that knowledge can be achieved and perhaps even imply that Socrates had a substantive view of his own. (One might think of Heidegger's or Gadamer's view that questioning takes place only from a preunderstanding of the matter in question.) The Stoics, then, can be understood as claiming to have achieved the knowledge implied by the Socratic profession of ignorance. On the other interpretation—that of the Pyrrhonians—Socratic cross-examination is always parasitic on substantive knowledge claims. Since it is always only reactive, it implies neither a substantive view on the part of the inquirer nor a possible goal or outcome; thus inquiry means more than merely open-mindedness. The inquirer is the one who resists dogmatism and the temptation to philosophize, and in this sense skepticism is a strategy that must constantly be deployed against those who, in Sedley's terms, hold beliefs, theoretical doctrines, tenets, or principles. Jonathan Barnes has put the point this way: "A Pyrrhonist's researches do not end in discovery; nor yet do they conclude that discovery is impossible. For they do not terminate at all: the researches continue and the researcher finds himself in a condition of [*epochē*]."[13] Inquiry in this continuing and therapeutic sense is always a parasitic and piecemeal affair, dependent entirely on the beliefs it needs to resist at the moment, and *epochē* is not a condition that is achieved once and for all by a general skeptical strategy. Rather, it must be continually perpetuated by deployment of counterarguments against philosophers. It is said that Arcesilaus would regularly encourage his students to attend the lectures of other schools so he would have fresh theses to argue against in order to keep debate alive and perpetuate suspense of assent.[14]

The closest contemporary analogue of the Pyrrhonist inquirer would be the deconstructionist strategy of someone such as Jacques Derrida. In "Différance," for example, Derrida describes his deconstruction of Hegel as "strategic and adventurous," explaining that it is a strategy without finality since it is not oriented toward a final goal, a *telos.*[15] Though the strategy does not imply a goal, it does have a purpose. Deconstructive tactics are deployed within a metaphysical text—Hegel's or Plato's, for example—in order to find within the text the thread that unravels the text and prevents it from achieving closure, thus constantly opening it up to the play of interpretations. Like the Pyrrhonist strategy, the deconstructive tactics have no life of their own and they do not achieve some global or completed condition as a result. Derrida characterized these deconstructive tactics of operating at the limit of metaphysics as "transgressing the limit." The tradition of metaphysics is structured around a series of binary oppositions—truth/fiction, reality/appearance, suprasensible/sensible, and so on—and a metaphysical system attempts to achieve a complete or total conception of reality—that is, to achieve closure. Deconstruction works at the limits of that conception by playing back and forth between those oppositions. In the interviews published under the title *Positions,* Derrida says that transgression is never a fait accompli since "transgression implies that the limit is always at work."[16] In the same way, the temptation to assent to the truth of some appearance, to hold beliefs—that is, the pull of philosophy—is always at work; thus *epochē* is never a fait accompli.

In a related way, Richard Rorty's attack on "epistemology-centered philosophy" in *Philosophy and the Mirror of Nature,* does not support an alternative epistemology or philosophical method. It is merely strategic and reactive. He contrasts epistemology-centered philosophy with what he calls edifying or abnormal philosophy. Epistemology-centered philosophy is concerned with securing the foundations of inquiry in order to guarantee that knowledge accurately represents reality. Edifying philosophy, however, is "reactive, having sense only as a protest against attempts to close off conversations by proposals for universal commensuration through the hypostatization of some privileged set of descriptions [of reality]. . . . The edifying philosophers are thus agreeing with Lessing's choice of the infinite *striving for* truth over 'all of Truth'." The goal of inquiry on this view is to keep inquiry going, "to see keeping a conversation going as a sufficient aim of philosophy, to see wisdom as consisting in the ability to sustain a conversation."[17] I will turn to an elaboration of these strategies against philosophy in the final chapter.

There are two points to be drawn from this interpretation of skeptics as inquirers or seekers. The first, suggested above, is to blunt the claim that Pyrrhonism is incoherent; that it is caught in the self-defeating paradox that inquiry implies the hope or possibility of coming to know. The point of the seeking is to keep the question on any matter open since that is what produces the suspension of belief and tranquility. The second point is that the skeptical strategies—their various tropes—are always deployed against substantive claims of the philosophy being opposed at the moment. Those claims can be opposed by counterarguments of equal weight without assent either to the premises or conclusions of the arguments advanced. Sextus made the point explicit: "If then, while the dogmatizer posits the matter of his dogma as substantial truth, the Sceptic enunciates his formulae so that they are virtually cancelled by themselves, he should not be said to dogmatize in his enunciation of them" (*Outlines,* p. 11). (It is not unlike Derrida's device of writing under erasure, in which a term of metaphysics is used at the same time that it is cancelled out.) Again, this means that the Pyrrhonist is not subject to the charge that he must at least assent to the premises of the counterarguments. In attempting to achieve quietude through the suspension of belief, "he states what appears to himself and announces his own impression in an undogmatic way, without making any positive assertion regarding the external reality" (*Outlines,* p. 11).[18]

In sum, the dogmatist is one who holds beliefs or assents to the truth of what is nonevident. The dogmatist is the philosopher. The philosopher's assent is found to be rash or hasty because it turns out that those beliefs can be opposed by opposite beliefs of equal weight. The holding of beliefs, then, results in mental unrest and disquiet in the face of counterarguments. However, the skeptic realizes that, confronted with counterarguments of equal weight, he is forced to suspend judgment and that this mental attitude of indifference with respect to the truth of any matter brings about quietude. Inquiry in contrast to philosophy, then, becomes a positive strategy to resist the rashness of dogmatism and to perpetuate *ataraxia* through *epochē,* restoring the appearances, instincts, customs, practices, and traditions of common life as the only guides for conduct.

## III

Later, I will turn to Hume's claim that one cannot live a life without belief. In preparation for that issue it is necessary to understand both what the Pyrrhonians meant by belief and to understand more fully what is meant by acting in conformity with appearance.

Myles Burnyeat and Michael Frede disagree on what it means for a skeptic to live without belief and whether the skeptic, on his own terms, has beliefs or not. Burnyeat argues that the skeptic cannot have both the condition of tranquillity he seeks and a total suspension of belief:

> if tranquillity is to be achieved, at some stage the sceptic's questing thoughts must come to a state of rest or equilibrium. There need be no finality to this achievement. . . . But *ataraxia* is hardly to be attained if he is not in some sense satisfied—so far—that no answers are forthcoming, that contrary claims are indeed equal. And my question is: How can Sextus then deny that this is something he believes? I do not think he can. Both the causes (reasoned arguments) of the state which Sextus calls appearance and its effects (tranquillity and the cessation of emotional disturbance) are such as to justify us in calling it a state of belief.[19]

I think that what I have argued with respect to the identification of the Pyrrhonist as inquirer—that the strategy of counterargument does not imply assent either to the premises or the conclusion of the argument offered—is enough to suggest why, *pace* Burnyeat, the causes of the state of appearance cannot reasonably be called beliefs. Sextus had admitted that in suspending belief skeptics "do not overthrow the affective sense-impressions which induce our assent involuntarily," and that "doubt does not concern the appearance itself but the account given of the appearance" (*Outlines,* p. 15). The complete answer to Burnyeat depends, then, on what Sextus meant by appearance and belief.

One common reading of the Pyrrhonist's notion of appearance is to interpret the appearance/reality distinction along the lines of the empiricist notion of sense data or sense impressions and the contrast between the immediate objects of consciousness and the extramental world. So construed, there would be little difference between the skeptic's acceptance of the appearance of things and the phenomenalist's claim that nature compels us to believe in the immediate impressions of sense. Roderick Chisholm[20] and Charlotte Stough[21] have given this narrow reading of the skeptic's notion of appearance. This interpretation of appearance is wrong for at least two reasons, however. First, since the skeptical strategy was dependent on the dogma being opposed at the moment, whatever appearance, as an epistemological term, meant for Sextus, it was only what it meant for the view being opposed. The Pyrrhonist need have no positive epistemological notion of appearance at all. (I will extend this point in terms of Frede's position shortly.)

Second, Sextus used the term "appearance" to cover a wide variety of conditions, including not only sense impressions in the narrow sense but also what appeared in thought or reason, garden-variety practices of daily life, natural instincts, instruction in the arts, and the laws and customs of society. When Sextus used the term narrowly to mean phenomena or sense impressions, it was usually within the context of arguing against or responding to a specific philosophical view, and it is natural and consistent with the Pyrrhonian strategy to borrow the epistemological terminology of the position being opposed. When, however, Sextus claimed that skeptics lived in accordance with appearance, the term either covered or was conjoined with nature, instinct, custom, the laws of one's country, instruction in the arts, and so forth. Avner Cohen has suggested that Sextus did not use the term in an epistemic sense at all,[22] but it is perhaps more accurate to say that, insofar as it was an epistemic notion, it was always borrowed from the epistemology of the dogmatist. The Pyrrhonist had no epistemology of his own, and the great variety of things that Sextus grouped under the head of "appearance" could not be considered an epistemological theory of appearance even in this broader sense, both because the skeptic would not want to assert anything even about appearances and because there is no textual evidence to suggest that the hodgepodge of things called appearances was intended to be complete.

What epistemological position was the Pyrrhonist opposing, then, in suspending belief? Frede has suggested that the skeptic's attack on the possibility of knowledge should be understood against the background of Stoic epistemology, since Pyrrhonism and Stoicism were rival movements in the second and first centuries B.C. The Stoics, like Socrates, Plato, and Aristotle, had connected morals and knowledge, claiming that the wise man could never be mistaken in moral matters. Stoic epistemology required a class of "rational impressions" which, by their very nature, could not be false. Rational impressions differ from affections of sense in that the latter are passive affections common to animals as well as men, whereas rational impressions are characterized by the act of assent. Frede explains: "Rational impressions have a propositional content, they are impressions to the effect that something is the case. . . . Thus rational impressions are thoughts which present themselves to the mind and which the mind either accepts or refuses to accept. To accept or give assent to a thought or impression is to have the belief that the proposition which forms the content of the impression is true, to refuse to accept a thought is to suspend judgment."[23] The issue between the Stoics and the Pyrrhonists was whether there were some rational impressions—cognitive impressions—which are self-certifying, thus which cannot possibly be false. The various skeptical modes or tropes can be seen as attacking this central doctrine of Stoic epistemology.

Though Frede finally concludes that the skeptics were unsuccessful in opposing cognitive impressions, what is important for my purpose is the sense of belief that is being opposed. For the Pyrrhonist, to have a belief is to assent to the truth of the content of an impression or thought. The strategy of counterarguments, then, aims at suspending assent to the truth or to the reality beyond what appears.

Though Pyrrhonism aimed at suspending belief in order to achieve mental health—quietude—it could not aim at suspending action. Sextus noted that the skeptic does have a standard for the conduct of life:

> Adhering, then, to appearances we live in accordance with the normal rules of life, undogmatically, seeing that we cannot remain wholly inactive. And it would seem that this regulation of life is fourfold, and that one part of it lies in the guidance of Nature, another in the constraint of the passions, another in the tradition of laws and customs, another in the instruction of the arts. Nature's guidance is that by which we are naturally capable of sensation and thought; constraint of the passions is that whereby hunger drives us to food and thirst to drink; tradition of customs and laws, that whereby we regard piety in the conduct of life as good, but impiety as evil; instruction of the arts, that whereby we are not inactive in such arts as we adopt. But we make all these statements undogmatically (*Outlines,* p. 17).

The skeptic, then, was prepared to accept and act on anything in common life but the claims of philosophers. It must be remembered, Sextus cautioned, that "we do not employ [doubt] universally about all things, but about those which are non-evident and are objects of dogmatic inquiry" (*Outlines,* p. 123). Consistent with doubt about the non-evident, they could be guided by thirst to seek drink, they could accept the benefits of medical practice (*Outlines,* p. 147) or other practical arts, they could accept the customary moral values and conduct their lives according to law. They might even accept the benefits of something like a science of appearances in the sense Kant would later give, so long as no judgment was made about truth beyond appearances. Thus the activity of doubt through counterargument was only directed at philosophical claims in order to perpetuate the condition of *epochē* which resulted in a life lived tranquilly in accordance with appearances, nature, instinct, the practical arts, tradition and custom. It is this final feature of Pyrrhonism—life lived in conformity with tradition and custom—that was taken up again in the sixteenth century.

## IV

Early modern skeptics, drawing equally from the Renaissance defense of practical wisdom against metaphysical speculation and from the rediscovery of the writings of Sextus, deployed skepticism as a weapon in the Counter-Reformation. Like the Pyrrhonian skeptics, they attacked the value of knowledge and praised ignorance as a positive condition, clearly recognizing the conservative consequence of Pyrrhonism. Richard Popkin has summarized this use of skepticism:

> since the complete sceptic had no positive views, he could not have the wrong views, and since the Pyrrhonist accepted the laws and customs of his community, he would accept Catholicism. . . . The marriage of the Cross of Christ and the doubts of Pyrrho was the perfect combination to provide the ideology of the French Counter-Reformation.[24]

This marriage of skepticism and Catholicism represented the first stage in the influence of skepticism in the early modern period. Doubts about the power of human reason had long been associated with the Christian defense of the necessity of faith against the pagan philosophers, but with the recovery of the Pyrrhonian skeptics through the writings of Sextus the various tropes and modes to undermine reason were joined to the skeptical attitude which favored conservatism and support for traditional authority.

The best case of wedding skepticism and Catholicism was Michel de Montaigne's essay, "Apology for Raymond Sebond," written around 1576.[25] Montaigne's praise of ignorance in the "Apology" presents the same sort of paradox as Rousseau's *First Discourse,* in that it was an unusually learned essay to support an apparently anti-intellectual conclusion. What was at issue in the essay for Montaigne, as for Rousseau, was not the possibility of knowledge but the desirability of knowledge for virtue. Though there were certain general skeptical themes in Montaigne's earliest essays—especially in "It Is Folly to Measure the True and False by Our Own Capacities"—the "Apology" was his most sustained skeptical work and it was clearly written under the influence of Sextus' *Outlines of Pyrrhonism.* Two years before writing the essay, Montaigne had translated the Spanish theologian Raymond Sebond's *Natural Theology.* In that work Sebond had claimed to demonstrate, among other things, the truth of the contents of the Scripture, relying only on unaided reason. The official purpose of the "Apology" was to defend Sebond against his critics.

Only a portion of the "Apology" was actually directed to a defense of Sebond, however. The rest was an extended attack on the possibility of knowledge and on the belief that knowledge could make humankind good. There had been two main objections to Sebond's rationalism: the first was the familiar one that religion ought to be grounded in faith rather than on reason; the second was the charge that Sebond's rationalist arguments themselves were extremely weak. The answer to the first charge, such as it was, actually occurred in defending Sebond against the second. Popkin has summarized Montaigne's strategy as follows. Montaigne shows that "since all reasoning is unsound, Sebond should not be blamed for his errors. . . . In order to excuse the weakness of Sebond's reasoning, Montaigne set out to show that nobody else's reasoning is any better."[26] Though this defense is clearly "damning with faint praise," as Craig Brush[27] has stated in his study of Montaigne, the means of accomplishing the defense and the conseqences to be drawn from it were extraordinary.

Montaigne's own account of how he intended to show that Sebond—mistaken though he was in his rationalism—was no worse off than anyone else was this: "The means I take to beat down this frenzy, and which seems fittest to me, is to crush and trample underfoot human arrogance and pride; to make them feel the inanity, the vanity and nothingness, of man; to wrest from their hands the puny weapons of their reason; to make them bow their heads and bite the ground beneath the authority and reverence of divine majesty" (*Apology,* p. 327). Sebond was to be defended by pointing up the inadequacy of man, and the skeptical arguments of Sextus would be used to accomplish the task.

Sextus, in the *Outlines of Pyrrhonism,* summarized the various modes or tropes by which the skeptic achieved and sustained the attitude of suspension of belief or indifference. Of these tropes, most had to do, one way or another, with the fallibility of the senses, either because of the difference of the organs of sense between humans and animals, or because of the different conditions and circumstances of sensation, or because of the nature of the objects of sensation. The other main argument the skeptics used was a form of relativism drawn from the diversity of human opinion and custom. The source of the skepticism was not mere diversity or fallibility of the senses, however. If it were just that, then Hume's remarks on the weakness of these sorts of skeptical arguments would have been correct. I will return to a more detailed account of Hume's rejection of Pyrrhonism shortly, but for now it is enough to say that it was not the *fact* of opposition or disagreement in matters of sensation or opinion that yielded the skeptical attitude. It rested on the impossibility of settling the disagreement between contrary views of equal weight. By what criterion was disagreement in matters of sensation or of opinion to be settled? And if some criterion were proposed, by what criterion was that criterion to be accepted? With characteristic precision, Sextus had presented this "problem of the criterion" thus:

> He who prefers one impression to another, or one "circumstance" to another, does so either uncritically and without proof or critically and with proof; but he can do this neither without these means . . . nor with them. For if he is to pass judgement on the impressions he must certainly judge them by a criterion; this criterion, then, he will declare to be true, or else false. But if false, he will be discredited; whereas, if he shall declare it to be true, he will state that the criterion is true either without proof or with proof. . . . The proof always requires a criterion to confirm it, and the criterion also a proof to demonstrate its truth; and neither can a proof be sound without the previous existence of a true criterion nor can the criterion be true without the previous confirmation of proof. So in this way both the criterion and the proof are involved in the circular process of reasoning, and thereby both are found to be untrustworthy. (*Outlines,* pp. 67–69)

The upshot of Sextus' rendering of the problem of the criterion was this: the attempt to settle conflicting impressions or conflicting opinions yields either an infinite regress of justification, demanding a criterion for the criterion for the criterion, and so on; or it involves a vicious circularity where what is justified by the criterion becomes the justification for the criterion itself; or acceptance of the criterion is merely arbitrary and dogmatic. Montaigne simply took this argument over, though he presented it in a much more careless and condensed fashion. His version of the problem of the criterion was reduced to this: "To judge the appearances that we receive of objects, we should need a judicatory instrument; to verify this instrument we need a demonstration, an instrument: thus we are in a circle" (*Apology,* p. 454).

Montaigne can hardly be seen, then, as contributing any new arguments to the skeptical literature, though his style of presentation makes the arguments unusually compelling. What is of interest to me, however, is that Montaigne is paradigmatic of early modern skepticism and that through Montaigne we can recover the practical significance of the skeptic's challenge. The significance for Montaigne was twofold: first, we could have no knowledge; second, and more important, even if we could, it would not make us happy. In terms of the second, consider a sample of Montaigne's case. "What good can we suppose it did Varro and Aristotle to know so many things? Did it exempt them from human discomforts? Were they freed from the accidents that oppress a porter? Did they derive from logic some consolation for the gout?" It should be clear from this that Montaigne, like Sextus, was opposing intellectual or philosophical knowledge, since, of course, various practical arts like medicine could provide consolation for the gout. Not only could philosophy provide no consolation for the gout, it could not make us virtuous either. A little later in the text he contended that "if anyone will sum us up by our actions and conduct, a greater number of excellent men will be found among the ignorant than among the learned: I mean in every sort of virtue" (*Apology,* pp. 358–59). The problem of the criterion became the basis for a general anti-intellectualism, both in the sense of opposing intellectualist doctrines about the nature of wisdom and in opposing doctrines about the value of the life of intellect. The strategy for rejecting the claims of intellect and reason was to break the connection between knowledge and virtue.

This motive was even more explicit in Montaigne's closest follower, Pierre Charron. For Charron, the wisdom to which virtue was tied was not derived from intellect or philosophy. Instead, virtue was the result of naturally acquired practical wisdom. "He that increaseth knowledge," Charron claimed, "increaseth sorrow. Ignorance is more fit remedy against all evil." He contended that not only were knowledge and wisdom different, they were almost never found together.

> Learning then and wisdom are things very different, and wisdom of the two the more excellent, more to be esteemed than science. For wisdom is necessary, profitable to all, universal, active, noble, honest, gracious, cheerful. Science is particular, unnecessary, seldom profitable, not active, servile, mechanical, melancholic, opinionated, presumptuous.[28]

More important even than the way Montaigne had used the skeptical strategies against the connection between knowledge and happiness was the consequence of this attack for reason and the connection between knowledge and virtue for the acceptance of the authority of nature, tradition, and custom. It had been common to portray Pyrrho as recommending a life in which one suspends all *action*—Hume even represented Pyrrhonism this way—but Montaigne reported that he found curious the portrayal of Pyrrho as "stupid and immobile, adopting a wild and unsocial way of life." Montaigne understood the implications of Pyrrhonian skepticism for practical affairs. His own account of the Pyrrhonians quoted the passage from Sextus nearly exactly: "As for the actions of life, they are of the common fashion in that. They lend and accommodate themselves to natural inclination, to the impulsion and constraint of passions, to the constitutions of laws and customs, and to the tradition of the arts" (*Apology,* p. 374). Relativist arguments about sense experience and custom and the problem of the criterion drawn from them were used to oppose the dogmatic pretensions of human reason, but the authority of the natural, the practical, the traditional, and the customary prevented a debilitating relativism.

It was this conservative consequence of the skeptical attitude which supported the authority of the Roman church. Pyrrhonian arguments served to justify traditional institutions and to accommodate people to their current situation. Though Montaigne would turn a critical eye toward the practices and values of ordinary life, in the hands of his followers the defense of ignorance became an apology for the existing order. Montaigne's own skepticism yielded an accommodation with a difference. While nobody's reasoning was any better than anyone else's, while no values, beliefs, laws, or institutions could withstand the skeptical attack, and while we must fall back on custom and tradition to provide the authority that reason could not secure, this was not for Montaigne an uncritical acquiescence. In his extraordinary study of Montaigne, Jean Starobinski has captured this critical acquiescence in a passage worth quoting at length because, in addition to the view of Montaigne it provides, it will serve to anticipate what I will develop as the deep challenge of Pyrrhonism.

> Once one has resolved to reject illusions and masks, no institution can withstand the skeptic's indictment: no social rule can prove that it is founded on an absolute standard of justice. The application of what Sextus Empiricus calls "the tenth way of the *epochē*" . . . shows that institutions, laws, customs, and convictions all contradict one another. But once doubt has wiped the slate clean, the mind finds nothing capable of establishing a higher authority. . . . In the face of abuses, cruelty, and torture, surely we must heed the protest of our natural sensibility. . . . The way to minimize the damage is to turn back from current abuses to prior custom, to usages and conventions justified by venerable age and long obedience. . . . While it is still permissible to fall back on custom and convention, this should be done without illusions as to what is arbitrary and perishable in tradition. With benevolent irony toward those who persist in placing all their "faith" in the past, Montaigne turns back to custom with his eyes open, seeing it for what it is: for him it is enough simply to feign respect, since it is only the outward form that matters.[29]

Montaigne's desire to take a critical stance toward custom and tradition notwithstanding, it is not at all clear that he could have both acquiescence and a critical standpoint. I will suggest in the final section of this chapter that this is part of what is deeply challenging about Pyrrhonism. Can a self-conscious acquiescence in common customs, institutions, beliefs, and values provide an adequate basis for the role of the nonphilosophical intellect or a place for social criticism, if the skeptical attack on the philosophical attempt to discover truth beyond the appearances is successful? I will argue in later chapters that the postmodern attack on the philosophical tradition poses the same sort of challenge for contemporary thought. My purpose in the remainder of this chapter is to chart how the moral thrust of Pyrrhonism and its practical consequences for the place of philosophy in culture is eclipsed by the epistemological turn of the seventeenth century.

In sum, there are two aspects of early modern skepticism that will be lost by post-Cartesian epistemology. First, the Pyrrhonians praised ignorance as a positive condition and attacked the desirability of knowledge for virtue. Second, Pyrrhonian skepticism was an inherently conservative moral stance because it eliminated the possibility of independent criteria for criticizing traditional authority. What the attitude of suspension of belief, or indifference on intellectual matters entailed was an acknowledgment of our natural and inevitable ignorance, and it resulted in acquiescence in traditional authority, custom, and current social practice as the only possible guides to conduct.

## V

Just as there were three phases to Pyrrhonian skepticism—the theory of doubt, the attitude of suspension of belief, and praise of the value of ignorance for common life—the seventeenth- and eighteenth-century responses to skepticism were in three phases. The first response—and the only one considered by most interpreters—was that of Bacon and Descartes to the epistemological arguments which underwrote the skeptic's theory of doubt. The second was Hume's attempt to reject the notion that one could live a life in which one suspended judgment. The third was the Enlightenment reaction to the praise of ignorance through a defense of the connection between the growth of knowledge and the progress of humankind and society. Though it is with the second response that I am now concerned—since if Hume's arguments are accepted Pyrrhonism presents no challenge for common life—brief comments are necessary about the first. I will turn to the Enlightenment response in Chapter 2.

The skepticism of Montaigne and Charron had been, in part, an extension and culmination of the Renaissance opposition to Scholasticism and the Scholastic preference for speculative over practical wisdom and for the contemplative over the active life. Francis Bacon and René Descartes shared the rejection of Scholastic philosophy but they opposed Pyrrhonism as well. Bacon had compared Pyrrhonian skeptics to "moody lovers who railed at their sweethearts but never leave them."[30] For all the differences between Bacon and Descartes, they agreed that skepticism was not to be taken as an indictment of philosophy as such, but rather was an indication that philosophy must begin anew.

Though the official purpose of Descartes' *Meditations* was the defeat of skepticism,[31] Descartes was curiously apologetic about devoting an entire meditation to developing skeptical arguments. In his reply to the second set of objections, he remarked that "he had long ago seen several books written by the Academics and Sceptics about this subject and felt some disgust in serving up again this stale dish."[32] What is interesting is the justification he gave for serving it up again: it was by way of these skeptical arguments that he was able to prove that the mind was more easily known than the body. The significance of skepticism, and his solution for it, was that the Pyrrhonian challenge to the reasonableness of belief and the problem of settling conflicting opinions came to rest on the possibility of certainty. Furthermore, the possibility of certainty was to be found in the nature of the mind—in the nature and status of foundational claims about items of consciousness considered in and of themselves. The point I wish to note is that by entangling questions about the reasonableness of belief and the possibility of knowledge in the issue of the nature of the mind, and by grounding knowledge in the immediacy of items of consciousness, the skeptical challenge after Descartes was transformed in a significant way. The challenge post-Cartesian skeptics issued turned not on the desirability of knowledge, the possibility of settling conflicting opinions, or the reasonableness of belief, but on the possibility of certainty and the question whether one could bridge the gap between conscious experience and the world as it is in itself. The challenge of skepticism after Descartes, that is, became one with the problem of the external world.

In the epistemological tradition motivated by Descartes, the connection between the epistemological and moral point of Pyrrhonism was severed. Subsequent skeptical arguments directed at the gap between ideas in the mind of the knower and the world independent of thought were of a far narrower and more purely theoretical sort than the Pyrrhonism of Sextus and Montaigne. Descartes had attempted to reestablish the authority of reason against the attacks of the Pyrrhonians. For the epistemological tradition after Descartes, however, the problem of the existence and nature of the external world swung entirely free of the deeper skepticism that had supported the view that ignorance was more conducive to a life of virtue than was knowledge. It would be surprising in the extreme if the contribution knowledge was to make to the good of humankind depended on a proof of the external world.

Oddly, it is in terms of a common interpretation of Hume's response to Pyrrhonism that this point can best be made. At the same time that Hume articulated the most thoroughgoing skeptical implications of the theory of ideas that had begun with Descartes, he also attempted to defeat Pyrrhonism by claiming that skepticism could have no consequences for action and conduct since one could not live a life without belief. On this reading, it appears that Hume had turned skepticism into a purely theoretical worry about the possibility of knowledge beyond the immediate data of sense, thereby stripping skepticism of any relevance for common life. Hume's relation to Pyrrhonism, however, is highly ambiguous. Though he explicitly argued against the possibility of achieving *epochē,* in many ways his philosophy is much more at home in the older skeptical tradition.

Richard Popkin has argued that Hume should be considered a modern Pyrrhonist.[33] More recently Donald Livingston has agreed that Popkin's view is correct as far as it goes, but he has extended that reading by recasting the role Pyrrhonism played in Hume's thought, concluding that Hume was a post-Pyrrhonian philosopher.[34] I shall argue that Hume's explicit attempt to defeat the second phase of the skeptical challenge was unsuccessful, but for reasons similar to those of Popkin and Livingston I interpret Hume's own view as illuminating the practical consequences of Pyrrhonism.

I think Hume both underestimated and misunderstood the force of the Pyrrhonian opposition to belief. The circumstantial explanation for Hume's misunderstanding is that he was mainly concerned to respond to the Pyrrhonian controversy of his own day and the version of Pyrrhonism then current in the work of someone such as Pierre Bayle.[35] This truncated version, however, was far less rich than the view presented by Sextus Empiricus. Agreeing with the Popkin-Livingston interpretation of Hume's own philosophy, I shall conclude that the failure to defeat the second phase of Pyrrhonism deepens the Pyrrhonian challenge.

## VI

Hume's attack against the Pyrrhonists was twofold. First, he claimed that the popular arguments for Pyrrhonism—arguments based on illusion, deception, and the fallibility of the senses—were trite and weak. Second, he asserted that, while the serious epistemological arguments that there was no rational support for belief in the external world, universal causality, the identity of the self, and so on, could not be refuted, they also could not be believed. Echoing Pascal, Hume concluded that while reason defeated the dogmatist, nature defeated the skeptic.[36]

The point over which Hume underestimated Pyrrhonism turns on what he thought were trite as opposed to profound arguments for skepticism. In section xii of the *Enquiry Concerning Human Understanding,* he dismissed one set of skeptical arguments as follows:

I need not insist upon the more trite topics, employed by the sceptics in all ages, against the evidence of sense; such as those which are derived from the imperfection and fallaciousness of our organs. . . . These sceptical topics indeed, are only sufficient to prove, that the senses alone are not implicitly to be depended on; but that we must correct their eviidence by reason, and by consideration, derived from the nature of the medium, the distance of object, and the disposition of the organ, in order to render them within their sphere, the proper *criteria* of truth and falsehood.[37]

The more profound argument for skepticism, not surprisingly, turns out to be Hume's own: there was no rational support for belief in the existence of the external world. What Hume missed, however, was that, for the Pyrrhonian skeptic, problems about evidence from the senses called into question the very notion of "the proper *criteria* of truth and falsehood" that Hume invoked against "the more trite topics." The point of the Pyrrhonists' counterarguments about sense impressions was not simply that sense impressions, considered in themselves, were not self-certifying. Though that was part of the issue between the Pyrrhonians and the Stoics concerning cognitive impressions, instances of illusion and relativity of sensory evidence were not raised to show the imperfection of the senses per se. Rather, these were introduced as instances of the more general problem of the criteria. Given that there was disagreement in the evidence of the senses, then—just as Hume insisted—criteria of truth and falsehood would be necessary to settle the disagreement. But the criteria themselves would require justification, and thus we are back to the original skeptical claim that the attempt to justify the criteria would either be infinite, circular, or arbitrary. By minimizing the significance of the issue that lay beneath the problem of sensory evidence and by shifting attention to the problematic relation between an impression and its cause, Hume was able to minimize the practical problem of settling conflicting opinions. The significant issue behind the "trite topics" was the equipollence of conflicting impressions or opinions in the absence of a criterion. It was this equipollence that produced a condition of suspension of assent to the truth of any opinion and the acceptance of appearances as the basis for action.

Hume's direct arguments against the possibility of living one's Pyrrhonism are contained in the following two passages from the *Enquiry:*

The great subverter of Pyrrhonism or the excessive principles of scepticism is action, and employment and the occupations of common life. These principles may flourish and triumph in the schools; where it is, indeed, difficult, if not impossible to refute them. But as soon as they leave the shade, and by the presence of the real objects, which actuate our passions and sentiments, are put in opposition to more powerful principles of our nature, they vanish like smoke, and leave the most determined sceptic in the same condition as other mortals. . . . For here is the chief and most confounding objection to excessive scepticism that no durable good can ever result from it. (*Enquiries,* pp. 158–59)

A Pyrrhonian cannot expect that his philosophy will have any constant influence on the mind: or if it had, that its influence would be beneficial to society. On the contrary, he must acknowledge, if he will acknowledge anything, that all human life must perish, were his principles universally and steadily to prevail. All discourse, all action would immediately cease; and men remain in total lethargy, till the necessities of nature, unsatisfied, put an end to their miserable existence. It is true; so fatal an event is very little to be dreaded. Nature is always too strong for principle. And though a Pyrrhonian may throw himself or others into momentary amazement and confusion by his profound reasonings, the first and most trivial event in life will put to flight all his doubts and scruples. (*Enquiries,* p. 160)

There are three distinguishable arguments in these passages. The first involved Hume's assumption—an assumption like the one about Pyrrho that Montaigne had recounted with such puzzlement—that the skeptic's suspension of judgment entailed a suspension of action. In this argument, however, Hume had simply misunderstood the force of Pyrrhonism by failing to recognize that instead of urging or resulting in a life of inactivity, the Pyrrhonian instead urged, as a consequence of his skepticism, that one act in conformity with the appearance of things and with custom. I have attempted to make clear above that the conservative thrust of Pyrrhonism for practical affairs is integral to the skeptical activity. Hume simply failed to take account of this aspect of Pyrrhonism.

The second argument was that no good could come to society from Pyrrhonism. Though this argument was directed at the skeptic's praise of the value of a life of ignorance, it was a promissory note Hume did not attempt to make good. It is to Enlightenment educational reformers and advocates of the idea that the growth of knowledge would yield the improvement of humankind that one must turn for support of this attack on Pyrrhonism.

The third and more serious argument was that the skeptic's doubts could not yield a mental condition of indifference or suspended assent because "Nature" rendered it impossible to live without belief. This argument was implied in the passage above and it was made explicit in the *Treatise on Human Nature.* According to Hume,

Nature, by an absolute and uncontroulable necessity has determin'd us to judge as well as to breathe and feel. . . . Whoever has taken the pains to refute the cavils of this *total* scepticism, has really disputed without an antagonist, and endeavour'd by arguments to establish a faculty, which nature has antecedently implanted in the mind, and render'd unavoidable.[38]

Hume's own epistemological analysis had shown that there was no rational ground for the belief that every effect had a cause, or that there was a world independent of thought, or that the same self endured through time. In that sense, he agreed with the purely epistemological basis for Pyrrhonism. Nevertheless, Hume concluded that we could not help but believe in universal causality, the existence of the external world, and the identity of the self because nature disposed us to do so. The central issue between Hume and the Pyrrhonian skeptics, then, turned on whether one was compelled by nature to have beliefs. And that issue turned on the notion of belief itself.

Hume's account of the nature of belief has been found to be notoriously unsatisfactory by commentators. Hume himself expressed dissatisfaction with it in the Appendix to the *Treatise.* He had claimed that a belief was "a more vivid and intense conception of an idea, proceeding from its relation to a present impression" (*Treatise,* p. 103). A belief differed from other ways of conceiving of an idea not in terms of some additional component of its content but in the same way that an idea differed from an impression. What is added to an idea that is believed is not a different idea, but a more forceful and intense conception which alters the effect of the idea on the mind. In the Appendix to the *Treatise,* Hume had written: "In my opinion, this dilemma is inevitable. Either the belief is some new idea, such as that of *reality* or *existence,* which we join to the simple conception of an object, or it is merely a peculiar *feeling* or *sentiment*" (*Treatise,* p. 623). He gave two reasons for rejecting the alternative that it was a new idea. First, he argued that we have no idea of existence or reality separable from the particular idea of any object. Second, if belief involved some additional idea of reality, then because we are able to combine and separate ideas any way we choose, it would follow, Hume argued, that it would be in our power to believe anything we pleased just by adding the new idea of existence to any given idea. If a belief is merely a feeling or sentiment that attaches to an idea and does not involve the addition of the idea of reality, then what is the nature of the feeling? According to Hume, beliefs "strike upon us with more force; they are more present to us; the mind has a firmer hold of them, and is more actuated and mov'd by them. It acquiesces in them; and, in a manner, fixes and reposes itself on them" (*Treatise,* p. 624).

Though consistency required that belief be defined merely psychologically in terms of differing force and vivacity, the result was that

Hume had no satisfactory way of distinguishing between belief, or assent to an idea, and denial; or between belief and all the other manners of entertaining an idea. Barry Stroud has pointed out the problem:

> If assent or belief is just a matter of having a lively idea before the mind, what is dissent or denial? It would seem to be a matter of having that idea before the mind in some different "manner". . . . But if denial is a completely different "manner of conceiving" from both belief and mere conception, and if all differences among "manner of conceiving" are just differences in degrees of force and vivacity, then denial will be just a matter of having an idea before the mind with yet a third degree of force and vivacity. . . . It is clear that, once we think not just about belief and conception, but about all the rest of the great variety of "attitudes" we can take with respect to a single idea, there is no plausibility at all in saying that they differ only in their degrees of force and vivacity.[39]

Though Hume defined belief in terms of the manner of its conception, the Pyrrhonists meant something quite different when they sought to suspend belief through the deployment of skeptical strategies. To have a belief was to assent to the truth of the propositional content of an idea. Thus a belief was more than a lively appearance. It was an *account* of the appearance to the effect that what appeared was true. Sextus made the point explicitly: "We do not overthrow the affective sense-impressions which induce our assent involuntarily; and these impressions are 'the appearances.' And when we question whether the underlying object is such as it appears, we grant the fact that it appears, and our doubt does not concern the appearance itself but the account given of that appearance" (*Outlines,* p. 15). If what Hume meant by claiming that nature compels us to judge was that we are naturally disposed to philosophy—to assert the truth or reality beyond what appears—the Pyrrhonists can agree, adding that it is because we are naturally disposed to philosophical investigation that skeptical strategies must continually be deployed to resist the temptation and to restore tranquillity. *Epochē* will not be achieved once and for all, because there will always be new temptations and new beliefs to oppose by counterarguments. For the Pyrrhonists, there is always work to be done.

Furthermore, Hume's claim that nature compels us to believe comes to about the same thing as the Pyrrhonists' claim that they assent to what is induced involuntarily and that they accept appearances. They differ only in how broadly or narrowly they define belief. If belief is the nonrational, natural effect of certain ideas on the mind that forms the basis for action, then, like Hume, the Pyrrhonists realize that one cannot help but accept such effects and act on them. If, however, the sense of belief at issue is the additional element of reality or existence, that is, if belief is what the Pyrrhonists understood by the term—the philosopher's assent to what is nonevident by giving an account of what appears—then Hume's skeptical arguments, like those of the Pyrrhonists, would call such beliefs into question. Hume failed to appreciate the fact that Pyrrhonism did not entail the suspension of assent to appearances or suspension of action. It did not entail the rejection of what nature compelled. The result is that Hume's was a merely verbal victory over Pyrrhonian skepticism. The Pyrrhonians used counter-arguments to undermine dogmatic assent to truth beyond appearance so they could perpetuate suspended judgment and accept and act on the way things appear. The second phase of the Pyrrhonian activity remains untouched by Hume's direct arguments against Pyrrhonism.

## VII

Far from defeating Pyrrhonism or rejecting its relevance for conduct, Hume's own position turned out to be far more at home in the older Pyrrhonist tradition. Though it is usual among interpreters to separate Hume's own brand of skepticism from the Pyrrhonian tradition, Richard Popkin has argued that Hume was the only consistent Pyrrhonist. Recently, Donald Livingston has referred to Hume as a post-Pyrrhonian, recognizing the significance of Pyrrhonism for what Livingston calls Hume's philosophy of common life. In this final section, I shall consider these interpretations of Hume in order to suggest what remains challenging and problematic about the Pyrrhonian tradition.

Hume's relation to the skeptical tradition was ambiguous at best. There are several sources for this ambiguity, which poses questions for an understanding of his relation to Pyrrhonism. The first concerns the connection between Hume the historian and Hume the philosopher. The common view among epistemologically oriented philosophers is to treat the author of *The History of England* and the *Treatise* as only coincidentally the same man. Insofar as an attempt is made to examine the connection of Hume's historical and philosophical writing, it is claimed either that Hume abandoned philosophy for history or that, given his epistemological view, his histories were "anti-historical."[40] Yet one of the themes that unites the historical and epistemological writings in Hume's thought was the skeptical tradition. From Sextus through Montaigne and Bayle, historical evidence had become the chief support to undermine confidence in the results of inquiry and the claims of reason. History provided sufficient examples of disagreement in everything from scientific theory to moral practice, and these disagreements cast the problem of the criterion in a more interesting and challenging way than problems of the relativity of sense impressions. The recognition of man's historical condition and the use of historical inquiry were weapons against dogmatism and rationalism. Though Hume had other interests to serve in his historical writings, he also appealed to history in issues ranging from the possibility of miracles to social contract theories of government. Furthermore, Hume's philosophy of history was important to his understanding of man. David Fate Norton has observed that it "is not merely that Hume's science of man is skeptically based, but that, like other skeptics' inquiries into man's nature and opinions, it is also historically based."[41] In the Introduction to the *Treatise* Hume made explicit that the "science of man" depended on "observation of human life . . . [and of] the common course of the world" (*Treatise,* p. xxiii).

An equal source of interpretative difficulty was Hume's paradoxical relation to the Enlightenment. On the one hand, he exemplified certain features of the Enlightenment in the extent to which he pushed the critical attitude. Yet, on the other, he turned that very critical spirit against rationalist and liberal political theory and against the confidence Enlightenment reformers had in the use of reason in the service of humankind. Though Hume and the Enlightenment reformers were joined in their opposition to the Pyrrhonists' praise of ignorance they were completely at odds over what ultimately defeated it. While someone like Condorcet attempted to reestablish the connection between knowledge and happiness through a defense of the claim that the growth of knowledge would bring about the improvement of humankind and society, Hume had claimed, of course, that it was nature, not reason, that defeated Pyrrhonism. In this sense, Hume was much closer to the conservatism of the Pyrrhonian skeptics and to Montaigne than to the Enlightenment liberal tradition.

Given the relation of Hume's epistemological and historical understanding of man and his stand toward central Enlightenment doctrines, the positive aspects of his philosophy seems more aligned with Pyrrhonism than opposed to it. Popkin has argued that Hume really showed how one lives in a Pyrrhonian universe, and that Hume was actually the only consistent Pyrrhonist. On Popkin's interpretation, the Pyrrhonism of Sextus was both too skeptical and too dogmatic. It was too dogmatic in thinking that one could or should suspend judgment on all matters. It was too skeptical by trying to remain undogmatic at all times. According to Popkin, the problem is that the ancient Pyrrhonians failed to separate considerations of the rational evidence for belief from considerations of the psychology of belief. He claims that Hume had found the proper balance between doubt and dogmatism by understanding the psychological impossibility of refraining from belief. Popkin concludes that "the Pyrrhonist ought to hold, as Hume did, that one believes when one must and one doubts when one must, though, on the epistemological level, no opinion of doubt or belief can be justified."[42]

Though I accept the Pyrrhonian interpretation of Hume and want to draw on Popkin's account to recast the challenge of Pyrrhonism, I think this way of contrasting Hume and the ancient Pyrrhonians is misleading for two reasons. First, I have suggested already that the skeptic's opposition to dogmatism should not be confused with dogmatism understood as unwarranted beliefs or intensely held opinions. In opposing the dogmatist, the skeptic is opposing the temptation to philosophize—the temptation to assert the truth beyond what appears at the moment. Second, and related to this, because the skeptical strategies were parasitic on substantive philosophical claims and because they were piecemeal, the strength of the skepticism depended on the strength of the doctrine being opposed. Jonathan Barnes has taken seriously the medical simile used by the Pyrrhonians and suggests that the thrust of the skeptical strategies and the resulting attitude of suspension of belief depend on the magnitude of the disease. "How much [*epochē*] does a man need for [*ataraxia*] or mental health? How far will a competent Pyrrhonist apply his Tropes. . . ? Plainly, it all depends on the disease. Serious mental conditions require strong remedies, minor maladies are righted by a simple argument or two. It is absurd to suppose that a Pyrrhonist can produce a single formula, applicable to all men in all conditions, or pronounce generally that every patient needs so much [*epochē*] or so many Tropes a day."[43] As with Popkin's account of Hume, the ancient Pyrrhonians accept appearances when they must, and they doubt as much as is required to restore *epochē* when faced with the current disquiet caused by whatever philosophical claims are at issue. Both Hume and the ancient Pyrrhonists, then, can be seen as providing a properly balanced and therapeutic skepticism, one which counteracts dogmatism and lends authority to natural inclination, tradition, and custom. Both are properly mitigated in their skeptical attitudes. It is this last point that I want to consider by way of Donald Livingston's interpretation of Hume.

Livingston is interested in the role Pyrrhonism played in Hume's natural history of philosophy, referring to it as a "Pyrrhonian illumination" which reveals the nature and limits of philosophy. I cannot do justice to the richness of Livingston's account of Hume, but a brief summary of his reading of Hume's dialectical account of false and true philosophy is necessary in order to set the Pyrrhonian challenge. The focus of Livingston's attention is part IV of book I of the *Treatise*—"Of the Sceptical and other Systems of Philosophy"—from which he develops Hume's view of the relation between perception and the public world.

It is usual in interpretations of Hume that focus primarily on part I of the first book of the *Treatise* to see Hume's epistemology and in particular his theory of perception as simply the extension of Locke's "new way of ideas." On this reading, Hume was a phenomenalist whose skepticism about the external world was the logical consequence of his theory of perception. Livingston reverses the relationship, however, arguing that Hume's doctrine of perception was not simply a more refined version of Locke. Instead, he thinks that Hume's doctrine of perception follows from, rather than entails, his conception of the limits of philosophical inquiry expressed in part IV. Thus Hume was interested in the problem of the external world not because of his theory of perception but because it was paradigmatically a philosophical problem whose analysis would ultimately vindicate the authority of common life—the popular world of instinct, custom, and tradition.

In the discussion of skepticism with regard to the senses, Hume had recounted the transition from dogmatism through skepticism as they gave way to the vulgar conception.

> Reason first appears in possession of the throne, prescribing laws, and imposing maxims. . . . Her enemy, therefore is oblig'd to take shelter under her protection. . . . But as it is suppos'd to be contradictory to reason, it gradually diminishes the force of that governing power, and its own at the same time; till at last they both vanish away to nothing. . . . 'Tis happy, therefore, that nature breaks the force of all sceptical arguments in time, and keeps them from having any considerable influence on the understanding. (*Treatise,* pp. 186–87).

The internal dynamic of this history is governed by two principles—Livingston calls them the ultimacy principle and the autonomy principle. On the one hand, philosophical thinking seeks the ultimate principle for the whole of reality. On the other, it supposes itself autonomous by declaring that it is irrational to accept any standard, principle, custom, or tradition of common life unless it has withstood critical philosophical reflection. These principles are at once integral to philosophical consciousness and are what drives philosophy to scepticism by totally alienating philosophical thinking from common life. On this reading, Pyrrhonism is not so much opposed to philosophical thinking as it is its inevitable outcome, just as in Heidegger's interpretation of Nietzsche the latter's nihilism was the inevitable outcome of Plato.

Hume's concern with the problem of the external world, then, can be understood within this natural history because it allowed him to examine the dialectical relation between three systems of thought: the popular or vulgar understanding of the world, which assumes that we perceive everyday public objects; phenomenalism, which assumes that we only perceive the mental images of private inner consciousness; and "the double existence" view, which attempts to relieve the dialectical tension between the other two by marking the distinction between appearance and reality as the distinction between private perceptions and objects in themselves. The problem of the external world allowed Hume to trace the natural history of philosophical consciousness out of the popular system, through the discovery of inner consciousness, to the bifurcated world of appearance and reality.

Livingston draws two lessons from this natural history of philosophy. First, Hume was able to show that phenomenalism and the double-existence view are incoherent since at the same time that they attempt to reject and replace the vulgar conception of the world, they presuppose it. Second, Hume was able to distinguish false and true philosophy. Each stage in this natural history was false philosophy because in its attempt to escape common life it failed to recognize that philosophical thinking can take place only within the framework of common life—the popular or vulgar conception of the world. What, then, was true philosophy for Hume? It was the philosophy that recognized the original authority of the common life. Hume's "Pyrrhonian illumination" was the discovery of the role Pyrrhonism played in true philosophy's abandonment of the autonomy principle and its recognition of the original authority of nature, custom, and tradition.

Hume's despair over the skeptical results of his analysis expressed at the conclusion of book I of the *Treatise* must be taken as genuine. However, he also recognized the advantages of a mitigated skepticism which joined him even more closely to the ancient Pyrrhonians and Montaigne. In the *Enquiry,* he wrote:

> There is, indeed, a more *mitigated* scepticism of *academical* philosophy, which may be both durable and useful, and which may, in part, be the result of this Pyrrhonism, or *excessive* scepticism. [This] mitigated scepticism, which may be of advantage to mankind, and which may be the natural result of Pyrrhonian doubts and scruples, is the limitation of our enquiries to such subjects as are best adapted to the narrow capacity of human understanding. . . . avoiding all distant and high enquiries, confin[ing] itself to common life, and to such subjects as fall under daily practice and experience. (*Enquiries,* pp. 161–62)

Mitigated skepticism, the outcome of the excesses of Pyrrhonism, allows us to avoid dogmatism by achieving a tranquil and balanced but not uncritical acceptance of the values, beliefs, and customs of common life.

Though the post-Pyrrhonian philosopher has abandoned the autonomy principle, Livingston claims that for Hume a revised version of the principle remains. Though philosophy cannot question the whole system of beliefs of common life, it can still function to call particular beliefs into question. In this way, the result of Hume's skepticism is like the result of Montaigne's. While it brings us back to the authority of common life, it does not support an uncritical acquiescence. However, if the result of Hume's mitigated skepticism is the vindication of the authority of the instincts, customs, and traditions of common life, and if one can only call into question specific beliefs and practices from *within* that framework, upon what basis can a critique of common life be erected? Hume's post-Pyrrhonian position simply pushes the problem to a higher level of concern. Whereas the Pyrrhonian sceptics accommodated us to the traditions, customs, and authority of the vulgar world; whereas Montaigne accepted the authority of tradition with his eyes open, the question posed by Hume's "Pyrrhonian illumination" is this: If philosophy cannot achieve a standpoint outside of the framework of common life, how can criticism or validation of traditions and institutions of the existing order avoid being arbitrary or ad hoc?

The final point I wish to make concerns this aspect of Livingston's interpretation of Hume as a "post-Pyrrhonian" philosopher. This point turns on the nature of Hume's conservatism in contrast to the conservative consequences of ancient Pyrrhonism. It is necessary to approach the question of Hume's conservatism cautiously for several reasons. The notion of conservatism itself is difficult to make precise because it is too easily identified with a mere defense of the status quo, and Livingston wants to claim that Hume's conservatism is not simply an uncritical acceptance of the framework of common life. In addition, conservatism is too often identified with a particular conservative thinker, Edmund Burke for example. Though it is generally acknowledged that Hume's philosophy was a form of conservatism, it is different in important ways from the political conservatism that followed the French Revolution. Hume's work contributed to the subsequent development of conservatism and to the liberal tradition as well. At the same time that he shared the conservatives' understanding of the importance of custom and tradition and their distrust of reform, he shared the liberals' distrust of religion and their respect for liberty and property.[44] What tied his philosophy most directly to the conservative tradition, however, was his opposition to rationalism in morals and politics. The most obvious context of this opposition was Hume's claim that reason is and ought to be the slave of the passions and that morality is more properly felt than judged. This clearly shared in conservative efforts to undermine rationalist claims of universal moral law.

Livingston has suggested that in its broadest sense the conservative tradition is "a doctrine of limits, in particular a doctrine of the limits beyond which philosophical criticism of social and political order cannot go,"[45] and in this sense Hume's post-Pyrrhonism is squarely in the conservative tradition. What Hume's "Pyrrhonian illumination" had shown was that there was no Archimedean point outside common life from which it can be either certified or criticized. This point, drawn from ancient Pyrrhonism and Hume, is the same point currently being made under the banner of "postmodernism." Jean-François Lyotard has defined postmodernity as an "incredulity toward metanarratives" and he states the central question of the postmodern condition thus: "Where, after the metanarratives, can legitimacy reside?"[46] If there is no standpoint outside of common life—no metanarrative—how can critique be made legitimate? It is too soon to argue for it here, but I submit that it is this question that joins the Pyrrhonian opposition to philosophy with the work of the late Michel Foucault, Richard Rorty, and Jacques Derrida. Each opposes the quest of Western philosophy for a metanarrative, a foundation, an Archimedean point outside of the web of power/knowledge relations, or the "conversation of the West," or discourse; and each has been criticized for eliminating the possibility of rationally grounded critique.

The connection can be elaborated briefly in terms of Foucault's last work. He had opposed the Enlightenment conviction that knowledge could exist only where power was absent, claiming in the way Nietzsche had that power and knowledge mutually imply one another. The result of conflating power and knowledge, however, is that there is no power-free foundation from which to criticize regimes of power. Both Jürgen Habermas and Charles Taylor have opposed Foucault for this result. Taylor, for example, charges that "the regime-relativity of truth means that we cannot raise the banner of truth against our own regime. . . . liberation in the name of 'truth' can only be the substitution of another system of power for this one."[47] I will turn to an examination of the issue between Foucault and his critics in Chapter 4 and to Rorty's attempt to have both an opposition to foundationalist philosophy and a place for social criticism in the final chapter.

My point in suggesting parallels between the challenge of Pyrrhonian skepticism, Montaigne and Hume's post-Pyrrhonism, and recent issues is to reinforce the importance of appreciating the coherence of Pyrrhonism as a moral stance that remains deeply problematic for us. Outside of the traditional conception of philosophy and its place in culture, on what basis can we question the instincts, customs, institutions, and traditions of common life? One possible answer to that question—the answer that will be taken up in Chapter 3—can be found in Rousseau's attack on the sciences, arts, and philosophy and his appeal to natural freedom and to sentiment as the foundation for a critique of modernity and modern forms of social relations. But it will be an answer with a price, since in separating freedom and morals from the progress of inquiry he too will challenge the traditional conception and role of philosophy.

# 2 Progress against Ignorance

In his *Essay on National Education,* La Chalotais had attacked the "apologists of ignorance," claiming that "the rudest and the most ignorant centuries have always been the most vicious and the most corrupt. Leave man without culture, ignorant and, consequently, insensible to his duties; he will become timid, superstitious and perhaps cruel. If he is not taught what is good, he will necessarily concern himself with what is bad. The mind and the heart cannot remain empty."[1] La Chalotais' attack on the skeptics was fairly typical of any number of treatises on education and proposals for educational reform during the French Enlightenment. Similar attacks and claims for the role of education had been made by Turgot and Condorcet.[2] Whereas Rousseau condemned the public education of his day as "fit only for making double men, always appearing to relate everything to others and never relating anything except to themselves alone,"[3] mainline Enlightenment thought supported public education as the source of social duty and personal autonomy.

Though typical for its time, the importance Enlightenment reformers attached to the philosophy of education located a concern for the role of education in our moral and social lives in a place it had not occupied at least since Plato's *Republic.*[4] Even when seen in relation to the seventeenth-century turn toward education, the Enlightenment conception of the connection between education, progress, and freedom was unique. Locke, for example, had applied the results of his epistemology to the education of children in *Some Thoughts Concerning Education,* and while this popular work was significant for the emphasis it placed on the process of education in freeing the mind to move easily from one subject to another, it is clear that Locke neither supported universal education—the book on education, after all, was directed to the education of a gentleman's son—nor drew the conclusion that education would foster emancipation.[5]

For the French educational reformers, the defense of education and the connection between education and progress was their response to the Pyrrhonian skeptics' attack on the desirability of knowledge. Those who praised ignorance would subject us to tyranny, superstition, and the authority of tradition. Condorcet had been careful to distinguish this Pyrrhonian skepticism from the Enlightenment practice of rational doubt and criticism in his *Sketch for a Historical Picture of the Progress of the Human Mind,* and he attacked Pyrrhonism this way: "This form of doubt, if it extends to ascertained truth, if it attacks the principles of morality, becomes either stupidity or madness, it favours ignorance and corruption."[6] He argued that the doctrine of the indefinite perfectibility of the human race was to be the final blow against "the comfortable indolence of absolute Pyrrhonism [which so despises] the human race as to teach it that the progress of knowledge would be not only useless but dangerous both to its happiness and to its freedom" (*Sketch,* p. 142).

Education, understood in terms of the spread of critical reason modeled on an application of scientific rationality to the moral sciences, would bring about our release from the enslavement of ignorance and would assure social progress. "Will not the free man's sense of his own dignity and a system of education built upon a deeper knowledge of our moral constitution, render common to almost every man those principles of strict and unsullied justice, those habits of an active and enlightened benevolence, of a fine and generous sensibility which nature has implanted in the hearts of all and whose flowering waits only upon the favourable influences of enlightenment and freedom?" (*Sketch,* p. 192). By locating the philosophy of education within the context of the spread of scientific rationality and placing both in the context of historical progress, the relationship between individual development and social progress, education and freedom, and scientific inquiry and emancipation received a unique formulation in the eighteenth century. The Enlightenment defense of progress—not post-Cartesian epistemology or Hume's direct attack on Pyrrhonism—constituted the significant response to the moral challenge of skepticism since it was aimed not so much at establishing the possibility of knowledge as at the necessity of knowledge for freedom.

The Pyrrhonian skeptics had called into question the connection between knowledge and virtue and they had supported custom, tradition, and appearance as the ground for conduct because reason was incapable of constituting a basis for criticizing social institutions. Rousseau would argue that education in science, arts, and philosophy stifled true freedom and transformed the genuine social bond based on esteem and goodwill into a social knot of reciprocal self-interests. By contrast, the Enlightenment defense of the connection between the growth of scientific knowledge, education, and freedom was an attempt to found a new source of legitimacy and to reestablish the connection between knowledge and morals. Whereas the Pyrrhonian skeptics had sought to sever the Socratic connection between knowledge and virtue by claiming that tranquility was achieved through a suspension of belief and acquiescence in the appearances, customs, and traditions of common life, and whereas Rousseau would locate virtue in the natural self antecedent to society and learning, the Enlightenment opposition to the skeptics was grounded in a defense of inquiry and education against the praise of ignorance which connected the progress of inquiry—both in the development of the individual and of human intelligence through the course of history—with the improvement of humankind and society. The moral goal of the Enlightenment was no longer virtue in the ancient sense or even happiness, though the utilitarian strand in eighteenth-century thought had set that as the goal. Instead, the goal was autonomy, and the growth of knowledge was emancipatory in that it was to produce our freedom.

In his essay on the question "What Is Enlightenment?" Kant had answered, "Enlightenment is man's emergence from his self-imposed immaturity. Immaturity is the inability to use one's understanding without guidance from another. This immaturity is self-imposed when its cause lies not in lack of understanding, but in lack of resolve and courage to use it without guidance from another. *Sapere Aude!* 'Have courage to use your own understanding!'—That is the motto of enlightenment."[7] The Enlightenment response to the skeptic's praise of ignorance—made explicit in Kant's essay—turned on these connected themes of knowledge, progress, and autonomy. My purpose in this chapter is to consider the nature of the Enlightenment response in terms of the coherence of the connection between these themes. I will focus the Enlightenment response to the Pyrrhonian challenge and anticipate Rousseau's attack on philosophy in terms of three issues: the identity of truth and utility in the pre-Enlightenment work of Francis Bacon; the connection of reason, the human sciences, and public good in the work of Condorcet; and Kant's linking of enlightenment, autonomy, and universal history. Clearly the period we designate as the Enlightenment was far richer and more varied than the selection of these themes would indicate. However, my purpose is not to exhaust the Enlightenment but to explore those themes that oppose the moral challenge of Pyrrhonism and that shape the challenge Pyrrhonism poses for us.

## I

In his classic study, *The Idea of Progress,* J. B. Bury summarized the Enlightenment belief in progress:

> The idea of human Progress . . . is a theory which involves a synthesis of the past and a prophecy of the future. It is based on an interpretation of history which regards men as slowly advancing—*pedetemtim progredientes*—in a definite and desirable direction, and infers that this progress will continue

indefinitely. It implies that . . . a condition of general happiness will ultimately be enjoyed, which will justify the whole process of civilization. . . . There is also a further implication. The process must be the necessary outcome of the psychical and social nature of man; it must not be at the mercy of any external will; otherwise there would be no guarantee of its continuance and its issue, and the idea of Progress would lapse into the idea of Providence.[8]

It has been a subject of scholarly debate lately whether belief in progress originated with the Enlightenment. The position taken by late nineteenth- and early twentieth-century historians—the position represented by Bury—was that while fragments of the idea may have existed in ancient and medieval thought, a fully articulated idea of progress had not existed prior to the eighteenth century. It is more common now, however, to find belief in progress present in various classical sources. Drawing on the work of a variety of classical scholars, for example, Robert Nisbet suggests that "we have come to see that the Greeks and Romans, contrary to conventional interpretation, did have a distinct awareness of a long past, did see a measure of progression of the arts and sciences and of man's estate on earth, and did on occasion refer to a future in which civilization would have gone well beyond what it was in their own time."[9]

The core of the Enlightenment conception of progress was the belief that the improvement of ourselves and society was inevitably connected with the progress of knowledge; it was this belief that knowledge and moral progress were *necessarily* connected that constituted their opposition to the skeptics' praise of ignorance for moral life. The controversy over the source of the idea of progress is, therefore, instructive for making this point. The two central features of the Enlightenment idea of progress in Bury's summary are that history was seen to be moving in a desirable direction and that this movement was brought about not by an external will but by ourselves. Kant had made both points in his "Idea for a Universal History With Cosmopolitan Intent." He thought that from the philosophical study of history one could "discover a guiding thread that can serve not only to clarify the thoroughly confused play of human affairs . . . it will also clear the way for . . . a comforting view of the future, one in which we represent from afar how the human species finally works its way up to that state where all the seeds nature has planted in it can be developed fully and in which the species' vocation here on earth can be fulfilled."[10] Though Kant had attributed our progress to Providence or nature, it was at best an ironic attribution. On the one hand, nature had decreed discord among humankind rather than harmony in order that we may develop our talents in the mill of conflict. On the other, nature's stinginess in the allocation of our physical abilities assured that what progress we made would be as a result of our own reason. In the third thesis of the "Universal History" he had stated that "Nature has willed that man, entirely by himself, produce everything that goes beyond the mechanical organization of his animal existence and partake in no other happiness or perfection than what he himself, independently of instinct, can secure through his own reason" ("Universal History," p. 31).

If one allows that progress is the result of the will of God rather than of the effort of ourselves, or if one agrees with Nisbet that the significance and survival of the belief of progress depends on the Judeo-Christian conception of the world and humanity, then indeed the belief in progress might be extended to a number of classical and medieval sources. But it was the denial of the effect of Providence that was distinctive about the Enlightenment conception of progress[11] and which allowed thinkers like Condorcet and Kant to map the success of science onto a conception of moral improvement, and to draw out the social implications of the growth of knowledge.[12] While some sort of idea of progress can certainly be attributed to the ancient and medieval world, the Enlightenment version of it was unique since it situated our moral development in a philosophy of history and supposed that moral or social progress would be achieved only through the growth of knowledge—that the life of reason was a necessary condition for realizing our moral end and the goal of history.[13]

Condorcet, the eighteenth century's most passionate propagandist for progress, had made the connection explicit in his *Sketch for the Progress of the Human Mind.* In the introduction he set the purpose of the proposed book: "we shall demonstrate how nature has joined together indissolubly the progress of knowledge and that of liberty, virtue and respect for the natural rights of man; and how these, the only real goods that we possess, though so often separated that they have even been held to be incompatible, must on the contrary become inseparable from the moment when enlightenment has attained a certain level" (*Sketch,* p. 10). After setting out the stages of progress his planned history would explore, he asked rhetorically: "do not all the observations which I propose to develop show the moral goodness of man, the necessary consequence of his constitution, is capable of infinite perfection like all his other faculties and that nature has linked together in an unbreakable chain truth, happiness and virtue" (*Sketch,* p. 193).

It is the last phrase that is fundamental: nature has linked together truth, happiness, and virtue. Involved in this linkage are several connected ideas. First, the success of science, both in terms of its own progress and its utility, established the methods of scientific inquiry as a new source of authority and foundation for legitimacy. Scientific reason was the paradigm of progress because progress was internal to the self-correcting methods of science; and it was the engine of progress because, in the manner of Francis Bacon's pragmatic account of the goal of science, it allowed us to achieve power over nature and ourselves. Charles Frankel has observed that the new position of authority science had achieved in the eighteenth century was justified on the basis of another quite distinct interpretation of science—one which situated the role of science in a metaphysical framework of movement toward a moral goal—and he argued that these distinct sanctions for scientific progress are inconsistent. I will claim, however, that the attempt to link knowledge and our moral and social improvement through the notion of progress in science depends on both sanctions, and that one source of the failure of the Enlightenment response to the Pyrrhonian challenge is the result of making progress rest on the nature of the scientific enterprise itself—that is, in removing the progress of science from a larger metaphysical backdrop.

It is worth remembering at this point that the Pyrrhonian opposition to philosophy was compatible with our living a life in accord with appearances broadly understood. But that broad notion of appearance also included our living according to sense impressions; thus it could be argued that the Pyrrhonian skeptic could accept the benefits of a science of appearances so long as no philosophical claims about truth beyond appearances were made. What makes the Enlightenment notion of the progress of science incompatible with the Pyrrhonian possibility of merely accepting uncritically a science of appearances was that Enlightenment thinkers situated science within the context of historical development in such a way as to link it with the goal of freedom. Outside of such a linkage, there is no basis for arguing against the Pyrrhonians that the course of science itself would produce virtue.

The second point is that the connection between truth, happiness, and virtue—the belief that scientific inquiry would bring about our moral and social development—depended on an assimilation of the philosophy of history and philosophy of education. This assimilation worked in both directions. For Condorcet, for example, the Lockean account of the development of knowledge in the individual was projected to the development of the species as a whole through history. But for Kant, it was assumed that the education of the individual was just the historical evolution of knowledge writ small. In his lectures on pedagogy, Kant had wondered "whether the education of the individual should imitate the development of the race in general through its various generations,"[14] and it is clear from the lectures and from his "Universal History" that he thought it should. Not only did this mean that the same rational methods that assured progress in science would result in the moral development of the individual—either by coming to know one's social duty, for Turgot, or from emulating the decision-making behavior of science, for Condorcet, or from realizing autonomy, for Kant—but the moral improvement of the individual was placed in the larger context of world historical development.

Third—and this is less explicit though more important—the scientific turn toward the control of nature produced, at the same time, the turn toward the human sciences. Ira O. Wade, in his study of the origins of the French Enlightenment, has observed that "thought cannot turn to the objects of the external world without at the same time reverting to itself. The truth it perceives in nature becomes in a way the truth in itself."[15] Locke, in the introduction to his *Essay Concerning Human Understanding,* had noted the usefulness of casting the same light on ourselves that our understanding casts on nature, but Hume had made a much stronger claim for the significance of the human sciences in the introduction to the *Treatise:* "'Tis evident, that all the sciences have a relation, greater or less, to human nature; and however wide any of them may seem to run from it, they still return back by one passage or another."[16] What was unique about the Enlightenment conception of progress, and therefore what is important about supporting Bury's account over Nisbet's, is that the Enlightenment conception of progress—unlike classical and medieval conceptions—brought the human sciences to a central position. Perhaps Condorcet's most significant contribution to eighteenth-century thought was his attempt to link the rational methods of natural science, the development of human studies, and the realization of public good. Not only was moral and social progress to be achieved through the development of our own capacities in history, but the study of nature found its way back to the study of ourselves, which in turn, would contribute to social progress.[17]

## II

In *After Virtue,* Alasdair MacIntyre provides an illuminating analysis of the reason the eighteenth-century justification for morality failed, and I shall draw on his analysis to suggest how the Enlightenment response to Pyrrhonian skepticism must fail for us. In characterizing the teleological moral scheme that dominated European intellectual history up to the Enlightenment, MacIntyre points to the fundamental contrast in pre-Enlightenment moral theory between human nature as it happened to be in its untutored condition and human nature as it could be if it realized its true essence. Our untutored state is initially discrepant and discordant, and it was the purpose of ethical precepts and instruction in practical reasoning to transform man as he was initially into man as he would be if he realized his *telos*. Each part of this scheme—untutored human nature, man's telos, and the function of instruction in bringing about the transition from one to the other—could only be understood, according to MacIntyre, in terms of each of the other parts. Against this interpretation of the pre-Enlightenment, MacIntyre diagnoses the failure of the Enlightenment in terms of its rejection of the notion of human telos that allowed the parts to hang together. According to MacIntyre,

> the joint effect of the secular rejection of both Protestant and Catholic theology and the scientific and philosophical rejection of Aristotelianism was to eliminate any notion of man-as-he-could-be-if-he-realized-his-*telos*. Since the whole point of ethics—both as a theoretical and a practical discipline—is to enable man to pass from his present state to his true end, the elimination of any notions of essential human nature and with it the abandonment of any notions of a *telos* leaves behind a moral scheme composed of the two remaining elements whose relationship becomes quite unclear.[18]

On MacIntyre's reading, eighteenth-century moral theory had to fail because at the same time that it inherited a moral scheme derived from a specific view of human telos, it rejected the very idea of man's essence in terms of which moral life was to be understood. I will suggest a related incoherence in the Enlightenment attempt to reestablish the connection between knowledge and moral life through the doctrine of progress. The failure, however, does not turn simply on the fact that eighteenth-century philosophy rejected the ancient conception of human telos. Rather, the conceptual role human telos had played was filled by a philosophy of history as progress; that is, the transition from our untutored and discordant condition to the realization of our true end was cast in terms of a teleological conception of the human species. Outside of that conception, the Enlightenment idea of progress fails to establish a necessary link between knowledge and our moral and social good.

The general structure of my argument will be this: For Plato and Aristotle knowledge was necessary for moral life because our virtue—our excellence—was to be achieved through the realization of our essence; and, since we are essentially knowers, our good was to be found in and through a life of inquiry. The Pyrrhonian skeptics, of course, had rejected the connection between knowledge and virtue. Through the idea of progress, the Enlightenment attempted to reconnect knowledge and virtue, but at the same time it had rejected the notion of human telos that made the connection intelligible for the Greeks. The difficulty, however, is not just that the eighteenth century had rejected the conception of human telos in favor of some Lockean *tabula rasa.* The mainline Enlightenment conception of freedom, worked out in terms of world-historical unfolding, was to bear the burden of supporting the connection between progress and the improvement of our moral and social condition. But within a teleological conception of history, the way reason or inquiry or knowledge or education was supposed to bring about our moral and social improvement developed in an essentially ambiguous way. From the tradition of Francis Bacon, knowledge gave us power over ourselves and nature for the improvement of our condition here on earth. From the tradition of Condorcet and Kant, the progress of knowledge brought about our autonomy and resulted in social progress. Within a larger religious or metaphysical framework—or within a teleological conception of history—knowledge, power, and freedom were merely different sides of a single conception of moral and social progress. Outside of that framework, however, they become incompatible goals.

I will develop this interpretation initially by looking to a precursor of the Enlightenment, considering how Bacon had directed the conception of knowledge away from the realization of our essence toward the acquisition of power over ourselves and nature. My purpose is to show how the identity of power and knowledge within Bacon's own view made sense only in terms of his belief that the aim of science was to realize the biblical promise of our dominion over the earth. Next, I will consider Condorcet's attempt to cast the methods of the natural sciences as the paradigm of social consensus and to link social science and the public good in terms of the metaphysical necessity of progress in history. Finally, I will consider how Kant developed his conceptions of moral and political freedom in terms of enlightenment and universal history.

## III

In *The Edge of Objectivity,* Charles C. Gillispie reduced the subjects of Francis Bacon's writings to three categories: demonstrations of the value and dignity of learning; analysis of the obstacles to it; and prescriptions for its reformation and advancement. In addition to the fact that Gillispie fails to include in this classification a great deal of Bacon's historical and religious writing, he dismisses the first category of Bacon's concerns, stating that "It is not, perhaps, necessary to insist much on the first point—indeed, it was not so necessary in the early seventeenth century as Bacon would imply. His pleas for learning generally took the form of a rather scornful repudiation of all that passed for such."[19] This assessment of the nature of Bacon's work—an assessment which, unfortunately, is far too common[20]—fails to appreciate the way Bacon's praise of learning constituted an important response to the Pyrrhonian challenge that ignorance rather than inquiry was more conducive to happiness. Furthermore, it fails to take seriously the relation between Bacon's pragmatic conception of science and his social vision, and the connection Bacon saw between God's revelation and the role of scientific method in realizing that vision. It was not because of something internal to science itself that Bacon defended the advancement of learning for the improvement of our condition. Rather, it was because he was convinced that science directed toward nature and toward works and operations was divinely sanctioned. In connecting science and revelation, Bacon can be seen as attempting to reconcile the project of the new science that aimed at understanding nature by analyzing it with the Renaissance project of being in accord with or being attuned to nature as a meaningful and purposeful order.[21]

Like Gillispie's, too many recent discussions of Bacon locate his importance merely in the epistemology of modern science, emphasizing the methodological contribution to science and treating his reorientation of the goal of science as a result of methodological considerations.[22] It is usual to credit Bacon with the defense of an inductive method against Aristotelianism and experimentalism, and to credit him with a pragmatic conception of knowledge and truth. While Bacon's contribution to the method of the new science was important, it had a broader context and purpose.

In *The New Organon,* Bacon had indeed opposed medieval conceptions of knowledge, dividing through, summing up, and attacking the science in his day by claiming that those who were engaged in science were either men of experiment or men of reason. The former were like ants. They merely collected and used. The latter were like spiders. They spun cobwebs out of their own substance. His own view, however, he compared to the bees: "the bee takes a middle course: it gathers its material from the flowers of the garden and the field, but transforms and digests it by a power of its own. Not unlike this is the true business of philosophy, for it neither relies solely or chiefly on the powers of the mind, nor does it take the matter which it gathers . . . as it finds it."[23] True philosophy—that is, Bacon's own method—neither flies from the senses and particulars nor merely gathers them up. Instead, the true method "derives axioms from the senses and particulars, rising by a gradual and unbroken ascent, so that it arrives at the most general axioms last of all" (*New Organon,* p. 333). While it is through this method that Bacon argued for a conception of science in which "human knowledge and human power meet in one" (*New Organon,* p. 331), my claim is that Bacon's contribution to the epistemology of modern science, his praise of learning, and his attack on the ancients were less a matter of introducing a new method than of achieving a reconciliation of the results of the new method for science with God's promise of man's dominion over the earth. The connection he made between scientific understanding and attunement with nature was made through the identity of truth and power, an identity sanctioned by the biblical promise, and it is within the context of this reconciliation that the new social vision of science must be understood.

In the opening paragraph of his book on Bacon, Benjamin Farrington summarized the social thrust of Bacon's project and his contribution to the modern age: "The story of Francis Bacon is that of a life devoted to a great idea. . . . The idea is a commonplace today, partly realized, partly tarnished, still often misunderstood. . . . It is simply that knowledge ought to bear fruits in works, that science ought to be applicable to industry, that men ought to organize themselves as a sacred duty to improve and transform the conditions of life."[24] As Farrington has claimed elsewhere, Bacon's opposition to the ancients was more a matter of moral indignation than epistemology.[25] Bacon's critique of the ancients, his reorientation of science, and his empirical method developed from religious and moral convictions. The significance of this point is that Bacon's response both to the barren state of the sciences of his day and the way his work constituted an answer to the skeptics' denigration of learning and their acquiescence in appearances makes sense because of the way he situated the advancement of learning, the identity of knowledge and power, and the social goal of science in a larger metaphysical or religious framework. Outside of that framework, we are left—as so many recent critics of the Enlightenment have argued—with an epistemology of mere prudence since control over nature would no longer receive its rationale within the more fundamental context of our sacred duty but would become an end in itself as domination pure and simple.

It will be helpful in developing this point to begin with the contrast between Bacon's attack on the ancients and his assessment of the goal of his own work. In "The Masculine Birth of Time"—an early work admittedly stronger in table-banging than argument—Bacon confronted the ancients as if he was bringing them before a court magistrate. He "dragged Plato before the bar" and accused his philosophy of being merely "scraps of borrowed information polished and strung together." The substance of his attack was this: "You gave out the falsehood that truth is, as it were, the native inhabitant of the human mind and need not come in from outside to take up its abode there; when you turned our minds away from observation, away from things to which it is impossible we should ever be sufficiently respectful and attentive; when you taught us to turn our mind's eye inward and grovel before our own blind and confused idols under the name of contemplative philosophy; then you truly dealt us a mortal blow."[26] Aristotle had fared no better: "that worst of sophists stupefied by his own unprofitable subtlety, the cheap dupe of words" ("Masculine Birth of Time," p. 62). Whereas Plato had turned our minds inward to grovel before our own idols, Aristotle had turned us toward words instead of works.

Compare this with what he had written in the preface to *The Great Instauration* of his own philosophy: "Of the business which is at hand I entreat men to believe that it is not an opinion to be held but a work to be done; and to be well assured that I am labouring to lay the foundation, not of any sect or doctrine, but of human utility and power."[27] From the very title of this work it is clear that Bacon's aim was to restore or reinstate the sacred goal of the sciences—a goal that had been corrupted and obscured by the ancients. The inwardness of contemplative knowledge had joined the Socratic claim that knowledge was necessary for virtue with the injunction to know thyself rather than nature. The preoccupation with words had turned us from industry and social duty to dialectic and the syllogism. By contrast, in the famous passage from Chapter 124 of *The New Organon* Bacon had concluded that "truth and utility are the very same thing."[28] Knowledge must be understood as outwardly directed empirical inquiry which aims at realizing our dominion over the earth. This point was made most interestingly in Bacon's explanation of the riddle of the Sphinx, in *Wisdom of the Ancients:* "Sphinx has no more than two kinds of riddles, one relating to the nature of things, the other to the nature of man; and correspondent to these, the prizes of solution are two kinds of empire—the empire over nature, and the empire over man. For the true and ultimate end of natural philosophy is dominion over natural things, natural bodies, and remedies, machines and numberless particulars."[29]

Bacon's rejection of a purely theoretical goal for science in favor of practical and socially oriented inquiry was, of course, part of a long tradition of opposition to the excesses of speculative metaphysics and contemplative philosophy. That opposition extended from the Augustinian tradition which gave priority to will over intellect, through the enthusiasm for civic life typical of Italian humanism, and even to the Pyrrhonian skeptics' attempt to reject the notion that virtue derived from intellect rather than from the practical wisdom of common life.

Within this tradition, it is tempting to interpret Bacon's identification of truth and utility, knowledge and power, understanding and industry, and his attack on the ancient disdain for practice and labor, as merely his embracing the opposite side of the theory/practice dichotomy—replacing an arid contemplative philosophy with an epistemology of prudence. If this is what Bacon's view comes to, then it is in principle compatible with the Pyrrhonian skeptics' resolve to live according to appearances and accept the practical benefits of instruction in the arts. What made Bacon's pragmatism a response to the moral challenge of Pyrrhonism, however, was the fact that his social orientation for science linked contemplation and action by connecting our own work toward the improvement of our condition with the glory of God—an attempt to have the practical benefits of science, human progress, and Providence all at once.

In the *Advancement of Learning,* Bacon had argued that the greatest source of error and obstacle to learning was the mistake about the end of knowledge. We have desired knowledge out of natural curiosity or for entertainment or for reputation or "as if there were sought in knowledge a couch, whereupon to rest a searching and restless spirit." By contrast he claimed: "this is that which will indeed dignify and exalt knowledge: if contemplation and action may be more nearly and straightly conjoined and united together," for "the glory of the Creator and the relief of man's estate."[30] In "Thoughts and Conclusions," as well as in numerous other places, Bacon made the connection between religion and science explicit. "Next to the word of God Natural Philosophy is the most certain cure for superstition and the most approved nutriment of faith. Its rightful station is as the accepted and loyal handmaid of religion, for religion reveals the will of God, Natural Philosophy His power."[31] And again "The rule of religion, that a man should show his faith by his works, holds good in natural philosophy too. Science also must be known by works. It is by the witness of works, rather than by logic or even observation, that truth is revealed and established. Whence it follows that the improvement of man's mind and the improvement of his lot are one and the same thing" ("Thoughts," p. 93).

Bacon's disdain for the ancient and medieval philosophers' preference for theoretical inquiry, then, did not turn on the argument that they preferred theory to practice. Paolo Rossi has argued that the whole of Bacon's work was directed at ushering in a technico-scientific culture and to do so it was necessary not only to break with historical tradition but to change an attitude toward the natural world. When the ancients posited the superiority of contemplative life over a life of work, this had constituted "resignation to nature rather than the conquest of nature."[32] Resignation to nature was a turn away from the biblical promise, and the fact that earlier theories did not issue in practical results, works, and industry, showed that they were *false* theories since truth was to be measured in terms of dominion over nature for the service of ourselves. My addition to this claim is that Bacon equally opposed the skeptics because, in merely accepting appearances, instruction in the arts, and the benefits and practices of common life, they failed to see beyond the appearances to the plan of God. What was required was a new beginning for inquiry—a great instauration. In his reorientation toward nature he had claimed, in *The New Organon,* that "the true signatures and marks set upon the works of creation" are found in nature (p. 334) and that works and operations were "pledges of truth" (p. 370); thus the results of inquiry directed toward nature through operations and experiment were more likely to demonstrate truth than a theoretical argument.

In sum, things as they really are carried the imprint of God, and when we turn from our own inner idols and from dialectical demonstrations to the things themselves, truth and utility, knowledge and power, theory and practice, contemplation and action converge as one. With this convergence, the connection between knowledge and the improvement of our condition on earth was no longer to be understood in terms of the realization of man's telos or inner essence, but rather it was to be understood in terms of the way our scientific inquiries realized God's promise, improving our condition through the convergence of knowledge, utility, and power.

## IV

In their belief in progress and their defense of the growth of science for the improvement of humankind, the French Enlightenment *philosophes* had retained Bacon's social vision but they looked elsewhere for their guarantee of progress. It was neither divine sanction nor, strictly speaking, the utility of science that would contribute to the improvement of our estate. Instead, it was the progressive nature of science itself, applied to history as a whole, that was to guarantee that the growth of scientific knowledge and the spread of scientific rationality would produce moral and social progress.

Condorcet's work emphasized three features of science that established it as the new source of authority and the basis for social progress. First, scientific methods of analysis and calculation were taken to be the paradigm of rational inquiry and the very model of progress, and the success of science was attributed to the fact that it was cumulative, self-correcting, and developmental. Second, the social structure of science—its egalitarian and open environment, the mechanisms of consensus, and the role of criticism—was taken as the model for rational social behavior generally, and thus was to become the basis for a conception of the social sciences that not only applied the methods of science to social reality but established the goal toward which enlightened society should develop—a goal articulated on the basis of rational consensus behavior. "This progress of the physical sciences which neither the passions nor self-interest can disturb, in which neither birth, nor profession, nor position are thought to confer on one the right to judge what one is not in a condition to understand, this inexorable progress cannot be contemplated by men of enlightenment without their wishing to make the other sciences follow the same path" (*Sketch,* p. 164). Third, science was the enemy of domination because the spread of critical rationality would undermine the authority of tyrants and tradition. Science was emancipatory since, with the spread of critical methods and their application to social reality, the only authority would be reason and truth.

Whereas Bacon had combined the social utility of science with a religious vision, Condorcet had attempted to develop the social implications of scientific rationality outside of the framework of divine sanction. He had attempted to justify the new authority of science in social life by placing the methods of science within a conception of history as the progress of reason against power rather than as the divinely sanctioned connection between truth and utility. I will suggest, however, that he had developed the social implications of the critical function of reason within an epistemology—the empiricist epistemology of Locke—that could not sustain its response to Pyrrhonism. More to the point, however, the coherence of his response to the Pyrrhonian praise of ignorance depended on the philosophy of history that supported his extension of scientific reason to social life. Without the support of historical progress against power, the bond between reason and virtue is again broken.

Condorcet's *Sketch for a Historical Picture of the Progress of the Human Mind* was merely the proposal for a book, yet it has come to stand as an exemplar for the Enlightenment faith in progress. He projected a book to be organized in ten stages, from the speculative history of the first stages of primitive and pastoral people to the last stage, the tenth, which forecast the progress to come. The conjectural parts of the *Sketch* were an application of theoretical observations about the development of individual intellect derived from Locke's sensationalist psychology, in which Condorcet projected individual development onto universal history. In the opening lines of the introduction to the *Sketch,* Condorcet had written:

> Man is born with the ability to receive sensations; to perceive them and to distinguish between various simple sensations of which they are composed; to remember, recognize and combine them; to compare these combinations; to apprehend what they have in common and the ways in which they differ; to attach signs to them all in order to recognize them more easily and to allow for the ready production of new combinations. (*Sketch,* p. 3).

From this clearly Lockean starting-point, Condorcet claimed that "progress is subject to the same general laws that can be observed in the development of the faculties of the individual, and it is indeed no more than the sum of that development realized in a large number of individuals joined together in society" (*Sketch,* p. 4).

Locke's impact on the French Enlightenment—evident throughout Condorcet's *Sketch*—has been well charted.[33] While Condorcet credited Descartes with bringing philosophy back to reason, he claimed that "Locke grasped the thread by which philosophy should be guided" (*Sketch,* p. 132). Locke's two great contributions were his "new way of ideas"—the method of analysis of ideas into simples—and, ironically, his realization of the limits of human understanding.

In terms of the first contribution, Condorcet projected a time when "this method [of analysis] was soon adopted by all philosophers and by applying it to moral science, to politics and to social economy, they were able to make almost as sure progress in theses sciences as they had in the natural sciences" (*Sketch,* p. 133). But not only would the extension of the method of analysis to the moral sciences result in progress comparable to that in the natural sciences, it would provide the mechanism for avoiding error and overcoming ignorance generally. The significance of Locke's second contribution was twofold. First, the limitation of human knowledge was turned into a virtue. Locke had set out in the *Essay Concerning Human Understanding* to "inquire into the original, certainty, and extent" of human knowledge in order to convince the mind to "be more cautious in meddling with things exceeding its comprehension; to stop when it is at the utmost extent of its tether; and to sit down in quiet ignorance of those things which, upon examination, are found to be beyond the reach of our capacity."[34] In turning from metaphysical issues that exceeded our reach and in restricting our inquiries to the limits of our experience, the progress of knowledge was to have a decidedly practical rationale and its utility was compensation for its limits. Second, the limitation of knowledge was the basis for opposition to dogmatism and thus a support for the liberal value of toleration in matters both epistemological and political. The political struggle against domination and dogmatism, of which the defense of toleration was a part, was to rest on an epistemology of limits.

Both of these consequences of the limits of knowledge can be illustrated by Locke's view of the nature and causes of ignorance. There were three causes of ignorance according to Locke: want of ideas; want of discoverable connections between ideas; and want of tracing and examining our ideas.[35] The first sort of ignorance was a result of our inability to have certain ideas because of the constitution of our faculties. With the second sort of ignorance, we lack ideas not because of the inadequacy of our faculties but because of the "remoteness or minuteness" of the subject matter. Locke claimed, for example, that because of the vastness of the universe and the fact that our knowledge could not extend beyond our own experience, there will remain "a huge abyss of ignorance" about the universe. Furthermore, because of the minuteness of the subject, we are incapable of having a science of bodies or of discovering the connection between mind and body. Each of these kinds of ignorance—ignorance through want of ideas or through want of discoverable connections—is absolute and unavoidable. We can respond to ignorance in these areas—in metaphysics, religion, and morals—not by a theory of knowledge but by "quiet ignorance" and toleration for conflicting opinions.[36] It is only the ignorance that results from inadequately tracing and analyzing our ideas and their connections that we can hope to overcome; within the limits of possible knowledge, the method of analyzing our ideas would guarantee the perfectibility of knowledge. This is the point that Condorcet drew from Locke and that was to serve as part of the response to Pyrrhonism. Analysis and calculation within the limits of knowledge were to be the weapons against the tyranny of ignorance and error.

The consequence, however, of Locke having set the limit and extent of human knowledge in terms of ideas arising from experience and their associations was, as Horkheimer has argued, a conception of reason that "has liquidated itself as an agency of ethical, moral, and religious insight."[37] The attempt, through a defense of toleration, to oppose both dogmatism and skepticism in those areas that exceed the limits of understanding was double-edged. If toleration was backed up by the methodological assumption that maximizing the competition of ideas will increase the chance for discovering the truth—as it was with John Stuart Mill later—then it made sense to extend the role of toleration in scientific inquiry to social reality. However, if toleration was a result of the limits of knowledge, that is, if it was urged because of the impossibility of settling conflicting opinions in those areas that exceed human understanding, then toleration becomes skepticism by another name, and in those areas where reason cannot settle conflicting opinions any opinion is as good as any other. Horkheimer has correctly observed that the idea of toleration is ambivalent since "on the one hand, tolerance means freedom from the rule of dogmatic authority; on the other, it furthers an attitude of neutrality toward all spiritual content, which it thus surrendered to relativism" (*Eclipse of Reason,* p. 19).[38] The consequence of the ambivalence of toleration for post-eighteenth-century culture has been analyzed by a variety of commentators from quite different political perspectives,[39] but is enough to note that the defense of toleration based on an epistemology of limits served less to defeat the skeptic's praise of ignorance than to legitimize it, since what the Pyrrhonian denied was the possibility of truth beyond appearances. Though Locke and Cordorcet had endorsed toleration as part of the critical function of reason, the effect was to constrict that function in proportion as the extent of knowledge was reduced.

For Condorcet, however, the extension of the methods of analysis and calculation to the moral sciences, and the consequences of the limits of knowledge for dogmatism, were to constitute only part of his response to the Pyrrhonian skeptic. The other part situated the success of science in a history of progress against power that was to establish the desirability of knowledge against the challenge of Pyrrhonism. The history of the progress of reason against power began in Condorcet's attempt to mediate conflicting views about the quality of earlier ages. In the second stage, where he speculated about the conditions of pastoral peoples, he observed:

> Some philosophers have pitied these savages, whilst others have praised them; what to some seems like wisdom and virtue, are by others branded as stupidity and idleness. The issue between these opposed attitudes will be resolved in the course of this book. We shall see why the progress of the mind has not always resulted in the progress of society towards happiness and virtue; how the combination of prejudice and error has polluted the good that should flow from knowledge but that depends more on its purity than on its extent. (*Sketch,* p. 24)

It is clear that the book was conceived at least in part as a response to Rousseau's *Discourses.* Rousseau had argued that progress in the arts and sciences had not contributed to virtue but had corrupted the self and society. The conclusion of the fourth stage obviously referred to Rousseau. "We shall prove that the eloquent declamations made against the arts and sciences are founded upon a mistaken application of history, and that, on the contrary, the progress of virtue has always gone hand in hand with that of enlightenment, just as the progress of corruption has always followed, or heralded, its decadence" (*Sketch,* p. 54). It is also clear that Condorcet was not arguing that a mere extension of knowledge would improve our condition. In fact the *Sketch* outlined a history of error and prejudice much more than a history of progress, and Condorcet connected the perpetuation of ignorance with domination. "[T]he way in which general errors are insinuated amongst people and are propagated, transmitted and perpetuated is all part of the historical picture of the progress of the human mind" (*Sketch,* p. 10).

A central theme of the *Sketch,* then, was the dialectical connection between ignorance, the progress of the sciences, and power.[40] Sounding a chord similar to Rousseau's in the *First Discourse,* he noted in the third stage of the *Sketch,* where he discussed early Greek science, that science would have remained in its infancy far longer had it not been for the fact that some families had made use of science as an instrument to gain power. "The progress of science was for them only a secondary aim, a means of perpetuating and extending their power. They sought truth only to spread error, and it is not strange that they found it so rarely" (*Sketch,* p. 36). In his discussion of China, he noted how the priestly caste had gained control of education "in order to train men to suffer more patiently the chains that had as it were, become identified with their existence, so that they were now without even the possibility of desiring to break them" (*Sketch,* p. 38). But unlike Rousseau's, his history of the progress of science was a history of the complicity of power and error, and of how science itself came to oppose power—a development of scientific reason from the service of power to the assertion of the authority of reason alone. Condorcet asserted that in the ninth stage, when the methods of analysis had spread from the natural sciences to public opinion, "force of persuasion on the part of governments, priestly intolerance, and even national prejudices, had all lost their deadly power to smother the voice of truth, and nothing could now protect the enemies of reason or the oppressors of freedom from a sentence to which the whole of Europe would soon subscribe" (*Sketch,* pp. 141–42).

Clearly the most hopeful aspect of Condorcet's historical vision was the progress of reason against power; because of that, the most troubling recent criticisms of Enlightenment values turn against this vision. In Horkheimer and Adorno's *Dialectic of Enlightenment,* for example, the triumph of reason over superstition and tyranny is indicted as merely the exchange of one form of tyranny for another. In Habermas's analysis of the relation between science, institutionalization, and government,[41] as well as in the sociology of scientific knowledge in the aftermath of Kuhn's history of science, the practice of science itself is treated in terms of relations of power. Foucault, in his analysis of modern power, exposed the complicity between the emergence of the human sciences and forms of discipline, coercion, and regimentation, and he did so within an analytic framework in which knowledge could not exist in the absence of power. I will return to these themes in later chapters both to develop the implications of recent attacks on Enlightenment values and to consider, in the final chapter, Richard Rorty's attempt to retain Enlightenment hope at the same time that he rejects the foundational and liberating project of philosophy and conceptions of human nature and universal history that sustained that hope for Condorcet.

Condorcet was able to support Enlightenment hope for the success of knowledge against power because of his conception of the necessity of progress in history. But just as MacIntyre has diagnosed the incoherence of the Enlightenment moral scheme in its rejection of the idea of a human telos that made the ancient scheme intelligible, our rejection of the teleological conception of history that gave voice to the hope for knowledge over power has reinstated the Pyrrhonian opposition to the liberating role of knowledge against power. The return of the Pyrrhonian challenge in Enlightenment terms can be seen in another way, in the Kantian attempt to connect knowledge, autonomy, and society in terms of universal history, and in the way our rejection of Kant's vision of universal history not only calls into question the progress of freedom but also the coherence of the relation between autonomy and community.

## V

It has been common—especially since Ernst Cassirer's elegant essay on Kant and Rousseau—to credit Rousseau with waking Kant from his moral slumber. While Kant had written that Rousseau taught him to respect mankind, the influence of Rousseau on Kant is at best paradoxical.[42] It is fairly easy to see how Kant extended Rousseau's notion of freedom as self-determination and self-dependency to an understanding of moral freedom in terms of rational beings as ends-in-themselves and of autonomy as self-legislation: "What else then can freedom of will be but autonomy—that is, the property which will has of being a law to itself?"[43] But Kant's departure from Rousseau was as significant as his indebtedness.[44] In his political and educational writings, he had characterized Rousseau's notion of freedom as "wild" or "raw" freedom to distinguish it from moral freedom. In his lecture notes on pedagogy, for example, he wrote of our original or natural instinct for freedom:

"this is not a noble instinct for freedom, as Rousseau and others maintain, but a certain rawness; for in this instance the animal has, so to speak, not yet developed the humanity within it" ("Pedagogy," p. 105); and in the "Universal History" he had claimed that culture was necessary for the transition from raw freedom to morality. While Rousseau had argued that culture leveled and degraded our original freedom, Kant had claimed that Nature, by willing discord and antagonism among us—the very sources of culture—had prevented that result and that the progress of the human species in history was the realization of the hidden plan of Nature to bring about freedom. Where Rousseau had rejected contract theories of government based on mutual self-interest and had argued that the progress of culture had replaced our true social bond with its mere appearance—a "knot" of reciprocal self-interests—Kant understood the origin of social relations and political freedom in terms of regulating and harmonizing conflicting self-interests. Whereas Rousseau had attempted to resolve the tension between self and society by recasting society in a way compatible with our original freedom, Kant had found in the tension itself—in our "unsocial sociability"—the very source of our progress and Nature's mechanism for achieving a universal cosmopolitan state. The source for Kant's departure from Rousseau as well as the basis for the success of Kant's response to Rousseau's attack on the connection between enlightenment, progress, and freedom is to be found in Kant's philosophy of history.

In the opening section of "The Idea of Universal History With Cosmopolitan Intent," Kant indicated the reason for his interest in the philosophy of history: human actions are the appearances of freedom of the will in history, and history allows us both "to hope that if we examine *the play of the human will's freedom in the large,* we can discover its course to conform to rules as well as to hope that what strikes us as complicated and unpredictable in the single individual may in the history of the entire species be discovered to be the steady progress and slow development of its original capacities" (p. 29). In the essay, and in the lectures on pedagogy, history is the progress of human freedom in the large, in which both the individual and the human species unconsciously proceed toward nature's end. The purpose of the essay was to find "a guiding thread" of history—"to discover whether there is some *natural objective* in this senseless course of human affairs, from which it may be possible to produce a history of creatures who proceed without a plan of their own but in conformity with some definite plan of nature's" ("Universal History," p. 30). The essay was developed in nine theses and led to the conclusion that the hidden plan of nature was the development toward "a universal *cosmopolitan state,* the womb in which all of the human species' original capacities will be developed" ("Universal History," p. 38). The realization of original human capacities in history is, in Lewis White Beck's phrase, "the dominance of morality over nature."[45]

The first thesis stated the basis for his teleological conception of nature: "All of a creature's natural capacities are destined to develop completely and in conformity with their end." If this were not so, then "we would no longer have a lawful but an aimlessly playing nature and hopeless chance takes the place of reason's guiding thread" ("Universal History," p. 30). Outside a teleological conception, history would present itself as incoherent. Though the source for the teleological conception was the projection of the development of individual capacities onto history, Kant thought that the completion in the development of our capacities in history will not be realized in any individual but only in the species as a whole. While Kant's philosophy of history is ironic in several respects, the most troubling is that his optimism for history and for the species does not extend equally to the individual. While we can achieve a degree of autonomy through self-legislation, individuals cannot hope to achieve the freedom that humanity as a whole will achieve through history. Individual autonomy ultimately makes sense only in terms of nature's plan for the progress of the species.

As I indicated when considering the controversy over the origin of the idea of progress, what was unique about the Enlightenment conception was that progress resulted not from the Divine Will but from our own effort through the growth of knowledge. While Kant wrote of progress resulting from nature's hidden plan through history, it turned out that that plan issued from the fact that nature had provided us only with what was minimally necessary for our survival, in order to assure that whatever progress was made, we achieved from the development and application of our own capacities. In addition to her stinginess, the means nature used in order that we develop entirely out of ourselves—we learn in the fourth thesis—is the *antagonism* between the individual and society. "I understand antagonism to mean men's *unsocial sociability,* i.e., their tendency to enter into society, combined, however, with a thoroughgoing resistance that constantly threatens to sunder this society" (pp. 31–32). The antagonism between self and society—what Hannah Arendt called "the secret ruse of nature"[46]—was, on Kant's view, essential for the development of our capacities and our progress toward a cosmopolitan state. The tension between our autonomy and community could not be resolved either on the side of extreme individualism or by the subordination of moral freedom to the sovereignty of the general will. Because our capacities could be developed and autonomy achieved only through antagonism, nature had prevented the resolution in terms of individualism. Furthermore, the result of suppressing autonomy in favor of sociability would be the very leveling out of individuality that, for Rousseau, in his criticism of the sciences and arts in the *First Discourse,* resulted from culture. With Kant, nature has prevented such a result as well. "Man wills concord; but nature better knows what is good for the species: she wills discord" ("Universal History," p. 32). Necessity compels us to give up unrestricted freedom since we cannot coexist for very long in wild freedom, but nature also decrees discord which prevents the individual from disolving into the social whole.

Two consequences follow from Kant's view of the antagonism of autonomy and community. First, the problem for the human species is how to achieve a civil society that "combines the greatest freedom, and thus a thoroughgoing antagonism among its members, with a precise determination and protection of the boundaries of this freedom, so that it can coexist with the freedom of others" ("Universal History," p. 33). Cassirer has set the problem for Kant's social philosophy this way: "The essential idea of social order consists not in bringing individual wills to a common level by force, but in preserving their individuality and hence their opposition, at the same time, however, defining the freedom of the individual in such a way that it discovers its own limits in other people."[47] Political freedom is the adjustment of autonomy to the needs of community. Second, it is out of this antagonism that Kant found the source of culture. "All the culture and art that adorn mankind, as well as the most beautiful social order, are fruits of unsociableness that is forced to discipline itself and thus through an imposed art to develop nature's seed completely" ("Universal History," p. 33). Contrary to Rousseau, culture was necessary for the transition from raw freedom to autonomy and, therefore, to morality.

Finally, just as nature had decreed antagonism between autonomy and sociability, it used this antagonism "even in the large societies and political bodies that are created through it, as a means for discovering a state of calm and security" ("Universal History," p. 34). On Kant's view, the history of the human species is the realization of the hidden plan of nature to bring about a final condition in which our capacities can be developed; and in seeing something of this plan of nature—the hidden thread of history—we are able to hasten its realization. That was the basis for Kant's optimism. "Although this body politic presently exists only in very rough outline, a feeling seems nonetheless to be already stirring among all its members who have an interest in the preservation of the whole, and this gives rise to the hope that, finally, after many revolutions of reform, nature's supreme objective—a universal *cosmopolitan state,* the womb in which all of the human species' original capacities will be developed—will at last come to be realized" ("Universal History," p. 38). The irony of Kant's optimism was that the ultimately desirable direction of history was the result of discord and conflict between individual and society and between peoples. His was a theodicy that vindicated the conflicts of our condition and the discord and antagonisms of culture that so troubled Rousseau in terms of nature's supreme objective.

Given Kant's notions of moral and political freedom and the secret plan of nature, the relation between autonomy and community can be understood in three ways that ultimately converge. Political community is a result of nature's hidden plan—the antagonism of our unsocial sociability—"since it is only in such a society that nature's highest objective, namely, the highest attainable development of mankind's capacities, can be achieved" ("Universal History," p. 33). At the basis of his conception of civil association is the notion of a social contract which restrains raw freedom and regulates conflicting interests through external coercion. But this notion of political community is merely a stage in the development of genuine community both because it is nature's mechanism for realizing a cosmopolitan state and because the idea of political association is consistent with what Kant referred to as an "ethical state of nature" in *Religion Within The Limits of Reason Alone.* Ethical community rests not on the social contract but on the demands of reason for morality and on the teleological conception of history. Because autonomy and morality are developed in terms of the demands of reason as such and the recognition of ourselves as rational agents, the law I give to myself is the law of all rational beings. In the *Groundwork of the Metaphysics of Morals,* Kant had made the point in terms of the Kingdom of Ends: "For rational beings all stand under the same *law* that each of them should treat himself and others, *never, merely, as a means,* but always *at the same time as an end in himself.* But by so doing there arises a systematic union of rational beings under common objective laws—that is, a kingdom" (*Groundwork,* p. 101). In *Religion Within The Limits of Reason Alone,* he made the point in terms of the transition from the ethical state of nature to the ethical commonwealth and the Kingdom of God, thus not only connecting the *I* of moral agency to the *we* of rational beings, but placing both within a teleological conception of the moral progress toward the Kingdom of God. "Now here we have a duty which is *sui generis,* not of men toward men, but of the human race toward itself. For the species of rational beings is objectively, in the idea of reason, destined for a social goal, namely, the promotion of the highest as a social good. . . . the highest moral good cannot be achieved merely by the exertions of the single individual toward his own moral perfection, but requires rather a union of such individuals into a whole toward the same goal."[48]

I need not explore the complexities of the relation between the political and ethical commonwealths or between autonomy and our duty to humanity as a whole, to make the general point of the relationship's dependence on the idea of progress toward the realization of the Kingdom of God or the cosmopolitan state. Outside of the goal of history, community is just the abstract recognition that we are brothers and sisters under the same categorical imperative which is far too thin a conception of community to support social solidarity;[49] and outside of such a conception of historical progress, civil society is just what Rousseau claimed it was—reciprocal self-interests and the appearance of community rather than a true social bond.[50] More recently Robert Paul Wolff has criticized this sort of individualistically based political theory because of the "serious confusion produced by the attempt to superimpose a collectivist sociology on an individualist liberal political philosophy";[51] and in perhaps the most penetrating critique of the political tradition of Kant and Rawls, Michael J. Sandel has claimed that a conception of autonomy and society that depends on the antecedent individuation of the autonomous subject cannot sustain a strong or constitutive sense of community.[52] In the same way that the coherence of power and knowledge for Bacon and scientific rationality and public good for Condorcet depend on the larger metaphysical and historical backdrop, the coherence of Kant's attempt to link emancipation, autonomy, and community depends on his universal history.

## VI

Our problem in the twentieth century is that we have inherited the Enlightenment conception of the connection between the growth of knowledge and the improvement of ourselves and society, as well as the Enlightenment conceptions of reason, autonomy, and hope for ourselves and the future, yet we have rejected the metaphysical structure and teleological conception of history that made the Enlightenment view plausible. We have retained eighteenth-century conceptions of freedom which have as their central feature the idea of individual self-determination, yet we seem no longer able—as Kant had been able within his universal history—to support both our autonomy and genuine community. The increase in power through the growth of knowledge appears increasingly to contribute to our unfreedom, and the application of scientific rationality to social reality appears to be at the expense of emancipation.

The success of the Enlightenment response to Pyrrhonism depended on the plausibility and coherence of the connections between knowledge and power, scientific reason and social reality, autonomy and community; but this response has been found to be deeply problematic in the absence of its supporting metaphysical and historical frame. In twentieth-century thought, the Enlightenment confidence in reason and progress has been called into question from a variety of directions. Horkheimer and Adorno have argued that the Enlightenment disenchanted the world, replacing myth with instrumental rationality; in so doing, it replaced one form of tyranny—the domination of dogmatism and superstition—with the tyranny of reason.[53] Heidegger, in his essays on technology and science, opposed the way technology, since the eighteenth century, projects all beings as resources, as "standing reserve" for the "total mobilization" of technology.[54] Gadamer has objected to the Enlightenment separation of reason from tradition, and he has sought to restore the historical nature of understanding and the authority of tradition as the source of values.[55] Michel Foucault has argued that the human sciences emerging from the Enlightenment were produced by, and themselves produced, distinctly modern and uniquely dangerous forms of power.[56] Alasdair MacIntyre has argued that the Enlightenment rejection of the older conception of man's telos and the virtues resulted in a fundamental incoherence in moral life that produced the unacceptable ethical alternatives of emotivism or Nietzschean nihilism.[57] Richard Rorty, in addition to his rejection of epistemology-centered philosophy, has opposed the Kantian basis for community and the connection between emancipation, historical progress, and cosmopolitanism.[58] This failure for twentieth-century thought of the Enlightenment project has reinstated the challenge of Pyrrhonian scepticism. In the following chapters, I will cast recent controversies concerning power, rationality, legitimacy, autonomy, and community in terms of the conflict over the Enlightenment project and the Pyrrhonian challenge to the place of philosophy for moral and social life.

# 3 Intellect and Culture

In the epistemological tradition after Descartes, skepticism was to lose its essentially moral aim, and the threat it posed for intellect was recast in theoretical rather than moral or social terms. The central challenge posed by skepticism in the epistemological literature after the seventeenth century—as a result of the infinite regress argument and the problem of the external world—was to the foundations of knowledge and the nature of representation rather than to the value of inquiry and the role of philosophy in common life. The practical or moral challenge of skepticism was to remain at work, however, not in the attacks on the foundations of knowledge but in attacks on the place of intellect and rational criticism in culture.

The place of reason in culture has been understood, at least since the eighteenth century, in terms of the role of the intellectual as critic of existing values, traditions, and institutions. That role had been made secure by grounding criticism in the nature of reason itself, or in terms of a philosophy of history as progress toward freedom, or in theories of human nature and natural rights, or on the basis of universal moral principles. To call the role of the intellectual as social critic into question served in one way or another as a challenge to the possibility of rationally grounded criticism of existing beliefs and values. In these terms the Pyrrhonian opposition to philosophy had both direct and indirect anti-intellectual consequences. Obviously, Pyrrhonian doubts about the value of the life of inquiry constituted direct opposition to the intellectual's claim for the necessity of rational criticism for the improvement of ourselves and society. Indirectly however, skepticism about the possibility of knowledge—even if not intended as a moral stance—provided aid and comfort to those outside of philosophy who attacked the life of intellect in order to establish some other source for wisdom than reason. In the first years of the Christian church, for example, disagreement among competing philosophical schools gave rise to skeptical arguments which undermined philosophy to make way for faith. In the Counter-Reformation, Pyrrhonism was placed in the service of vindicating the traditional authority of the Roman church. Since the seventeenth century, doubts about the possibility of certainty have been used variously to support truths of heart, sentiment, and the practical wisdom of the plain man against the claims of the intellect.

Because various forms of anti-intellectualism have become so much a part of contemporary life, the skeptical views that underwrite it and call philosophy and the life of reason into question are all the more troubling and challenging. Our recent history is marked by anti-intellectual attacks by fundamentalist preachers and populist politicians as much as by despots. But one must be careful about the charge of anti-intellectualism. Morton White has observed that "one of the more obvious features of the epithet 'anti-intellectualist' is its ambiguity."[1] It refers both to those who are hostile to intellectuals and the value of learning and to those who, like Pascal or William James, oppose certain intellectualist or cognitivist doctrines about the proper source of truth. White designates those who reject cognitivist doctrines of truth "anti-intellectualists" to distinguish them from those who are hostile to the life of intellect itself. Anti-intellectualists do not urge the abandonment of the life of learning; instead, they claim other sources for truth than cognition—sentiment perhaps, or revelation, or intuition, or nature. While this does not entail an attack on the role of philosophy in culture, it can serve to motivate it. It is not just the anti-intellectuals themselves who endanger the life of reason and against whom philosophy must assert itself. Both the indirect attack on reason in favor of other sources of wisdom and the direct hostility to intellectuals aid and abet irrationalism, emotionalism, and intolerance.

Leszek Kolakowski has cut the ambiguity of opposition to intellect at a slightly different but overlapping angle in terms of attacks on the claims for the universality of reason. On the one hand, such attacks may be launched against the view that some specific principles of reason and rules of verification apply to every possible subject matter. On the other, they may be attacks on the view that principles of reason apply equally to all human beings in every culture or every age. The first kind of attack on the universality of reason is not in itself culturally dangerous. Its most recent example could be more properly described as an attack on "scientism"—a rejection of the notion that the principles and methods of empirical scientific inquiry are the paradigm for all forms of knowledge. Other versions would include as diverse a range of opinions as support for revelation as a valid source of knowledge against rationalism in theology, opposition to the reduction of all reason to instrumental or procedural reason, and the claim that understanding in the human sciences is different in principle from explanation in the natural sciences. The second sort of attack, however, implies a pluralistic conception of rationality which runs the risk of undermining the possibility or the need for reasonable dialogue and rational consensus among alternative cultures or competing systems of belief. Criticism of the universality of reason in this second sense fosters a pernicious relativism on the one hand and invites dogmatism and fanaticism on the other.[2] It is the sort of danger that is thought to result from the "new philosophy of science" that follows the work of Thomas Kuhn, or from anthropological research which supports rational pluralism, or from the antihumanism of Heidegger or Foucault, or from such antifoundationalist and postmodernist writers as Jacques Derrida and Richard Rorty.

Philosophy has opposed the political tyrant, the fundamentalist preacher, and the populist demagogue by encouraging an even greater spread of reason to social reality in the name of freedom and social improvement. But when reason itself is charged with complicity in our social decay and the degradation of true freedom, philosophy must oppose the anti-intellectual by reestablishing the necessity of the life of reason for a life of virtue. I will turn to the relation between rational pluralism and relativism in later chapters. In this chapter, I will initiate the connection between skepticism, anti-intellectualism, and opposition to the traditional place of philosophy in culture by considering the case of Jean-Jacques Rousseau.

In the work that made Rousseau famous, the *Discourse on the Sciences and Arts,* he identified "a taste for philosophy" with vice rather than virtue and he argued against the mainline Enlightenment faith that the spread of reason and progress of knowledge would contribute to individual autonomy and the improvement of society. This first discourse has rarely been taken seriously by commentators, but I intend to bring it to the interpretative center, not only in order to understand the connection between Rousseau's critique of modernity and his view of freedom and genuine social relations but to use it as a case study of one sort of anti-intellectual challenge to the place of philosophy in culture. I will begin by considering the interpretive dilemma posed by Rousseau's critique of the sciences and arts, and I will place his critique in the larger context of a challenge to the traditional role of philosophy. After an initial exposition of his arguments, I will situate them between Pyrrhonism and the mainline Enlightenment view of the connection between knowledge and freedom. Finally, I will turn to a more careful consideration of the connection between his critique of the sciences, arts, and philosophy and his conception of the self and social relations in order to explore the connection between skepticism and anti-intellectualism and to set the stage for the emergence of this theme in recent discussions of power, rationality, and legitimacy.

## I

In Voltaire's well-known letter to Rousseau acknowledging receipt of his second discourse, the *Discourse on the Origin and Foundations of*

*Inequality,* Voltaire had written: "I have received your new book against mankind. I thank you for it. . . . You paint in most faithful colours the horrors of human society, from which ignorance and weakness expect so much pleasure. So much intelligence has never been used to seek to make us stupid. One is tempted to walk on all fours after reading your book."[3] Voltaire's assessment of this and Rousseau's earlier *Discourse on the Sciences and Arts* has been widely shared. In the *First Discourse* Rousseau opposed the Enlightenment conviction that progress in the arts and sciences contributed to the improvement of ourselves and society, and in the *Second Discourse* he located the source of inequality in modern forms of social organization and the requirements of intellect and culture. In these two *Discourses* he appeared to support a primitive individualism in opposition to the mainline Enlightenment conviction that public policy, modeled on progress in the sciences, arts, and philosophy, would produce an autonomous self and social equality. His condemnation of the place of learning in modern life had the ring of a dangerous anti-intellectualism in contrast to the Enlightenment confidence in the role of reason and philosophy in opposing tyranny and superstition.

Rousseau has posed many paradoxes for his readers, not the least of them being what to make of an apparently philosophical treatise on why learning and philosophy were destructive of virtue and a source of inequality. It is tempting to think that he was not opposed to philosophy at all, but only opposed to prevailing philosophical views. We will see a similar paradox in the final chapter, with the postmodernist attempt to end the philosophical tradition without becoming forever entangled in it as just another philosophical view. Though Rousseau's criticism has the form of a philosophical treatise, I shall argue that his aim was to oppose the traditional conception of philosophy since it led us away from nature and tradition, and that there is no inconsistency between the form and substance of his criticism.

Also paradoxical, Rousseau's conception of the wholeness and independence of the self antecedent to society, developed in the *Discourses,* appears to stand in contradiction to his view of the self as a fractional unity of the social body and of the absolutism of the general will in *The Social Contract.* And the *Discourses* appear to represent a self-defeating contradiction in Rousseau's own intellectual life as well. At the same time that he condemned the sciences and arts, he wrote plays and music and pursued a career as "a man of letters." While he viewed philosophy as an instance of the corruption of the modern self and attacked it for "loosening the social bond" and while he denied any intent to be a philosopher, he wrote philosophical treatises. He criticized the role of the intellectual in improving the morals of individuals or society, but he himself produced a thoroughgoing critique of corrupt social institutions in order to recast society in a form more suited to the true humanity of its members. How seriously are we to take his skepticism about the value of the sciences, arts, and philosophy and his hostility to the intellectual? Are we to dismiss his opposition to intellectual endeavor on the grounds of inconsistence with his more fully developed social theory? Is his attack on the corrupting effect of learning merely a local attack on French high culture of his day, or can it sustain the more general claim about the relation between knowledge and morals? To answer these questions it is necessary to explore the relation between his opposition to learning and the demands of culture and his conceptions of the self and society.

In 1749, the Academy of Dijon had proposed an essay competition for the following year on the question "Has the progress of the sciences and arts done more to corrupt morals or improve them?" Rousseau had only recently come to Paris, had been befriended by Diderot, and was involved in the *Encyclopédie* project. His reputation as a man of letters had not yet been made. He later described in his *Confessions* the effect the announcement of the question proposed by the Academy had had on him. "One day I took the *Mercure de France* and, glancing through it as I walked, I came upon this question. . . . The moment I read this I beheld another universe and became another man."[4]

Though Rousseau won the prize and secured his reputation with the *Discourse on the Sciences and Arts,* his own judgment of the work—and the judgment of commentators—makes it difficult to understand how, from the question and the subsequent essay, he "beheld another universe and became another man." In a "Foreword" added to the essay later he had asked: "What is celebrity? Here is the unfortunate work to which I owe mine. Certainly this piece, which won me a prize and made me famous, is at best mediocre, and I dare add that it is one of the slightest of this whole collection. What an abyss of miseries the author would have avoided if only this first written work had been received as it deserved to be!"[5] In the *Confessions* he had written that "the work. . . . though full of strength and fervour, is completely lacking in logic and order. Of all those that have proceeded from my pen it is the most feebly argued, the most deficient in proportion and harmony" (pp. 328–29).

Commentators have generally shared Rousseau's judgment of the work and dismissed it as an "occasional piece" contrived to achieve notoriety. Even so sympathetic a reader of Rousseau as Ernst Cassirer has called it "a mere rhetorical display piece" suggesting that it has "lost its hold on us; it no longer has the overwhelming power over us that it had on his contemporaries."[6] Bronislaw Baczko has explained the surprising negative answer Rousseau gave to the prize question in terms of the requirements for success in a society in which scandal was a social institution.[7] Robert Wokler has written that he "find[s] it difficult to disagree with Rousseau's own assessment of the text. Its rhetorical flourishes may well have merited the prize for which it was composed, but it seems to me much the least elegant, least consistent, least profound, and—despite the fuss that it stirred—least original of all his celebrated writings."[8]

Regardless of stylistic defects and regardless of how the *First Discourse* had figured in Rousseau's initiation as a man of letters, the theme of the essay—the role of the sciences, arts, and philosophy in the corruption of the self and of genuine social relations—was integral to the whole of Rousseau's thought, and the arguments of the essay are ones he returned to and elaborated on several other occasions. In bringing Rousseau's critique of the sciences, arts, and philosophy to the interpretive center, I want to suggest an essential relationship between the arguments first advanced in *Discourse on the Sciences and Arts* and Rousseau's subsequent conception of the self, freedom, and society. Those arguments are positioned between his conception of the self and the nature of society in a way that made possible the discovery of the true self anterior to culture at the same time that they provided a criticism of contract theories of society based on mutual benefit, a criticism which, in turn, revealed a conception of social relations that was true to the self free of the demands of culture. The way that this analysis of the demands of culture conditioned his view of the self and his subsequent recasting of society in *The Social Contract,* can be usefully structured in terms of a brief digression on Hannah Arendt's illuminating analysis of the transformation of the public and private realms in modern thought. It will also serve to anticipate the theme of autonomy and community that will emerge as the outcome of Richard Rorty's opposition to philosophy that I will turn to in the final chapter.

In *The Human Condition,* Arendt provided an account of how the rise of "the social realm" in the modern age had displaced the public realm at the same time that it invaded and redefined the private, and we can understand Rousseau's critique of modern society and the demands of culture in terms of Arendt's notion of the rise of the social realm in contrast to the private and the public. Her analysis began with the Greek distinction between the *polis* and the private domain of the household. The private was the sphere of necessity in which housekeeping administered the needs and requirements of life. The polis, on the other hand, was the realm of freedom—the public realm in which citizens met as equals. Her argument was that the emergence of society in the modern age transformed the distinction between private and public in a significant way. "The emergence of society—the rise of housekeeping, its activities, problems, and organizational devices—from the shadowy interior of the household into the light of the public sphere, has not only blurred the old borderline between private and political, it has also changed almost beyond recognition the meaning of the two terms and their significance for the life of the individual and the citizen."[9] The public domain had been not only the realm in which everything is "seen and heard by everybody and has the widest possible publicity" (*Human Condition,* p. 50); it signified the world common to all as distinct from one's private household. The public realm—the common world—is what gathered people together, relating them one to another. But the common world was not a world without diversity. In fact, Arendt wrote that "Being seen and being heard by others derive their significance from the fact that everybody sees and hears from a different position. . . . Only where things can be seen by many in a variety of aspects without changing their identity, so that those who are gathered around them know they see sameness in utter diversity, can worldly reality truly and reliably appear" (*Human Condition,* p. 57). In contrast to the public, society—growing out of the requirements for the administration of the household—levels out the plurality of the common world, "expect[ing] from each of its members a certain kind of behavior, imposing innumerable and various rules, all which tend to 'normalize' its members, to make them behave, to exclude spontaneous action or outstanding achievement" (*Human Condition,* p. 40).

At the same time that society produces the disappearance of the public realm, it invades and transforms the private. In the modern age, privacy is no longer understood in contrast to the public—that is, as the privation of the world of citizens—but in contrast to the social. It becomes the sphere of the "intimate," a sense of the private that must be secured and protected against the ever-expanding social realm, and Arendt credited Rousseau, more than any other modern thinker, with the discovery of the intimate. On Arendt's account, with the expansion of the social, not only was the private transformed, the common world was lost and in its place is "the unnatural conformism of a mass society."

In Arendt's terms, then, Rousseau's criticism of the sciences, arts, and philosophy can be seen as a diagnosis of the way the requirements of intellect and culture level out genuine individuality; and that diagnosis allowed him to discover an intimate or innermost conception of the self free from the requirements of society. Using that discovery, the task of *The Social Contract* was to recast the public realm—the creation of a public person—in a way that, unlike the requirements of culture, did not level out differences and did not exist at the expense of the genuinely autonomous self. The task, as Rousseau himself had presented it, was to find that form of association in which we enter society yet remain as free as before. I will claim that the arguments of the *First Discourse* are crucial both for the discovery of the true self and for recasting the public realm. Given the significance of Rousseau's conceptions of the self and society, then, we should take seriously the way the arguments of the *First Discourse* contribute to their formation.

Rousseau's view of freedom was, of course, at odds with the conception of freedom we identify with the Enlightenment. Whereas for Condorcet or Kant, freedom was the *achievement* of enlightenment, Rousseau argued that progress in the arts and sciences contributed to the degradation of the self and stifled that freedom which existed antecedent to society and progress. His attack on the corruption of modern society and the complicity of the sciences, arts and philosophy in that corruption, served to reveal and support a conception of the self and freedom that was the antithesis of the Enlightenment conception; it also was the antithesis of Enlightenment faith in the value of intellect or philosophy in realizing freedom.

Though Rousseau's critique of learning and society is significant in its own terms, it becomes all the more interesting when approached from the context of recent critiques of modernity and the modern conception of the self. Michel Foucault's last work, for example, was concerned with the way the modern conception of the self as an individual subject—the conception central to the emergence of the human sciences since the Enlightenment—resulted from and contributes to a uniquely dangerous form of power.[10] Like Rousseau, Foucault rejected the Enlightenment view that the sciences liberate the self, and he criticized modernity for "normalizing" and leveling out the marginal and producing our unfreedom. Richard Rorty has opposed the traditional conception of philosophy inherited from Plato—especially since Kant—that casts it in the role of "tribunal of reason" before which all inquiry must be judged, and in his recent work he has implied a conception of values that is not tied to the traditional notion of philosophy that attempts to secure the foundations of morals.[11] Because the traditional conception of philosophy and the central themes of the Enlightenment—the connections between reason, progress, and freedom—have been so much under attack in contemporary thought—by Heidegger and the Frankfurt School as well as by Arendt, Foucault, and Rorty—the arguments advanced in the *First Discourse* take on added significance. Though Cassirer was no doubt correct in 1950 when he wrote that the arguments of the *First Discourse* had lost their hold, for those of us troubled by recent critiques of philosophy, modernity, and the Enlightenment, they still constitute a challenge.

## II

The arguments of the *First Discourse* are deceptively straightforward. They are presented in summary fashion early in the first part of the essay, and are developed and defended in the remainder in two ways: first, through a series of historical arguments which were intended to support the claim that "our souls have been corrupted in proportion to the advancement of our sciences and arts toward perfection" (*Discourse,* p. 39); and second, through an analysis of the nature of the arts and sciences themselves which purported to show—beyond the "historical inductions"—that corruption *must* follow from their progress. The summary passage is this:

> the sciences, letters, and arts . . . spread garlands of flowers over the iron chains with which men are burdened, stifle in them the sense of that original liberty for which they seemed to be born, make them love their slavery, and turn them into what is called civilized peoples. Need raised thrones; the sciences and arts have strengthened them. . . . civilized peoples, cultivate talents: happy slaves, you owe to them that delicate and refined taste on which you pride yourselves; that softness of character and urbanity of customs . . . in a word, the semblance of all the virtues without the possession of any. (*Discourse,* p. 36)

Though Rousseau said that the arts and sciences make us love our chains, he did not think they were a mere cosmetic gloss on our slavery. The charges go much deeper. What was behind these charges became clear in the Preface to *Narcisse.* There he connected a taste for philosophy with the modern view of society in which one pursues the happiness of others in order to pursue one's own: "of all the truths I offer here to the consideration of wise men, this one is the most astonishing and the most cruel. Our writers like to regard absolutely everything as 'the political masterpiece of the century': the sciences, the arts, luxury, commerce, laws—and all other bonds which, in tightening the social knot with the force of personal interest, make men mutually dependent, give them reciprocal needs and common interests, and require that all pursue the happiness of others in order to be able to pursue their own."[12] The general point is that social relations based on mutual benefit make us dependent, and the requirements of civilized culture gloss that dependency thus obscuring the fact that we have achieved neither true freedom nor true community.

Michael Sandel has recently distinguished something like the sense of social relations criticized by Rousseau—what Sandel calls an instrumental account of community—from a stronger or constitutive sense of society, and the distinction will be useful for interpreting Rousseau. In the instrumental sense of community, "the subjects of co-operation are assumed to be governed by self-interested motivations alone, and the good of community consists solely in the advantages individuals derive from co-operating in pursuit of their egoistic ends;"[13] but in the strong sense, being a part of society or community is a central part of one's self-understanding as a moral agent. Although Sandel's distinction is part of an argument directed against the individualistically based liberal political theory of Kant and Rawls—an argument that liberal political theory cannot sustain this strong sense of community—one can read Rousseau as agreeing with Sandel about the inadequacies of a merely instrumental sense of society. And in these terms, Rousseau's criticism of an instrumental conception of social relations provided the basis for his attempt to develop a constitutive conception of society that was true to individual autonomy. The critical thrust of Rousseau's account was that the instrumental conception of society that was modeled, for example, on commercial interests substituted true freedom and a genuine social bond for their mere appearance—self-interest and mutual benefit.

Implied by this criticism was not only an attack on social philosophy that attempts to found social relations on contractual arrangements between self-interested parties, but also a significant redefinition of vice and virtue. Rousseau's innovation was the identification of vice with need, dependency, and the demands of culture, and his identification of virtue with true freedom.[14] I will return to a fuller account of this redefinition shortly. For now it is important to realize the initial point that the life of intellect played a double role in his diagnosis of the viciousness of modern society. First, it was born of unfree social relations—relations of need and dependency—and it reinforced them, destroying a genuine social bond. Second, it replaced true freedom—self-love and self-sufficiency—with mere self-interest.

Ronald Grimsley has written that as arguments or as historical demonstrations Rousseau's *Discourse* is not particularly impressive. "The significance of the *Discours* does not lie in what it seeks to prove but in what it actually says about the position of man in contemporary society; the manner of Rousseau's demonstration is far less important than his intuitive perception of a deep-seated malady which was hidden from most of his contemporaries and to which he himself was made sensitive by his particular personality and position as an 'outsider' living in a alien environment."[15] Though Grimsley is right about the interest of Rousseau's insights into contemporary society, I shall suggest in Section IV that when the arguments of the *First Discourse* are situated in the more general context of Rousseau's conception of the self and freedom, they are indeed impressive and they pose a serious challenge to the role of philosophy in the service of freedom. For now the point needs making that if the significance of the *First Discourse* were to rest simply on his insights into modern society—insights that were not particularly original since he shared them with Montaigne, Hobbes, Mandeville, and many others[16]—the essay would deserve the neglect so often accorded it. It is not the perception of the corruption of modernity but his genealogy of that corruption that makes the arguments of the essay important.

Grimsley is also right in noting the relationship between Rousseau's own position with respect to contemporary society and his criticism of it. In few other writers was there so intimate a connection between the inner life of the author and the substance of his thought. Rousseau's acute sense of his place at the margins of modern society was the starting-point for his critique. At the end of his life he had written: "I am now alone on earth, no longer having any brother, neighbor, friend, or society other than myself. The most sociable and the most loving of humans had been proscribed from society by an unanimous agreement."[17] And though he was referring to his most recent condition of exclusion, he had always been and felt himself an "outsider."[18] What he had written of Molière's misanthrope in the letter to d'Alembert on the theatre could be said equally of himself: "who then is the misanthrope of Molière? A good man who detests the morals of his age and the viciousness of his contemporaries; who, precisely because he loves his fellow creatures, hates in them the evils they do to one another."[19]

It was his position at the margin of society—his own resistance to the leveling-out effects of learning and the dependency required by culture—that was the fulcrum of his critique. Just as he had, in his autobiographical writings, attempted to come to terms with the tension between himself and his social circumstances, his critique of modernity was an attempt to reconcile the virtuous self—that is, true freedom—with the requirements of society.[20] His attack on the sciences, arts, and philosophy, and his analysis of the origins of inequality constituted the negative phase of that project. The *Discourses,* by their identification of the viciousness of modern society with an unfree self and corrupt social relations, aimed at uncovering true freedom in what was natural to the self independent of society. His philosophy of education in *Emile* and his view of society in *The Social Contract* were the constructive part of his attempt to reconcile self with society by recasting society in terms of freedom.

Equally important for my purpose, the arguments of the *First Discourse* and the development of those arguments in the Preface to his play *Narcisse* and in the "Letter to M. d'Alembert on the Theater" laid a foundation for criticizing society and realizing freedom. That effort constituted a serious alternative both to Pyrrhonian skepticism, which appeared to eliminate a basis for social criticism, and to the mainline Enlightenment conviction that liberation of the individual could be achieved only through the progress of reason. The Pyrrhonian skeptics had opposed the dogma of philosophy and merely acquiesced in the customs and traditions of daily life. Condorcet and Kant, each in their own way, had attempted to establish the authority of rational critique as the tribunal before which every belief and institution must be judged. In his attack on progress in the sciences and the arts, Rousseau—by resisting the requirements of culture—sought to uncover the authority of *nature,* by which modernity was to be judged and self and society were to be reconciled. In this sense, his apparently philosophical treatises were opposed to the philosophical theme, expounded since Plato, that virtue was to be found only in the philosophical attempt to transcend sentiment or tradition. His alternative, which was opposed both to Pyrrhonism and the Enlightenment, attacked the life of intellect in order to recover virtue and recast society in terms of freedom.

Before we turn to a more careful analysis of his arguments, it is necessary to fill out the way his position is situated between Pyrrhonism and the Enlightenment. In the final section, I will return to the issue of his social marginality and to the problem of anti-intellectualism.

## III

In condemning the sciences, arts, and a taste for philosophy, Rousseau defined his own project in opposition to philosophy. A typical passage from the *First Discourse* sums up his attitude toward philosophy:

> [W]hat is philosophy? What do the writings of the best known philosophers contain? What are the teachings of these lovers of wisdom? To listen to them, would one not take them for a troop of charlatans, each crying from his own spot on the public square: Come to me, I alone do not deceive. One holds that there are no bodies and that everything is appearance. Another that there is no substance other than matter, nor any God but the world. This one suggests that there are neither virtues nor vices and that moral good and evil are chimeras. That one that men are wolves and can devour one another with clear conscience. O great philosophers, why don't you save these profitable

lessons for your friends and children; you would soon reap the reward, and we would have no fear of finding among ourselves any of your followers. (*Discourses,* p. 60)

I think we can get a sense of Rousseau's view of his own work in terms of what he wrote of the "Profession of Faith of the Savoyard Vicar" in *Emile:* "I am not a great philosopher, and I care little to be one. But I sometimes have good sense, and I always love the truth. I do not want to argue with you or even attempt to convince you. It is enough for me to reveal to you what I think in the simplicity of my heart."[21] In a related remark it is also clear what Rousseau's view of his own work was in contrast to that of "great philosophers" and what he hoped to reveal: "As for me—I who have no system to maintain, I, a simple and true man who is carried away by the fury of no party and does not aspire to the honor of being chief of a sect, I who am content with the place in which God has put me, I see nothing, except for Him that is better than my species. And if I had to choose my place in the order of beings, what more could I choose than to be a man?" (*Emile,* p. 278).

The significance of these remarks in the context of the arguments of the *First Discourse* is that Rousseau, unlike the philosophes of the French Enlightenment, saw philosophy standing in opposition to our true selves. The rejection of philosophy was part of the project of restoring virtue, which he now identified with our true freedom. His were not books against mankind, as Voltaire would have it, but books that attack the claims of philosophy in order to recover the true self.

Though Rousseau condemned philosophy in the *First Discourse* and wondered whether knowledge and virtue might not be incompatible, he also opposed "a dangerous Pyrrhonism." His attack on progress in the sciences and arts shared many Pyrrhonian themes, but he opposed the possibility of a sustained skepticism in much the way that Hume had. In the "Profession of Faith of the Savoyard Vicar," Rousseau wrote: "I was in that frame of mind of uncertainty and doubt that Descartes demands for the quest for truth. This state is hardly made to last. It is disturbing and painful. It is only the self-interest of vice or laziness of soul which leaves us in it" (*Emile,* p. 267). The Savoyard Vicar had asked: "How can one systematically and in good faith be a skeptic? I cannot understand it. These skeptic philosophers either do not exist or are the unhappiest of men. Doubt about the things it is important for us to know is too violent a state for the human mind, which does not hold out in this state for long" (*Emile,* p. 268). Like Hume, Rousseau acknowledged the initial benefit of skeptical doubt to combat dogmatic philosophy, but also like Hume he believed that nature prevented us from remaining in such a condition. Furthermore, striking a tone rather like that of Locke in the introduction to his *Essay Concerning Human Understanding,* Rousseau understood that the benefit of skepticism was "to learn to limit my researches to what was immediately related to my interest, [and] to leave myself in a profound ignorance of all the rest" (*Emile,* p. 269).

With the Pyrrhonian skeptics, he opposed philosophy by doubting the necessity of knowledge for virtue. As in Hume's post-Pyrrhonism, sustained doubt was resolved by the acceptance of nature and sentiment. Whereas Descartes had resolved only to accept those ideas as certain that were clear and distinct, the methodological starting point for Rousseau was "to accept as evident all knowledge to which in the sincerity of my heart I cannot refuse my consent" (*Emile,* p. 270)—the simplicity and immediacy of sentiment rather than the self-evidence of rational principle was to be his foundation. And, ironically, he thought that his principle of yielding to sentiment was confirmed by reason itself. In contrast to what Kant would later argue, Rousseau claimed that "I know only that truth is in things and not in the mind which judges them, and that the less of myself I put in the judgments I make, the more sure I am of approaching the truth. Thus my rule of yielding to sentiment more than reason is confirmed by reason itself" (*Emile,* p. 272).

He had challenged the possibility of sustained uncertainty, yet in the *First Discourse,* in the Preface to his play *Narcisse,* and in the "Letter to M. d'Alembert on the Theatre" he had exposed the role of knowledge in the corruption of the self and modern society. In *Emile* he had claimed that "We can be men without being scholars" (*Emile,* p. 290). In the context of his attack on learning, Rousseau seemed to be saying something much stronger: "We can be men only if we are not scholars." In the Preface to *Narcisse,* he concluded that "reflection can only make [man] unhappy, without making him either wiser or better. . . . [we] have to maintain a wary guard against the sciences; and, above all, against those savants whose sententious and dogmatic maxims would soon teach men to scorn both their usages and their laws" ("Preface," p. 550–51).

The French Enlightenment had surely been the age of the intellectual par excellence. The philosophes believed and practiced what Kant later summed up in the Preface to the *Critique of Pure Reason:* "Our age is, in especial degree, the age of criticism, and to criticism everything must submit."[22] Rousseau's argument against the value of the arts and sciences and his rejection of that taste for philosophy which undermines custom and traditional morality must be understood in that context. His was no crude anti-intellectualism, but it was an anti-intellectualism nonetheless. For that reason, his *First Discourse* poses a problem for philosophy. It was not contrived merely to shock and amuse,[23] nor can it be dismissed as inconsistent with the rest of Rousseau's work. His resolve to yield to sentiment and his conception of what was natural and original to the self prior to the corruption of modern society provided an alternative to the philosophical claim that knowledge was necessary for virtue and an Archimedean point from which to criticize modernity. If philosophy is to reassert itself against anti-intellectualism and claim a role in the process of liberating the self, it must reckon with Rousseau's arguments, so it is necessary to give them more careful attention.

## IV

The *First Discourse* was structured around two sorts of arguments: first, Rousseau offered a series of "historical inductions"—the cases of Egypt, Athens, China, Rome, and so forth—in support of his claim that those cultures in which the sciences and arts had flourished were also the ones that were the weakest and most corrupt; and second, he provided an account of the arts and sciences themselves that aimed to show why such weakness and corruption was a *necessary* consequence of their progress. Most critics have focused on the historical arguments and found them unpersuasive, concluding—as Rousseau himself knew—that at best they supported only a coincidental connection between progress of the sciences and arts and social corruption. When it comes to the claim that one is a necessary consequence of the other, either it is suggested that Rousseau had failed to make good on the claim or that he was equivocal between the arguments that the arts and sciences were the cause of the corruptions of society or the much weaker claim that they were merely an effect.[24]

My suggestion, however, is that the thrust of Rousseau's criticism lies not in the causal role of the sciences, arts, and philosophy in the corruption of the self and society. Rather, he criticized them as extreme examples of the inequality and corruption of the self and social relations which had become the norm in modern society.

The first link he found between philosophy and corruption was the relationship it reinforced between intellectual endeavor, admiration for talent, and moral and political inequality. Though it was not developed in detail until the *Discourse on the Origin and Foundations of Inequality,* the theme of this *Second Discourse* was foreshadowed in the first. Having catalogued various ways in which the sciences and arts had contributed to the dissolution of morals, Rousseau had asked rhetorically: "What brings about all these abuses if not the disastrous inequality introduced among men by the distinction of talents and the debasement of virtues? That is the most evident effect of all our studies and the most dangerous of all their consequences" (*Discourses,* p. 58). In the *Second Discourse,* Rousseau had distinguished between natural or physical inequality that resulted from differences in health, strength, age, qualities of mind, and so forth; and moral or political inequality—"the different privileges that some men enjoy to the prejudice of others, such as to be richer, more honored, more powerful than they or even to make themselves obeyed by them" (*Discourses,* p. 101). The purpose of the *Second Discourse* was to show how the latter sort of inequality originated out of social organization; and, of course, the device for tracing the progress of moral inequality was the conception of the state of nature.

Rousseau acknowledged that other philosophers had sought the origins of society by going back to the state of nature, but he claimed that none but him had reached it. They had attributed to natural man and the state of nature all that they found corrupt and vicious in contemporary society. "All of them, finally, speaking continually of need, avarice, oppression, desires, and pride, have carried over to the state of nature ideas they had acquired in society: They spoke about savage man and they described civil man" (*Discourses,* p. 102). He could agree that Hobbes's portrait of man driven by self-interest accurately represented civilized man. But Rousseau, like Condorcet, denied that it accurately described human beings in the state of nature.[25] "Stripping this being . . . of all the supernatural gifts he could have received and of all the artificial faculties he could only have acquired by long progress" (*Discourse,* p. 105), Rousseau painted an altogether different picture.

Rousseau's device of the state of nature worked roughly like Descartes' hypothetical doubt—it eliminated everything accidental or unessential to human nature in order to focus clearly on what was original, in the way that Cartesian doubt stripped away everything that was merely probable in order to reveal what was clear and distinct about the *cogito.* The conjecture of a state of nature was not designed to identify a condition historically anterior to the corruption of modern life, though Rousseau sometimes appeared to use it that way. It did not seek to recover some pristine past to which we might hope to return. Instead, it revealed one pole of a tension between the self and others that exists in modern life[26] and that Rousseau had captured in the opening chapter of *The Social Contract*—"Man was born free, and he is everywhere in chains" (p. 49).

In its original condition, the freedom of the self consists in its wholeness and self-sufficiency. Freedom is not so much independence from others or independence of any social arrangements, since that would define it entirely negatively and in terms of external conditions. On Rousseau's account, freedom is an internal completeness. In *Emile,* for example, he wrote: "Natural man is entirely for himself. He is numerical unity, the absolute whole which is relative only to itself or its kind" (p. 39). He called this form of internal unity and self-love that is natural to man *amour de soi.* It arises entirely from within the self and is distinct from that corrupt form of self-love—*amour-propre*—which is the result of seeing ourselves in relation to others. Rousseau's notion of *amour-propre* thus had features similar to Nietzsche's notion of *ressentiment* in *The Genealogy of Morals,* where he distinguished master morality from slave morality. The values of master morality arose from within—from an affirmation of oneself. *Ressentiment,* according to Nietzsche, was the source of slave values—values that arose by negating what was other than or outside oneself. For Rousseau, because the self was defined in terms of others, *amour-propre* was self-interest as opposed to self-love. Not only was it the source of inevitable conflict with others, it becomes the source of our alienation from ourselves. "The wicked man fears and flees himself. He cheers himself by rushing outside of himself. . . . By contrast, the serenity of the just man is internal. . . . He is as gay alone as in the midst of a circle. He does not draw his contentment from those who come near him" (*Emile,* p. 288).

The unfree self—the self of modern society—is the self defined by its relation to others. This corrupt form of self-love arises hand-in-hand with a corrupt form of social relations. Rousseau's analysis of the role of the sciences and arts in the corruption of modern society in the *Discourses* aimed at showing how the true social bond based on esteem and good will between self-dependent individuals was replaced by a "social knot" which tied us together through dependency, need, and reciprocal interests with the result that we appear to act out of an interest in others but always actually relate everything to ourselves alone. True freedom and true social duty are replaced by their appearance—self-interest and social relations cast on the model of commercial relations.

It is standard to oppose Rousseau by arguing that there is a contradiction between his apparently intensely individualistic conception of freedom in the *Discourses* and *Emile,* and the absolutism of the public person suggested by his notion of the general will in *The Social Contract.* We cannot resolve the contradiction either by rejecting his conception of freedom or by minimizing the role of the social pact in our moral transformation. I think we must take seriously Rousseau's own formulation of this problem that *The Social Contract* was supposed to answer: "How to find a form of association . . . under which each individual, while uniting himself with the others, obeys no one but himself, and remains free as before" (*Contract,* p. 60). If what is essential to our freedom is not so much our separation from others but our self-containment and personal wholeness, then freedom need not be at odds with genuine social relations or a conception of the general will. The problem for Rousseau—and for Kant later—was how to integrate this conception of freedom or autonomy with that of social order. What appears as a contradiction in Rousseau is, in part, his recognition of the deep tension that exists in social life. In society, we are both for ourselves and for others, and the positive phase of Rousseau's project aimed at a form of association that resolved the tension in a way that created a genuine social whole consistent with self-dependency.[27]

It is not my purpose to say whether Rousseau succeeded in making good this vision. My aim is to place the arguments against the sciences, arts, and philosophy at the center of Rousseau's account of the failure of modernity to resolve the tension. The significance of the two *Discourses* is Rousseau's diagnosis of how modern society had attempted to resolve the tension by creating "double men"—ones who give the appearance of acting out of the interest of others while acting only for themselves and who found society on relations of reciprocal interests rather than on social duty. On Rousseau's account, such a resolution yields neither true autonomy nor true community. In *Emile,* he had written that "the good man orders himself in relation to the whole, and the wicked one orders the whole in relation to himself" (p. 292). The failure of modern society was seen in its attempt to give wickedness the appearance of virtue. His opposition to the Enlightenment faith in the connection between the progress of learning and the improvement of ourselves and society finds in the sciences and arts an unusually clear example of the failure of modern society.

In both the first and second *Discourses* Rousseau was acutely conscious of the failure of modern social theory to resolve the tension between self and society, and together the *Discourses* served as a partial diagnosis of the failure. His claim that the sciences, arts, and philosophy are born of vice was the claim that they are possible only within a social arrangement based on mutual needs—in this case, the needs of the mind rather than the body—and the desire for pleasure and approval that attends them. Thus the sciences, arts, and philosophy, just as much as commercial relations, bind us through dependency rather than esteem and good will. This point needs to be developed.

The result of considering only what was essential to the self in the state of nature and of identifying virtue with the freedom of the self in its original condition was that the various talents and capacities associated with intellectual endeavors were shown to be artificial and, therefore, not essential for virtue. In the Preface to *Narcisse,* however, Rousseau argued not only that knowledge was not essential for virtue, he claimed in two connected arguments that intellectual endeavor was actually destructive of virtue. First, the source for an interest in arts, letters, and philosophy was a desire for distinction, thus intellectual endeavor annihilated a love of duty and true virtue. In this argument, the criticism of philosophy, I think, is just an instance of the more general analysis of *amour-propre.* Second, talent in arts, letters, and philosophy was praised and rewarded when, in fact, it was something one had by accident. To think, therefore, that virtue was achieved through inquiry, connected virtue to the accidental rather than the essential. But it was not just that individuals pursued philosophy out of vanity, or that philosophers supported conceptions of freedom and social theory based on self-interest, or even that they were praised for the talents they had by accident. Progress in the sciences, arts, and philosophy reflected and reinforced the wickedness of modern morals.

This last point can be developed in terms of Rousseau's criticism of the theatre. In the letter to d'Alembert,[28] Rousseau had argued that the theater cannot be expected to change morals since it merely follows, reflects, and intensifies public sentiment. "The love of the [morally] beautiful is a sentiment as natural to the human heart as the love of self; it is not born out of an arrangement of scenes" ("Letter," p. 20). Though much of the criticism was specific to the drama and to the theater as entertainment, this point can be extended to the sciences and arts generally. Because they are born of need—albeit the needs of the mind rather than of the body—and the social relations proper to fulfillment of needs, they reflect, in the name of virtue and social duty, its exterior appearance. They are the most extreme example of *amour-propre.* Not only did Rousseau think they divert us from the love of the morally beautiful that is natural to us, they are an instance of our enslavement. In a footnote in the *First Discourse* where he had observed that princes promote pleasures as so many chains that bind the people, Rousseau had asked rhetorically: "Indeed, what yoke could be imposed on men who need nothing?" (p. 36n). But since the sciences, arts, and philosophy are born of and reinforce relations of dependency, they cannot serve the cause of freedom; instead, they "spread garlands of flowers over the iron chains" with which we are burdened.

## V

Finally, it is necessary to consider how Rousseau's skepticism about the value of knowledge is a problematic anti-intellectualism that poses a challenge to philosophy. First, in what sense is Rousseau's indictment of learning a form of anti-intellectualism? The answer is not straightforward, and it is partly as a result of that—because his was no simple-minded hostility to intellectuals—that Rousseau poses a problem for philosophy. Rousseau was obviously an anti-intellectualist in Morton White's sense of the term—supporting sentiment rather than reason as the criterion for truth—but his hostility to the life of intellect was paradoxical at best. At the same time that he was critical of the arts and sciences and could write, as he had in *Emile,* "take away our fatal progress, take away our errors and our vices, take away the work of man, and everything is good" (p. 282), he praised the few great thinkers who "raise monuments to the glory of human intellect" (*Discourses,* p. 63). It is tempting to think that Rousseau's hostility to the life of intellect is only apparent—that he was only attacking the effect of learning on the common herd of humanity and that he was opposing the way this common learning levels out individuality and genius. Though there is evidence in the texts to support this view, his anti-intellectualism was both real and general. While part of his criticism of learning was that it leveled out originality—stamping everyone from the same mold—he believed that even the work of the few great thinkers could not improve morality and, in fact, was antithetical to virtue and social duty.

Though he expressed admiration for the few great thinkers, he did not suppress his hostility for the intellectuals of his day, and it is significant that our notion of the intellectual is closely bound up with the role of philosophy and rational criticism in liberal social theory assigned by Rousseau's Enlightenment contemporaries. It is that notion that was opposed by Rousseau. The intellectual calls everything into question, standing opposed to tradition, subjecting it and the existing order to rational scrutiny in order to liberate us from tyranny and superstition.[29] The Enlightenment hope of liberation from tradition and sentiment, however, was enslavement in disguise. Rousseau's position aimed to secure natural sentiment and tradition against claims for the priority of reason, and he had in fact urged that we be on guard against those who would undermine custom and tradition. He warned that "customs are the moral life of a people, and as soon as they cease to respect them, there is no rule but the passions, no restraint but the laws" ("Preface," pp. 550–51). But Rousseau—unlike the Pyrrhonism of Sextus or the use made of Pyrrhonism in the sixteenth century in the support of the traditional authority of the Roman church—did not eliminate a basis for opposing social values and institutions. The *First Discourse* was just such an opposition. It was an opposition that was made possible, in part, by Rousseau's own marginal status, and it was not grounded in terms of the Enlightenment claims for the centrality of the intellectual in culture—since that resulted in the leveling of genius that Rousseau had attributed to the sciences and letters; nor could it be grounded in the progress of scientific reason or in the Platonic demand that we transcend the beliefs and practices of common life. Instead it was grounded in what sentiment revealed—a conception of the self and freedom untainted by the corruption of learning and society.

His hostility to the life of intellect operated, then, at several levels at once. He did indeed despise French high culture of his day. That culture, elevating the status of the intellectual and the role of the sciences and letters, replaced virtue with its mere appearance and assured that all minds would be stamped in the same mold. He opposed the philosophical theories which attempted to resolve the tension between the individual and society in terms of harmonizing self-interests. He opposed rationalist claims for the priority of reason over sentiment and tradition. He opposed the view that the progress of inquiry was necessary for virtue and argued that, in fact, they were antithetical. There is a problem posed by his criticism of the role of intellect and reason, as well as by his criticism of the modern conception of the self and virtue that he made from his position at the margin of culture—a position that allowed him to recover tradition and discover a conception of the self that sentiment revealed. It is not just that his attack on the progress of learning might give aid and comfort to irrationalism—though it had that effect. What is at risk is the traditional conception of philosophy itself for understanding the place of the intellectual in culture. Not only did Rousseau deny philosophy the central critical role in liberating the self it had held since Plato, and not only did he criticize the practice of philosophy as paradigmatic of and a contributor to that very corruption of the self and false freedom that he had found in modern society, his own way of opposing modernity had the effect of marginalizing the nature of cultural criticism. Not only his personal circumstances but his form of criticism suggested a model for cultural criticism based not on the notion of critic as cultural overseer who brings all beliefs and values before the norms of reason but on the notion of critic as outsider who calls those norms of reason into question. It is to this theme of the marginality of cultural criticism suggested by the nature of Rousseau's criticism in the *Discourses* that I shall return in the final chapter, since I think Richard Rorty's opposition to the traditional conception of philosophy and his notion of the edifying thinker as a peripheral and abnormal thinker share this shift of the critical function of intellect from the center to the margin.

# 4 Knowledge and Power

Since Bacon and the Enlightenment, we have been accustomed to think of the relation of power to knowledge in two ways. First, following Bacon's utilitarian account of science, we have related power to knowledge as effect to cause. The growth of science will give us power over ourselves and nature. Second, following the liberal tradition of Locke and Condorcet, we have opposed power to knowledge in the sense that knowledge can exist only in the absence of repression or coercion. The importance the Enlightenment attached to the moral or human sciences can be understood in terms of both of these ways in which power is related to knowledge. Whereas the growth of scientific knowledge could be repressed by the exercise of power, the extension of its methods to the human sciences and its application to social reality would eventually free us from the tyranny of princes, prejudice, and ignorance. The hope of the Enlightenment was that the application of scientific reason to the human disciplines would yield success with respect to our moral and social improvement comparable to success in the natural sciences with respect to our control over nature.

Though we tend to think of someone such as Condorcet in terms of this Enlightenment hope, we find it even in an otherwise ambivalent Enlightenment enthusiast such as David Hume. It is clear that Hume's turn to the human sciences sprang both from epistemological and moral motives. Epistemologically, it arose from the insight that all of the sciences rest ultimately on the science of man. Morally, it arose from the conviction that understanding human understanding would contribute to our improved condition. The opening sentence of his *Enquiry Concerning Human Understanding* contrasted two approaches to moral philosophy—the one which takes us to be born for action, the other as born for reason—but Hume quickly acknowledged that while each approach has its peculiar merit, both contribute to "the entertainment, instruction, and reformation of mankind."[1] He observed that no matter how remote abstract philosophy might become from matters of business and common life, "the genius of philosophy, if carefully cultivated by several, must gradually diffuse itself throughout every art and calling," and with the diffusion of the moral or the human sciences, whether abstract or practical, "[t]he politician will acquire greater foresight and subtility . . . the lawyer more method and finer principles . . .

the general more regularity in his discipline, and more caution in his plans and operations" (*Enquiries,* p. 10).

This Enlightenment view of the human sciences and their relation to the improvement of ourselves and society has come under attack in recent thought from two directions: first, in terms of opposition to the attempt to model the human sciences on the methods and aims of the natural sciences; and second, in terms of opposition to the view that knowledge in the human sciences will free us by giving us power over ourselves.

Opposition to the reduction of the human to the natural sciences is usually treated as an ontological and methodological dispute. Treated this way, the issue is whether there is something special about human beings that makes them fundamentally different from the objects of the natural sciences, and whether such differences, if they exist, have consequences with respect to method. In a recent version of the debate, for example, Charles Taylor has claimed that human beings are self-interpreting, and therefore that a study with human beings as its subject could never achieve an interest-free decontextualization of its subject matter in the way that Galileo had made possible for physics. Taylor has argued that a social science attempting to reconstruct social reality on the model of the natural sciences would exclude from it the fact that social reality is constructed out of intersubjective and common meanings, and that while the natural sciences can eschew context or subject-related properties, the kind of understanding required in the human sciences cannot.[2]

Against this view one could argue as, for example, Mary Hesse has[3] that it is wrong to think that the natural sciences have achieved the decontextualization of their subject matter in the way that positivism and logical empiricism had led us to believe, and that there is no ontological or methodological distinction between the natural and human sciences since the natural sciences must also be approached interpretively. Or one could argue, as Richard Rorty has,[4] that one could achieve the same sort of decontextualized account of human beings as Galileo made possible for physics if one wanted; that nothing about human beings would prevent developing the sort of description which treats human beings as objects. For Rorty the difference between the human and natural sciences is not ontological or methodological but merely pragmatic.

Another way of looking at the controversy over the relation between the natural and human sciences is as a political dispute. On this view, the issue turns on the Enlightenment hope that the human sciences would produce our freedom. According to one line of thought, for example, the reduction of the methods of the human sciences to those of the natural sciences, far from liberating us from tyranny and superstition, has shaped the human sciences as tools to repress real human interests and has placed the human sciences in the service of power. On this view, the spread of scientific reason to social reality merely replaced one form of domination with another. This is the view of certain Frankfurt School "critical social theorists" who argue for a distinction between the natural and human sciences by maintaining that the aim of understanding in the human sciences—unlike explanation in the natural sciences—should be emancipation from false consciousness or from ideologically distorted conceptions of ourselves.[5]

The work of Michel Foucault has important implications for both ways of viewing the controversy. In *The Order of Things,* the ontological dispute is taken as just a wearisome series of possible moves in a game made possible by the Enlightenment concept of "man" (a technical term for Foucault that I shall explain shortly) central to the emergence of the human sciences. In *Discipline and Punish,* in *The History of Sexuality,* vol. 1, and in the interviews and lectures published as *Power/Knowledge,* he argued that what made the human sciences possible was not an advance of reason into the domain of human behavior and social reality, but the emergence of new forms of coercive and disciplinary techniques for control and regimentation of our bodies. Unlike the Frankfurt social theorists, however, Foucault did not think that we could be liberated from the complicity of power and knowledge. Instead, he argued that knowledge could not exist where power is absent, nor power in the absence of knowledge. By juxtaposing power and knowledge as "power/knowledge," by understanding power/knowledge as a grid or web of relations that structures all of our actions, by rejecting the possibility that knowledge could provide independent normative criteria for criticizing regimes of power, and by arguing that an analysis of modern forms of power will not emancipate us from forms of power/knowledge in the way the liberal and Marxist traditions had envisioned, Foucault's work has been seen by many as the antithesis of Enlightenment hope. I think, therefore, that the question concerning Enlightenment commitment to the place of the human sciences in the project of freedom can be brought to focus in the confrontation between the work of Foucault and his critics.

The ambiguity and denseness of Foucault's work lends a certain amount of support for the charges that he is anti-Enlightenment. His analysis of power appears not to be able to support a philosophically grounded political stance against modern forms of repression, and his work provides no hope for a power-free and improved future. In his archaeological works on madness, the clinic, and the human sciences, it is clear that while he was interested in the emergence and transformation of large-scale historical systems, his work was not a philosophy of history which offered a vision of either historical progress or decay. In his genealogical works on the prison and sexuality, he described his work as a "felicitous positivism" and he eschewed any normative framework for criticizing regimes of power, knowledge, and truth.

Yet—and this is the interpretive dilemma—his writing is highly charged politically and clearly politically engaged, and his own political activity mirrored his analysis in many ways. Like most recent French intellectuals, his philosophical work was inevitably situated in the context of leftist politics, yet his personal views did not fit easily into any particular slot on the political spectrum. He rejected any connection between his own biography and his work, stating that he tried "to write as if he had no face," but his personal involvement in the cause of prisoners, the insane, and homosexuals paralleled his analysis of systems of exclusion and normalization that target the marginal and the abnormal in society for intervention and control. The dilemma posed by Foucault's work turns on the connection between his analysis of the human sciences and of modern forms of power, and the place of a critique of society in the goal of emancipation and autonomy.

## I

Foucault took up the question "What Is Enlightenment?"[6] by returning to Kant's formulation. The apparent motivation for Foucault was to respond to what he called in that essay "the blackmail of the Enlightenment." This blackmail was characterized by the assumption that in criticizing modernity one must either be for or against Enlightenment values. Though the target of the essay was probably Jürgen Habermas, I think it suggests the basis for a response to a wider set of critics.

Habermas had not commented on Foucault's work directly until after Foucault's death. In a short memorial essay, "Taking Aim At the Heart of the Present," Habermas reports what is probably for us the lost intellectual opportunity of the decade. He had been invited by Foucault to discuss Kant's essay, "What Is Enlightenment?" but was unable to attend. In this brief reflection on Foucault, Habermas notes the paradox in Foucault's account of Kant's essay. On the one hand, Foucault discovered in Kant the philosopher who transformed philosophy into a critique of the present and Foucault aligned himself with that Kantian spirit. Yet on the other hand, Foucault's own work constituted a sustained criticism of modernity and of Kant. Habermas put the question this paradox raises this way: "How can Foucault's self-understanding as a thinker in the tradition of the Enlightenment be compatible with his unmistakable criticism of this very form of knowledge of modernity?"[7] Habermas observes that Foucault was in the predicament of "being rich in values and able in action, yet at the same time asking what makes the ethical questions possible at all," and Habermas recognizes that this predicament was the source of charges by "self-styled pragmatists or critical theorists or academic social democrats" ("Taking Aim," p. 6) that Foucault owed us a normative standpoint from which to criticize power and ground social action. Though in this brief memorial Habermas understands the tension in Foucault's work and appreciates that this sort of criticism does not do it justice, his own previous asides about Foucault fall into this category of criticism.

In "The Entwinement of Myth and Enlightenment: Re-Reading *Dialectic of Enlightenment,*"[8] Habermas made a passing reference to Foucault, including him among those Habermas accuses of engaging in a "total critique of modernity." In "Modernity versus Postmodernity"[9] he included Foucault, along with Derrida and others, among the "young conservatives." Though I will sort out these charges more carefully, a rough approximation of their force is that Foucault provided an analysis of modernity that at the same time eliminated the possibility of criticizing it. Along similar lines Nancy Fraser, in an illuminating paper, has argued that Foucault's work vacillates between a condemnation of modernity and political activism and an analysis of power that eliminates the possibility of normative criteria for criticizing power.[10] Charles Taylor has argued that Foucault's analysis of modernity allows no escape from power into freedom.[11] Richard Rorty has characterized Foucault as a cynical social observer who "pours cold water on any hopes for reform."[12]

My purpose in this chapter is to construct a confrontation between Foucault and these critics over the question of the Enlightenment connection between social criticism and freedom. I will argue that Foucault's critics have incorrectly located the problem posed by his work, and I will formulate what I think are the questions that one must ask of it. To do so, I will begin by filling out Fraser's criticism since it will illuminate the relation between Foucault's genealogical method in his last works and his analysis of power. Then I will return to the criticism of Habermas and the related criticism offered by Charles Taylor. Against their interpretation of Foucault I will disentangle the antihumanist thrust of his work from the Enlightenment values to which he remained committed. I will argue that, pace Habermas and Taylor, there is in Foucault's later work the suggestion of a sense of emancipation and autonomy—a sense which couples a Nietzschean notion of autonomy as self-creation with a Stoic or Kantian notion of self-mastery. I will conclude by considering Rorty's charge concerning the possibility—given Foucault's analysis of modernity—of social hope and social solidarity. Whether his view of autonomy is finally adequate or not, I will suggest that Foucault's critique of modernity can be seen as an attempt to avoid the view that social criticism is possible only in terms of an ahistorical ground, independent normative framework, or transcendental standpoint; and at the same time, it can be read as an attempt to avoid lapsing into a conservative acquiescence or accommodation to the current regime of power, as Habermas and Taylor have charged. It is this that ties him to what I have called the Pyrrhonian challenge.

## II

The issue Fraser brings to focus in Foucault's analysis of modern forms of power/knowledge is this: how is it possible for Foucault to provide a politically involved critique of modern forms of power when his analysis has as one of its consequences a suspension of a normative framework for criticizing regimes of power? She sums up this dilemma in the following way:

> Foucault vacillates between two equally inadequate stances. On the one hand, he adopts a concept of power which permits him no condemnation of any objectionable features of modernity. But at the same time, and on the other hand, his rhetoric betrays the conviction that modernity is utterly without redeeming features. Clearly what Foucault needs and needs desperately are normative criteria for distinguishing acceptable from unacceptable forms of power. As it stands now, the unquestionably original and valuable dimensions of his work stand in danger of being misunderstood for lack of an adequate normative perspective. ("Foucault on Modern Power," p. 286)

Though Fraser does not distinguish them explicitly, there are at least three levels on which this dilemma arises. First, Foucault often suggested that his analysis was normatively neutral—a felicitous positivism as he sometimes put it—yet his rhetoric was anything but neutral and unengaged and, I shall argue, his method of analysis was, by its very nature, politically situated. Second, while it is clear that Foucault considered the effects of modern forms of power/knowledge the most serious danger of the present age, he eschewed a normative basis for answering the question "Why is it dangerous?" and in the absence of a normative framework, he seems unable to counter someone who thought that modern forms of discipline, regulation, and normalization might be a good thing. Third, though Foucault himself was active in various political struggles, his analysis seems to provide no philosophically grounded basis for political action—at least no grounding in the name of a conception of the good for society as a whole. The dilemma Fraser poses comes to this: either Foucault's analysis was merely a methodological suspension of the normative in order to see the phenomena of power in a new way, thus clearing the way for an alternative normative framework; or he had suspended the normative altogether, committing himself to a relativism by which normative assessment and nonarbitrary political opposition to the existing order are impossible.

What I shall suggest initially is that this sort of criticism makes sense only within the traditional understanding of the relation between power and knowledge that Foucault's work aims to undermine. As a consequence, to challenge Foucault to produce a normative framework or to charge him with relativism in the absence of such a framework is to fail to appreciate that his analysis—like the Nietzschean and postmodernist opposition to philosophy—was aimed at undermining the very philosophical framework that structures our alternatives as either grounded criticism or relativism and arbitrariness. A first approximation of my argument is this: if having a normative framework means having a standpoint outside of power/knowledge relations from which to make judgments of legitimate or illegitimate exercises of power, then Foucault has no normative framework. But this does not mean that his analysis of power is neutral or that his opposition to modern forms of power is relative or arbitrary. To suggest why, it is important to note initially that one thrust of Foucault's work—from *Madness and Civilization* through *The History of Sexuality* and *The Use of Pleasure*—was the shattering of the binary opposition between such normative categories as the sane and the insane, the healthy and the sick, the normal and the abnormal, the legitimate and the illegitimate upon which normative judgments are made. But like Nietzsche and the postmoderns, Foucault did not oppose these normative categories by supporting one side of the opposition over the other. Instead, his work opposed the way the Western philosophical tradition has been structured in terms of the oppositions between reality and appearance, truth and fiction, knowledge and power, and so on, and especially opposed the way social analysis has been structured in terms of normative "dividing practices." Now it seems to me that the dilemma Fraser poses for Foucault's work is structured by one of the very dividing practices against which Foucault's analysis is directed. I will fill out this argument in what follows by considering the genealogical method Foucault employed in his works on power in order to show the danger he saw in these dividing practices, and to show how the politically situated nature of his analysis offers social criticism without recourse to binary oppositions or an independent normative framework.

## III

At the conclusion of the first chapter of *Discipline and Punish,* Foucault had anticipated his reader's question of why he was interested in writing the history of the prison. "Simply because I am interested in the past? No, if one means by that writing a history of the past in terms of the present. Yes, if one means writing a history of the present."[13] The initial key for understanding the politically situated nature of Foucault's writing is to be found in understanding what he meant by writing the history of the present.

To begin with, writing the history of the present was not an attempt to write a history by projecting present meanings and concerns on the past. Furthermore, he was not attempting to recover the "truth" of the past in order to understand the present. On Foucault's view, there is no true past from which to lay tracks to the present. There is, however, a connection between present concerns and history, between an understanding of the past and our present condition, that I will get at by considering his genealogical method in broad outline.

Methodologically, Foucault's work can be divided into the archaeological studies of *Madness and Civilization, The Birth of the Clinic, The Order of Things,* and *The Archaeology of Knowledge* on the one hand, and the genealogical studies of *Discipline and Punish, The History of Sexuality,* volume 1, and *The Use of Pleasure* on the other.[14] Foucault's genealogy, or his history of the present, obviously owes much to his interpretation of Nietzsche, but it is enough for my purpose to notice very general features of his indebtedness. The general point is that genealogical analysis must necessarily begin from its situation in our present condition. This is not simply the truism that one always writes history from one's own place in it, but rather, that genealogical analysis is self-consciously situated in the present. For Foucault, this means that his genealogy of modern forms of power was situated within the very web of power it analyzed, and it took a specific stand on the way modern forms of power structure our present condition. That is, it began from a recognition of current dangers. It is worth noticing at this point that Foucault's use of the term "dangers" to describe our current condition is problematic since what he seemed to want was a term of alarm that was not included in a normative category. Part of the reason why his use of the term "dangers" to describe our present condition was not a term of normative evaluation was his claim that since everything is structured in terms of relations of power, then *everything* is dangerous. Yet while everything may be thought to be dangerous, he nevertheless believed that there was something uniquely dangerous about modernity, and the question was whether he could express this without recourse to normative distinctions. This is just another way of expressing the thrust of Fraser's concern.

There are three aspects of this genealogical stance within and toward our present dangers that are important for my purpose. First, because the genealogist is necessarily writing the history of the present from *within,* genealogy can provide no standpoint or meta-story about that history; that is, Foucault's interest in the generative process of modern forms of power was not couched in a philosophy of history as either progress or decay and, therefore, it can provide no historical framework for judging better or worse power/knowledge regimes.

My second point develops indirectly from what is a misleading but illuminating reading of what Foucault meant by the history of the present. Michael Roth has made much of the fact that in his earlier books Foucault claimed that he was on the edge of an impending rupture or shift in the structures of experience that made possible his archaeology of madness, medical experience, or the human sciences. In the introduction to *The Birth of the Clinic,* for example, Foucault had written that "a new experience of disease is coming into being that will make possible a historical and critical understanding of old experience,"[15] and in the final sections of *The Order of Things* he claimed to be able to reveal the invention of "man" and the sciences of man because man is nearing an end.[16] From this, Roth concludes that "Foucault . . . is writing a history of the present in order to make the present into past."[17] What is not quite right about this interpretation is that it situates Foucault's work in terms of the future—that is, in terms of the dissolution of the present for some future condition. Furthermore, Foucault made no similar claims about writing at the edge of an impending rupture of experience in the works on the prison and sexuality; and though he sometimes alluded to the possibility of forms of power/knowledge different from modern forms, there is no evidence that he held out much hope for the demise of the present power/knowledge regime. It is the present, not a vision of the future, that situates the genealogy. Alan Sheridan struck the right tone when he wrote that "His passion is to seek out the new, that which is coming to birth in the present—a present that most of us are unable to see because we see it through the eyes of the past, or through the eyes of a 'future' that is a projection of the past."[18] I will return to this idea of critique as a specific stand toward the present in terms of Foucault's discussion of Kant and the Enlightenment. For now it is enough to note that the genealogy is a specific stand toward and critique of the present which aims at seeing the present for what it is.

The third point is that the genealogy is not arbitrarily situated. Because the genealogy of power is caught in the web of disciplinary technologies, struggles, domination, and normalization that it traces, it is able to see the current danger, and for that reason it is not objective or neutral history because it is politically involved from the start. It is not arbitrary or incidental that the prison was selected for study, for example. It was studied because, as Foucault said in a conversation with Deleuze, in the prison, "for once, power does not hide or mask itself."[19] And of course, it is selected precisely to make the point that, with the emergence of modern forms of power, ours is a carceral society.

As with the genealogy of a family, the lines one traces in the history of the present are not neutrally selected, nor are they arbitrary. Since the genealogy of the prison is self-consciously situated in the dangers of modern power it seeks to expose, to demand independent normative criteria for accessing power or, in the absence of those criteria, to charge that the analysis is relative or arbitrary, both misunderstands the nature of his history of the present and does not adequately appreciate that, as with Nietzsche, the genealogy aims to undermine the sorts of binary oppositions in which the charge is formulated. This response, however, only touches the demand that Foucault produce normative criteria for evaluating power/knowledge regimes. It does not explicitly get at the more fundamental background concern that motivated Fraser's argument or the criticism of Habermas and Taylor. Is there any sense that Foucault's analysis can provide a philosophical basis for political action which can free us from the current power/knowledge regime? I will turn to that question by filling out the criticisms of Habermas and Taylor.

## IV

Habermas presents two variants of what he calls "the totalizing, self-referential critique" of the Enlightenment. The first is Horkheimer and Adorno's critique of the Enlightenment, and the second is Nietzsche's genealogy of the Western philosophical tradition; and in an aside during his discussion of them, he includes Foucault among those who engage in a totalizing critique.

In their influential *Dialectic of Enlightenment,* first published in 1944, Horkheimer and Adorno had argued that the Enlightenment confrontation with myth in the name of liberation had disenchanted the world and transformed liberation into domination: "Myth turned into enlightenment, and nature into mere objectivity. Men pay for the increase of their power with alienation from that over which they exercise power. Enlightenment behaves towards things as a dictator toward men."[20] Against their analysis of the Enlightenment, Habermas claims that "they take that which Enlightenment did to myth and turn it back onto the process of Enlightenment itself. Critique becomes total: it turns against reason as the foundation of its own analysis" ("Myth and Enlightenment," pp. 21–22). Thus, according to Habermas, there is a self-referential paradox involved in their total opposition to the Enlightenment since, in turning against the Enlightenment demand that everything be subjected to rational criticism, their critique turns against itself, stripping itself of its possibility as a rational critique of the Enlightenment.

For similar reasons he asks in his account of Nietzsche, "If . . . all proper claims to validity are devalued and if the underlying value-judgments are mere expressions of claims to power rather than validity, according to what standards should critique then differentiate? It must at least be able to discriminate between a power which *deserves* to be esteemed and a power which *deserves* to be disparaged" ("Myth and Enlightenment," p. 27). And he makes this same point in his aside about Foucault:

> Foucault . . . replaced the model of repression and emancipation developed by Marx and Freud with a pluralism of power/discourse formations. These formations intersect and succeed one another and can be differentiated according to their style and intensity. They cannot, however, be judged in terms of validity which was possible in the case of the repression and emancipation of conscious as opposed to unconscious conflict resolutions. ("Myth and Enlightenment," p. 29)

Thus for Nietzsche and Foucault alike, their total critique of modernity—in this case their rejection of an evaluative framework—is self-referentially paradoxical since in opposing the notion that values can be judged in terms of their validity they eliminate the possibility of a critical basis for emancipation from the modern forms of power.

In Habermas's paper "Modernity versus Postmodernity" Foucault is included in another sort of criticism of those who oppose modernity. There, Habermas sets the problem facing the critique of modernity this way: "should we try to hold on to the *intentions* of the Enlightenment, feeble as they may be, or should we declare the entire project of modernity a lost cause?" (p. 9). Among those who declare it a lost cause, he distinguishes the old conservatives who view the modern world "with sadness and recommend a withdrawal to a position *anterior* to modernity"; the neoconservatives who welcome modernity as long as it carries forward "technical progress, capitalist growth and rational administration"; and the young conservatives who, on the basis of modernistic attitudes, "justify an irreconcilable anti-modernism" (p. 13). He includes Foucault among the young conservatives.[21] Though they claim to be postmodern, Habermas says that the young conservatives are merely antimodern.

There are two parts to this charge. First, in offering a total critique of modernity, they have merely negated modernity, and in the process their critique turns on itself, stripping itself of emancipatory force. Second, the negation takes place in modernism's own terms: rather than breaking with modernism, they give new life to the structures of modernity they negate. The first part of this claim is the same as that against Horkheimer and Adorno. The second can be illuminated in terms of Habermas's analysis of the mistake of the surrealist negation of modernism in art. The surrealists' attempt to collapse the distinctions between art and life and between appearance and reality served actually to reinstate the binary oppositions they sought to level out. "All these undertakings have proved themselves to be sort of nonsense experiments. These experiments have served to bring back to life, and to illuminate all the more glaringly, exactly those structures of art which they were meant to dissolve" ("Modernity," p. 10).

Habermas's point about antimodernism is, I think, similar to Heidegger's assessment of Nietzsche in relation to the metaphysical tradition. On Heidegger's reading, Nietzsche had attempted to achieve a postmetaphysical position through the transvaluation of value, but he merely revalued the subordinate terms of the binary oppositions—truth/fiction, real/apparent, reason/sense, and so on—that define metaphysics. Thus Nietzsche represented merely the reversal of Platonism and the extreme possibility of metaphysics.[22] Interpreted along this line, the young conservatives are antimodern in the sense that they are just modernism's dark underside. These two parts of Habermas's account of the young conservatives, taken together, indicate that merely to negate modernity by a total critique is simultaneously to remain within the modern framework and to eliminate a basis for emancipation from that framework through rational criticism.

Like Habermas, Charles Taylor has structured his criticism of Foucault in terms of opposition to Enlightenment commitments. For Taylor, the issue turns on Foucault's repudiation of the Enlightenment connection between truth and freedom. That repudiation is grounded in Foucault's Nietzschean stance toward truth and in his eschewal of normative criteria for assessing exercises of power. Taylor summarizes his reading of Foucault as follows: "[For Foucault] the idea of a liberating truth is a profound illusion. There is no truth that can be espoused, defended, or rescued against systems of power. On the contrary, each such system defines its own variant of truth. And there is no escape from power into freedom" ("Foucault on Freedom and Truth," pp. 152–53). In terms of this reading, Taylor's argument is that Foucault's stand toward modernity is incoherent. This charge is developed around two main issues: the first is Taylor's claim that an analysis of power must leave room for freedom and truth; and the second is that Foucault's Nietzschean view of the regime-relativity of truth provides no basis for criticizing our own regime in the name of truth, or for thinking that the transformation of one regime to another could be an advance of truth or freedom.[23]

The thrust of Taylor's charge of incoherence, then, is similar to the criticisms offered by Habermas. The opposition to modernity self-destructs, since it opposes the very framework of values upon which such an opposition could be mounted. These criticisms, of course, emerge from a deeper background in the stances of Habermas and Taylor toward Enlightenment commitments, and at least a brief sketch will illuminate what they think is at stake. For Habermas, it derives in part from his analysis of the transformation of the emancipatory intent of the Enlightenment by positivism, and in part from his own analysis of adult autonomy through an empirical theory of communicative competency. In "Dogmatism, Reason, and Decision," for example, Habermas considers how, in the eighteenth century, the relation between theory and practice developed in terms of reason taking up the interest in liberation as its own, and how emancipation by critical insight into relations of power was transformed by positivism through the interlocking development of science, technology, industry, and administration.[24] In this transformation, decision becomes external to the cognitive interest of reason in liberation; practical and technological powers are conflated; action is confused with control; and rational consensus is replaced by administration. Though Habermas's account of the result of these conflations is not unlike Foucault's account of the emergence of disciplinary power, or biopower, and normalization, Habermas views this transformation of the Enlightenment as a bastardization of its emancipatory intent, and in his own work he returns to the cognitive interest of reason in liberation in order to develop a conception of rationality based on a theory of communicative competence. For Taylor, the opposition to Foucault is involved in his own position in the controversy over the relation between the natural and human sciences, in his view that because we are self-interpreting beings the human sciences must be hermeneutic, in his views concerning the compatibility of pluralistic conceptions of rationality and meaningful evaluation of alternative systems of values, and in his attempt to provide a basis for understanding political behavior in terms of shared meanings of agents and notions of autonomy and rationality.[25]

The way in which Habermas and Taylor shape their criticism of Foucault, then, against the background of their own attempt to use certain Enlightenment views implies that Foucault's views must be anti-Enlightenment, and because of that they claim that he can offer no hope for the liberating role of rational criticism. What I wish to show, however, is that in returning again to Kant's answer to the question "What is Enlightenment?" Foucault provided the basis for developing a response to what he thought of as this "blackmail of the Enlightenment." That response will sharpen the issue between Foucault on the one hand, and Habermas and Taylor on the other.

## V

Though Kant was not the first to reflect on his own present, Foucault interpreted Kant's essay as posing a new problem because of the way he addressed the concern about the present age. He was not attempting to situate the present through a historical event to which it belonged or through its contribution to a future achievement. "He is looking for a difference: What difference does today introduce with respect to yesterday? ("Enlightenment," p. 34). The difference Kant identified was that the age of Enlightenment was a "way out" or an "escape" from immaturity. In Foucault's account of Kant, reflecting on the Enlightenment as a way out was not only reflecting on the present age, but was "reflecting on the contemporary status of his own enterprise" ("Enlightenment," p. 38). He was reflecting on the role of critique in the escape from tutelage. This interpretation of the status of Kant's question provided Foucault with the basis for outlining "the attitude of modernity" and its connection with the Enlightenment.

In most recent concerns with the issue of modernity and postmodernity, modernity has been identified with Cartesian subjectivity, or with the Kantian "Copernican revolution," or with the authoritative place of science, or with the culmination of the metaphysical tradition begun by Plato, or with some combination or variation of these themes. However, it is to Charles Baudelaire's consciousness of modernity, through the figure of the *dandy,* that Foucault turned in order to characterize modernity. For Foucault, as for Baudelaire, modernity was understood as a particular mode of relation to the present. In "The Painter of Modern Life," Baudelaire had contrasted the modern painter with the idle spectator. Though they both are involved in the present occasion, the painter looks for something more than the fleeting moment of the present. "This 'something else' that he seeks is what we may be allowed to call 'modernity'. . . . His business is to separate from contemporary fashion whatever it may contain of poetry within history; to extract the eternal from the ephemeral."[26] On Foucault's reading of Baudelaire, the attitude of modernity lies in the will to "heroize" the present, to grasp the "heroic" aspect of the present moment. But Foucault claimed that it was an ironic heroization in that "what is real is confronted with the practice of a liberty that simultaneously respects and violates it" ("Enlightenment," p. 41). It is an attitude to the present that transforms it not by destroying it but by grasping it for what it is.

It should not surprise us that this characterization of Baudelaire's consciousness of modernity is roughly the same as Foucault's own description of his genealogical method as a "history of the present" in *Discipline and Punish.* This is a history that seeks neither to explain the present in terms of the past nor to interpret the past on the basis of present issues; instead, it seeks to grasp the present *as* present. With Baudelaire, this attitude toward the present was connected with the realization of oneself not simply as caught up in the flux of the moment but as an object for elaboration—what, for Baudelaire, was the dandy who makes himself a work of art. Baudelaire had asked, "What . . . is this ruling passion that has turned into a creed and created its own skilled tyrants? What is this unwritten constitution that has created so haughty a cast? It is, above all, a burning need to acquire originality, within the apparent bounds of convention. It is a sort of cult of oneself" ("Painter," pp. 55–56). As Foucault put it, the dandy "is the man who tries to invent himself. This modernity does not 'liberate man in his being'; it compels him to face the task of producing himself" ("Enlightenment," p. 42).

What connects Foucault to modernity and the Enlightenment, then, is not a set of doctrines but an attitude toward the present, a "philosophical ethos" that he called "a principle of critique and a permanent creation of ourselves in our autonomy" ("Enlightenment," p. 44). Negatively stated, this ethos is the refusal of Enlightenment blackmail. Foucault thought the blackmail rested on the confusion of the Enlightenment with humanism. Whereas he thought the Enlightenment was, fundamentally, a certain reflective attitude toward the present, he identified humanism with a set of themes, always tied to value judgments, which he saw standing opposed to and in a state of tension with the Enlightenment.

Though humanism encompasses various movements and refers to a number of historical periods, Foucault's notion of humanism and his opposition to it was connected with the concept of "man" and the human sciences that emerged in the nineteenth century. Before returning to Foucault's positive account of the permanent critique of the present and how this provides a basis for confronting Habermas and Taylor, I shall fill out what he meant by humanism and his criticism of it. My purpose in the following section will not be to adjudicate the dispute but to set the terms of Foucault's side in the confrontation.

## VI

In an essay, "The Subject and Power," Foucault reflected on the organizing theme of his work. "My objective . . . has been to create a history of the different modes by which, in our culture, human beings are made subjects."[27] Humanism was his term for the various ways we turn ourselves into subjects. In one way his history of ourselves as subjects was a part of the general opposition to humanism as the privileging of the subject that would include Heidegger,the structuralists, Jacques Lacan, Derrida, and Deleuze.[28] But the term "subject" carried a double meaning for him, and his analysis traded on both senses. On the one hand, humanism covered the way we privilege ourselves as subjects for the possibility of representation; on the other, it covered the way in which we are subjected—that is, the way modern forms of power turn us into docile bodies. His history of ourselves as subjects was an analysis of forms of inquiry which have tried to give the study of human beings the status of a science; of norms and "dividing practices" such as the sane and the insane, the sick and the healthy, by which we objectify ourselves; and of the ways we turn ourselves into "deep selves," as in the domain of sexuality or the Christian confessional. His opposition to humanism was bound up with this history of ourselves as subjects and its connection with the emergence of the human sciences. In this sense, it was not the Enlightenment that he opposed but humanism.

There are two related parts to his opposition to humanism. In *The Order of Things,* Foucault claimed that the human sciences are essentially unstable because the concept of "man" that emerged from Kant into the nineteenth century and gave rise to the human sciences was unstable. In *Discipline and Punish* and *The History of Sexuality,* he was concerned not with the instability of the human sciences but with the way they are made possible by and contribute to a uniquely dangerous form of power. It will be necessary to consider both parts of his antihumanism.

Foucault's "archaeology of the human sciences" began, of course, with an ingenious analysis of Velazquez's painting, *Las Meninas,* which served for Foucault as an exemplar of the age of representation—"the representation, as it were, of Classical representation" (*Order of Things,* p. 16). Nothing is stable in the Velasquez painting: subject and object, spectator and model, representer and representation are constantly reversing roles. In its tension, Foucault interpreted the whole painting as pointing to vacant space, to "an essential void: the necessary disappearance of that which is its foundation—of the person it resembles and the person in whose eyes it is only a resemblance" (*Order of Things,* p. 16). In his analysis of the painting, this place toward which the painting points in its instability is the place of the king. The king, however, is both the condition for the possibility of the scene being represented and is necessarily elided. In much the way that Derrida deconstructed Hegel through *différance*—where the "a" is present but silent—Foucault found in the Velasquez painting the absent thread that unraveled the Classical age, since the possibility of representation depended on that which could not itself be represented.

The painting served as the exemplar of the unraveling and eclipse of the Classical age, and with that eclipse "man appears in his ambiguous position as an object of knowledge and a subject that knows: enslaved sovereign, observed spectator, he appears in the place belonging to the king, which was assigned to him in advance by *Las Meninas*" (*Order of Things,* p. 312). Man, then, was Foucault's technical term for the modern subject who is at once condition for knowing and object of knowledge—both subject and docile body—and humanism was identified with the emergence of a science of man. The Classical age had excluded the possibility of a science of man because it concealed the condition for the possibility of representation, and thus could not call man into question. When the relation between sign and signified lost its transparency, man appeared as the one in whom knowledge is made possible.[29] The sciences of man began in the realization that man is finite because he cannot represent to himself that which makes representation possible; however, the Kantian revolution—Foucault called it "the analytic of finitude"—transformed man's finitude into a triumph. That finitude, which makes possible the sciences of man, was *not* taken as a limit since man became the ground for knowledge as the condition of its possibility. Man was cast in a privileged position as sovereign subject, a position unlike those assigned by Renaissance humanism or by Classical rationalism. On Foucault's analysis, though, it was a position that was essentially unstable.

Man appeared, in the analytic of finitude, as "a strange empirico-transcendental doublet." He appeared as both an object of knowledge and the one in whom knowledge was made possible. On Foucault's reading, Kant's awaking from his dogmatic slumber was just the beginning of the "anthropological sleep." The human sciences were destined to play out a predetermined set of permutations opened up by a conception of man as a doublet—in Foucault's terms, by the repetition of the positive in the fundamental: where "in succession the transcendental repeat[s] the empirical, the cogito repeat[s] the unthought, and the return of the origin repeat[s] its retreat" (*Order of Things,* p. 316).[30] Humanism, as Foucault understood it, exhausts itself in an endless back and forth from one side to the other of man and his doubles: from man as the condition for the possibility of knowledge to man as himself an object in the empirical field; from man's attempt to become intelligible to himself to the unthought that makes intelligibility possible; from man as historical to man as what makes history possible. Humanism, or the analytic of finitude, then, is "warped and twisted forms of reflection"; and all those forms of reflection that take man as the starting point, that talk of man's liberation, that attempt to reach the truth about man are caught up in the instability and futility of man and his doubles.

In *Discipline and Punish, The History of Sexuality,* and the lectures and interviews published under the title *Power/Knowledge,* Foucault was concerned not with the impossibility of the human sciences but with their complicity in the emergence and maintenance of uniquely modern forms of discipline, control, and normalization which turned us into docile bodies. One such form of modern power that Foucault analyzed in the works on the prison and sexuality was biopower. Briefly put, biopower is a modern form of power/knowledge which combines disciplinary techniques for optimizing administration of bodies with regulatory controls over biological processes for the management of life.[31] Biopower functions by normalization, that is, it functions globally by subjecting everything to norms, thus dividing and colonizing every aspect of life to maximize utility at the same time that it maximizes the docility of the body.[32] Normalization in Foucault's analysis is similar to rationalization in Weber's analysis or to various other accounts of the leveling-out effect of modern administrative society. But what is uniquely dangerous about normalization is more similar to "total mobilization" in Heidegger's analysis of technology as "enframing." Its danger—just like the danger Heidegger saw with technology—consists in the fact that everything becomes a target for normalization, just as technology orders everything as a resource, as "standing-reserve." What turns out to make biopower such a danger is not only that it simultaneously maximizes utility and docility but that every attempt to resist it is to be targeted for further intervention and normalization, and thus resistance contributes to biopower's continuation and success.

The general character of Foucault's account of biopower is well known: it is productive rather then merely repressive; it is capillary, decentralized, and omnipresent; it operates through coercion, surveillance, and discipline at the level of micropractices rather than merely through class domination or ideological distortion; and it is intentional and strategically deployed but nonsubjective, i.e., it is strategies without strategists.[33] Furthermore, biopower is fundamentally different from the classical conceptions of power: different especially from a liberal analysis of power in terms of rights exchanged between the sovereign or the law and its subjects; from the Marxists' view which situates the analysis of power in the material basis of class struggle and oppression; and from the Freudian-inspired analysis of power as repressive of true interests.[34] In each of these analyses, power is conceived of as repressive and the analysis of power is developed in terms of its legitimate or illegitimate exercise.

Foucault opposed these analyses, but in opposing them he did not claim that power was not repressive or that the emergence of biopower had superseded the power of the sovereign and the law. Rather, his analysis revealed that biopower's success depended on its coexistence and complicity with what he called juridical-sovereign power.[35] Furthermore, an analysis of power in terms of repression and within the framework of legitimacy and illegitimacy was part of the "dividing practices" through which biopower normalized and succeeded. Foucault summarized his point in the "Two Lectures": "I believe that the notion of repression remains a juridical-disciplinary notion whatever critical use one would make of it. To this extent the critical application of the notion of repression is found to be vitiated and nullified from the outset by the twofold juridical and disciplinary reference it contains to sovereignty on the one hand and to normalization on the other" (*Power/Knowledge,* p. 108). Since the success of disciplinary strategies in normalizing society depended on a superimposed juridical theory of power that conceals the actual operations of biopower, it turns out that liberal, Marxist, and Freudian critiques themselves contribute to normalization insofar as they are structured by a juridical view and by the categories of repression and resistance.

Foucault's antihumanism, then, followed from his analysis of how the emergence of the human sciences constituted man as an unstable doublet as well as from the complicity of the human sciences with a uniquely dangerous form of power—dangerous because it operates totally and globally, leveling out every aspect of ourselves by subjecting everything from illness to sex to norms which make us targets for the further deployment of discipline and intervention. In terms of Foucault's antihumanism, then, and his analysis of the complicity of juridical conceptions of power in the success of normalization, I think that he could have claimed that Habermas and Taylor are not only caught up in the futility of the doubles—Habermas's empirical theory of communication competency as the reverse of a transcendental grounding of rationality and Taylor's grounding of political rationality in the self-interpreting character of human beings and in intersubjective meanings as a privileging of man—but that they are part of the very danger of normalization itself.

## IV

In the essay on Kant's "What Is Enlightenment?" Foucault characterized negatively the philosophical ethos that aligned him with the Enlightenment, in terms of his refusal to submit to the intellectual blackmail that demanded one be either for or against the Enlightenment; and he developed the sense in which he remained connected to the Enlightenment by disentangling it from humanism. His positive characterization, however, was in terms of what he called a "limit-attitude" involved in his notion of a permanent critique of the present. About this attitude he cautioned, "We are not talking about a gesture of rejection. We have to move beyond the outside/inside alternative; we have to be at the frontiers. Criticism indeed consists of analyzing and reflection upon limits. . . . The point, in brief, is to transform the critique conducted in the form of necessary limitation into a practical critique that takes the form of a possible transgression" ("Enlightenment," p. 45).

This idea of a critique which transgresses the limits—an idea of considerable interest in Foucault's early work but not explicitly involved in the genealogical works on the prison and sexuality—and the connection between this "limit-attitude" and the emancipatory thrust of the Enlightenment constitute the basis, I think, for formulating a more positive response to Habermas's criticism of Foucault as a young conservative and to Taylor's claim that Foucault's work provides for no means of escape from power into freedom. The issue between Foucault and his critics will be seen to turn not on whether he was against the goal of Enlightenment but on his ideas about the nature of critique and the nature of autonomy that are suggested by his later works. I will claim that in eschewing the framework of legitimacy and truth in analyzing power, Foucault did not eschew the goal of liberation, though clearly his notions of liberation and autonomy are implied rather than explicit.

From the positive way he formulated his relation to the Enlightenment, liberation can be understood as an attitude toward ourselves and the present which is a genealogy of the limits that are imposed on us by evaluative norms and a transgression of those limits that opens the possibility of going beyond them.

The initial focus in sorting out this notion of transgression and its connection to emancipation and autonomy is what Foucault meant by a permanent critique of ourselves at the limit. This notion—which, despite other important differences between them, seems similar to the deconstructionist results of Derrida—was intended to suggest how criticism of limit-contrasts like normal/abnormal, sane/insane, and so on can be opened up as a plenitude of possibilities for self-elaboration which not only liberates the self from the leveling effects of normalization but compels us to face the task of producing ourselves. This implies a coupling of a Nietzschean notion of freedom as self-creation with a Stoic and Kantian notion (suggested by Foucault's work on Greek ethics in *The Use of Pleasure*) of autonomy as self-mastery and self-rule. I will fill out this suggestion shortly, but for now the point to be made is that the issue we must decide in the confrontation between Foucault and his critics is not whether he is for or against the Enlightenment but whether this notion of maturity as self-creation and self-mastery is plausible, and furthermore whether it can support the Enlightenment goal of community.

In an early essay on George Bataille, Foucault analyzed the eroticism of Bataille's work as an experience of limits and their transgression. Of this experience Foucault had written that "transgression has its entire space in the line it crosses. The play of limits and transgression seems to be regulated by a simple obstinacy: transgression incessantly crosses and recrosses a line which closes up behind it in a wave of extremely short duration, and thus it is made to return once more right to the horizon of the uncrossable."[36] He continued: "Transgression is not related to the limit as black to white, the prohibited to the lawful, the outside to the inside, or as the open area of a building to its enclosed spaces" ("Transgression," p. 35). What this suggests is that in understanding criticism of the present as transgressing the limiting or dividing practices that form the human sciences and contribute to normalization, Foucault should not be thought of as supporting terms that constitute one side of the limit—the insane, the abnormal, the illegitimate, the relative—against the terms that form the other side of the limit. He was not merely reversing the traditional hierarchy. Instead, transgression "forces the limit to face the fact of its imminent disappearance," and it opens the limit onto the limitless ("Transgression," p. 34). That is, the permanent critique of the present as a limit-attitude aims at undercutting the possibility of drawing the line; thus it opens up a plenitude of possibilities.

In unpacking this rather dense formulation, it will be helpful to focus on two aspects: first, the transgressive move itself which will provide a basis for meeting Habermas's charge that Foucault was merely antimodern and Taylor's charge that his Nietzschean relativism provided no basis for criticizing our own regime; and, second, the limitless possibilities opened up by transgressing the limit, an aspect that will provide a basis for meeting Habermas's charge that Foucault is a young conservative and Taylor's charge that Foucault can offer no hope of an advance of freedom.

A first approximation of my argument is this: In juxtaposing power and knowledge as power/knowledge, Foucault's genealogical analysis of the prison and of sexuality operates at the limit, neither opposing power to knowledge nor seeking their separation. To claim that Foucault's critique is merely antimodern, as Habermas does, is to mistakenly think that the genealogy supports one side of the binary opposition over the other, that Foucault was just reversing the limit rather than opening it up. To charge that Foucault's relativism with respect to power/knowledge regimes provides no basis for critique of the current regime, as Taylor claims, is to fail to appreciate the sense in which Foucault's "limit-attitude" and trangression are liberating.

Given what I have called the genealogical stance, it must be recalled that the genealogy of power/knowledge was neither a meta-account of power nor was it a prelude to an escape from power/knowledge to power-free relations. Since power/knowledge constitutes the field of struggle of all our actions, there is no power-free foundation from which to criticize and there is no post–power/knowledge regime that the genealogy could open up. Thus for Foucault, as with Derrida, transgression was not to be thought of as an act which, once accomplished, allows one to move permanently beyond the limit. Derrida makes the point in terms of his deconstruction of metaphysical texts in the interviews published as *Positions:* "There is *not* a transgression, if one understands by that a pure and simple landing into a beyond of metaphysics. . . . by means of the work done on one side and the other of the limit the field inside is modified, and a transgression [is] produced that consequently is nowhere present as a *fait accompli*. . . . Transgression implies that the limit is always at work."[37] For Derrida, we are always pulled by metaphysics, thus deconstructive strategies must be continually deployed against the closure of metaphysical drag. I have already connected this deconstructive strategy to the Pyrrhonian strategy of constantly opposing philosophical claims in order to achieve mental health in relation to the appearances of common life. In a similar way for Foucault, since one is always caught up in the web of power/knowledge—since one can never divorce knowledge from power—there is no post–power/knowledge regime to which genealogical analysis can contribute. There are always dangers to resist, thus resistance must be understood in terms of a permanent critique rather than as an escape from power.

In addition, while Foucault's genealogy of biopower is neither normative nor neutral—to be either would place his analysis in terms of the binary oppositions through which normalizing power operates and would reabsorb his analysis in the way that an analysis of power as repressive is absorbed—this does not mean that the analysis is not liberating. In revealing the way biopower operates in our practice, for example, genealogy liberates but not by releasing an autonomous self from repression or through progress toward the achievement of the self as a goal. Instead it opens up the limit; it prevents the leveling out or closure of normalizing power, freeing us to create ourselves in our autonomy.[38] For Foucault, maturity is our permanent self-creation, and liberation comes through the Nietzschean realization that everything is possible.

This sense of maturity as our self-creation—which connects Foucault to Baudelaire's notion of the dandy—suggests an understanding of the achievement of our maturity that is not grounded in the humanist notion of man as an autonomous subject. But at the same time that he understood autonomy as permanent self-creation, Foucault remained connected to the Kantian notion of maturity as the rule of self by self. This is apparently part of the motivational theme of Foucault's second volume in the series on sexuality, a project that was reshaped by his interest in the Greek concern with the techniques of self-care and self-mastery. In an interview with Dreyfus and Rabinow about this work, Foucault discussed the similarity between the problem we face in elaborating a basis for conduct and that faced by the Greeks. "Recent liberation movements suffer from the fact that they cannot find any principle on which to base the elaboration of ethics. They need an ethics, but they cannot find any other ethics than an ethics founded on so-called scientific knowledge of what the self is, what desire is, what the unconscious is, and so on."[39] What his work on the Greeks revealed was a response to a similar problem which he thought did not depend on constituting the self as an autonomous subject and did not contribute to totalization and normalization. Though he was clear in the interview that he in no way proposed the Greek concern with mastery of self as an alternative to our current plight, it is also clear that he saw something preferable in it: "I don't think one can find any normalization in, for instance, the Stoic ethics. The reason is, I think, that the principal aim, the principal target of this kind of ethics was an aesthetic one" (*Beyond Structuralism,* p. 230). In *The Use of Pleasure,* the point in examining Greek ethics is made explicit: "In what does [the critical work of thought] consist, if not in the endeavor to know how and to what extent it might be possible to think differently, instead of legitimizing what is already known?"[40]

In considering the way the Greeks constituted themselves as ethical subjects with regard to pleasure, Foucault's analysis presented an alternative to the modern conception of the self and thus suggests the possibility of thinking of ourselves differently. The Greek notion of the self was understood in terms of moderation and self-mastery, not in terms of an ethical subject regulated by formal codes prescribing the forbidden and the permitted, or, as with the Christian confessional or Freudian analysis, in terms of a "deep" self whose relation to itself was one of self-decipherment. Unlike the modern notion of the ethical subject, the moderate self of the Greeks was not understood in terms of codes or norms, or in terms of control of hidden desires. Instead, it was concerned with an art of existence: "those intentional and voluntary actions by which men not only set themselves rules of conduct, but also seek to transform themselves, to change themselves in their singular being, and to make their life into an *oeuvre*" (*Use of Pleasure,* pp. 10–11). What is suggested by the permanent critique of ourselves as a limit-attitude and a transgression of the limits, as well as by the alternative of the Greeks, is a *style* of existence and the possibility of our willing to live a beautiful life; a life whose moral value "does not depend either on one's being in conformity with a code of behavior, or on an effort of purification" (*Use of Pleasure,* p. 85), but on being master of one's self. This, it seems to me, connects with a Kantian notion of autonomy directed not at freeing us from relations of power but at enabling us to be lawgivers for ourselves.

I need not dwell on the work on Greek ethics to make the general point I wish to make. In his genealogy of the modern self as subject, Foucault's work points toward the possibility of a non-normalized self but it does not emancipate in the sense of recovering the historically antecedent self, as with Rousseau, or of realizing the mature self as a goal, as with Kant. Autonomy applies to neither past nor future; it is a mode of our relation to the present. Though critique of the present will not provide for an escape from power/knowledge into freedom, as Taylor would require, neither does it result in acquiescence or accommodation to the current power/knowledge regime, as Taylor's and Habermas's criticism suggests. It seems that, much in the way Heidegger's analysis of the essence of technology aimed at achieving a free relation with it, one that neither resists it nor is swept along by it, Foucault's analysis of power/knowledge suggests a conception of the mature self that is free in relation to normalizing power, a self that creates itself in its possibilities.

## V

I have suggested that Habermas and Taylor have incorrectly located the problem with Foucault's work by failing to appreciate the way in which his critique of the human sciences and the analysis of modern power is connected with the Enlightenment goal of autonomy. He had opposed both the traditional philosophical project of grounding critique in an independent normative framework and in the binary oppositions that have structured philosophical analysis, without the conservative result that we live in conformity with the existing order. Though Foucault's work avoids the charge of conservatism and points toward a sense of maturity not grounded in the modern notion of the autonomous self as subject, I will suggest in this final section that this account—an account that identifies normalization and unfreedom, and that connects liberation with transgression and connects maturity with self-creation—remains deeply problematic for other reasons. These reasons are related to the Enlightenment view of the place of the intellectual in social action and the role of reason in achieving moral or political community.

Before turning to those issues, I want to raise two general but related points that arise from the conception of the self that seems to result from Foucault's work. The first can be made indirectly through the postmodern theme of the end of the metaphysical tradition. Any number of different stances toward metaphysics have been grouped under the banner of postmetaphysics or postmodernism or the end of philosophy. For Heidegger, for example, the end of metaphysics does not mean its termination but the realization of its limit or extreme possibility. Yet he thought that there was something more original left at the limit of metaphysics for what he termed "thinking" as opposed to philosophy. Derrida, likewise, does not seek to terminate metaphysics but, unlike Heidegger, he does not seek something more original. Instead, he writes within metaphysics in order to find in the metaphysical text itself that which prevents it from achieving closure. Deconstruction seeks to keep philosophy going by continually opening up the text to a play of interpretations. Richard Rorty's opposition to the philosophical tradition is ambivalent. On the one hand, he shares with Derrida the attempt to prevent closure in order to keep what he calls "the conversation of the West" going; on the other, there is the sense that, unlike Derrida, one can turn one's back on the metaphysical tradition and quit doing philosophy whenever one likes. There is in Rorty a kind of meta-philosophy of boredom that allows for an end of philosophy in the sense of its termination and that justifies a withdrawal, not to some position anterior to metaphysics as with Heidegger, but to a position where one simply refuses to be involved in the philosophical conversation. My suggestion is that, considered by itself, the Nietzschean theme of autonomy as self-creation, a theme common to Rorty and Foucault, seems to suggest that liberation from closure or normalization is achieved by withdrawing from social action, much in the way in which a certain sort of post-modern critique of philosophy is consistent with a complete disengagement from the philosophical tradition. I shall argue in the final chapter that Rorty avoids this result by coupling a Nietzschean notion of the self with Dewey's notion of community. But for Foucault, opposition to normalization by permanent critique and self-creation is consistent either with anarchistic, local forms of resistance or with a withdrawal from the scene of politics altogether. It certainly cannot be a satisfactory conclusion if our escape from tutelage means a withdrawal from the struggle against power. It is only within the context of some other view of the self—the Kantian self as moral agent or as member of a community, for example—that he can tie the notion of autonomy to social action. Otherwise, though Foucault's work may suggest a notion of emancipation, there will remain merely an ad hoc connection between political action and his genealogy of modern forms of power.

Second, Foucault's notions of autonomy and an aesthetics of existence may not have escaped humanism and normalization after all. In the *Intimate Journals,* Baudelaire had entered a line about the dandy that could well be the motto for the self as a work of art: "To be a great man and a saint by *one's own standards,* that is all that matters."[41] That line sums up what, in *The Use of Pleasure,* Foucault seems to have meant by an aesthetic of existence in which one makes one's life an *oeuvre.* If this does not privilege the conscious subject of Descartes and Kant, it at least fosters "a cult of self," in Baudelaire's phrase. So understood, it has all the appearance of being merely another instance of the "individual vs. society" controversy that has structured much of modern social theory. Rousseau attempted to resolve that opposition by recovering a notion of freedom as wholeness and self-sufficiency, criticizing the way culture levels out individuality; but he was able to integrate the self and society because that conception of freedom became the basis for restructuring society in such a way that we enter into social relations yet remain as free as before. Kant had understood moral agency to be constituted by our membership in a moral community and he had connected maturity and community by a philosophy of history as progress toward a cosmopolitan state. If an aesthetics of existence is not integrated into a notion of community, though, not only will there be the problem that we are freed from normalizing power only by withdrawing from social action—neither resisting the current regime of power nor being carried along by it—but the "cult of self" will be simply one side of the binary opposition of individual against society. But if this is what it comes to, Foucault has not escaped humanism after all, and his view of the self runs the risk of being re-colonized by normalizing power.

These general points can be made more directly and concretely by considering Rorty's claim that Foucault's view cannot support a sense of social solidarity because of Foucault's view of the role of the intellectual and his opposition to grounding political action in any notion of society as a whole. Rorty has put the criticism this way:

> Foucault once said that he would like to write "so as to have no face." He forbids himself the tone of the liberal sort of thinker who says to his fellow citizens: *We* know that there must be a better way to do things than this; let us look for it together." There is no "we" to be found in Foucault's writing. . . . It is this remoteness which reminds one of the conservative who pours cold water on hopes for reform, who affects to look at problems of his fellow citizens with the eye of the future historian. Writing "the history of the present," rather than suggestions about how our children might inhabit a better world gives up not just on the notion of a common human nature, and on that of "the subject," but on our untheoretical sense of social solidarity.[42]

Now on Foucault's account, both the traditional idea of the intellectual in political struggle and the idea of political action grounded in terms of society are, themselves, part of normalization, and for that reason Foucault could not support Rorty's sense of social solidarity and social hope. On the point of the role of the intellectual, Foucault remarked in a conversation with Deleuze that "Intellectuals are themselves agents of this system of power—the idea of their responsibility for 'consciousness' and discourse forms part of the system. The intellectual's role is no longer to place himself 'somewhat ahead and to the side' in order to express the stifled truth of the collectivity."[43] His opposition to the traditional role of the intellectual in political criticism, it turns out, resulted from an assimilation of the epistemological and the political in that he opposed the role of the intellectual in political struggle for exactly the same reasons that he opposed the foundational role of the Cartesian-Kantian subject. The intellectual as the one who represents social consciousness is just an instance of the conscious subject as the condition for the possibility of representation of reality. In the conversation with Deleuze, Deleuze asserts and Foucault agrees, "representation no longer exists; there is only action" (*Language, Counter-Memory, Practice,* p. 206). While he remained tied to the Enlightenment themes of critique and autonomy, he rejected the Enlightenment view of the intellectual as representative conscience and critic of society.

Rorty's demand for social solidarity, according to Foucault's line of thought, also stands in the way of the struggle against power. In Foucault's conversation under the title "Revolutionary Action: Until Now" one of the participants remarks: "I cannot believe that the movement must remain at its present state, as this vague, unsubstantial, underground ideology that refuses to endorse any form of social work or community service, any action that requires going beyond the immediate group." To this Foucault responded:

> To speak of the "whole of society" apart from the only form it has ever taken is to transform our past into a dream. . . . I believe that this is asking a great deal, that it means imposing impossible conditions on our actions because this notion functions in a manner that prohibits the actualization, success and perpetuation of those projects. "The whole of society" is precisely that which should not be considered except as something to be destroyed. And then, we can only hope that it will never exist again.[44]

Of all the dark parts of Foucault's analysis, this is clearly the darkest. Social solidarity, too, is a part of normalizing power.

Nevertheless, while Foucault points to a notion of maturity in terms of self-creation, and while he opposes the idea of "society as a whole" or social solidarity as a foundation for political resistance, there seems to be some sense in his later work that he attached importance to one's relation to others and to social reciprocity, but it is not at all clear that he can have both self-mastery and reciprocity. In the interview with Dreyfus and Rabinow, for example, Foucault pointed out that while the Greeks had a notion of self-mastery that was not tied to the conscious subject, their ethics of pleasure had no place for mutual recognition and a reciprocal relation with the other, and that was the danger. This point was best illustrated in his discussion of Greek attitudes toward marital fidelity. According to Foucault, one's fidelity to one's spouse did not depend on a sense of duty to the spouse but resulted from the duty to have authority over one's pleasure. What the work on the Greeks does suggest, however, is our need for a notion of self-creation that also has a place for mutual recognition; and it is not clear that Foucault's notion of autonomy—fragmentary as it is—can support both self-creation and mutual recognition.

The issue I have attempted to focus between Foucault and his critics, then, turns not on the Enlightenment commitment to the goal of autonomy and critique but on the nature of critique and the nature of autonomy. Foucault's genealogy, like Nietzschean nihilism, offers a notion of autonomy as transgression of limits and as self-creation in the face of a permanent critique of the present. It is not the conservative accommodation to our current condition or to current regimes of power. Although Foucault's work resists this line of criticism from Habermas and Taylor, there are still serious problems with it. At the same time that his critique of modernity remains connected with the goal of the Enlightenment and illuminates our understanding of the present, it suggests a notion of liberation and autonomy that cannot support social hope and the Enlightenment goal of moral community.

# 5 Relativism, Dogmatism, and Rationality

Since the seventeenth century rationality has been understood through a matrix of relations between "truth," "objectivity," "certainty," and "reality." Proper to this conception, philosophy has been the quest for the permanent, foundational, ahistorical framework from which to secure truth and objective knowledge of the real, and its task has been thought to be guaranteed by the nature and universality of reason itself. Thus to call the universality of reason into question undermines this foundational project and puts philosophy itself into question. The problematic nature of rationality and the role of philosophy proper to it has been the common theme that unites a number of important topics and problems in recent philosophy. Since the work of Thomas Kuhn, the rationality of science—which has served since the Enlightenment as the paradigm of reason generally—has been brought into question by an understanding of scientific change and the growth of knowledge that proceeds through paradigm shifts and revolutions rather than by linear progression. In the debate between realists and antirealists—a debate spawned not only by recent philosophy of science but also by the work of Quine, Putnam, Davidson, and others in the philosophy of language—the relation between rationality and realism has been a central issue. Work in the philosophy of social sciences like that of Peter Winch has made the univocality of reason a fundamental concern for recent anthropology and social theory, as Western social scientists attempt to avoid enthnocentrism when interpreting alien cultures and to avoid cultural chauvinism in applying Western values. In addition, challenge to the rationality of belief and, therefore, to the possibility of reason has become the focus of epistemological considerations along with concern over skeptical arguments like those of Peter Unger.

Because the post-seventeenth-century conception of the universality of reason as the tribunal before which all beliefs and values are to be judged goes hand in hand with the notion of philosophy as foundational, and because the problematic nature of this conception of rationality is the overarching theme of so many crucial debates in recent philosophy, the defense of rationality against its challengers is, at the deepest level, a defense of the traditional conception of philosophy and its place in culture. It has appeared that philosophy must reassert itself against recent criticism of the traditional conception of rationality;

otherwise, we are left with irrationality in our beliefs and arbitrariness or dogmatism with respect to our values.

Recent defenses of reason and its connection with truth, objectivity, and reality can be usefully read, I think, as attempts to steer between the companion threats of dogmatism and relativism. The problematic is provided by two sorts of skeptical challenge. On the one hand, the skeptic challenges us to justify our commitment to reason itself. On the other, the challenge is to justify the rationality of our ultimate commitments; or, less artificially, to justify the rationality of our beliefs, values, or theories in the face of alternative and alien beliefs and values. Recent reaction to these skeptical challenges has issued in attempts to take the curse off relativism by offering heady arguments about radically alternative conceptual schemes and incommensurable ways of seeing the world, by urging rational pluralism and creative nihilism. Alternately, it has produced attempts to mitigate dogmatic commitment in the name of "critical rationality" by equally heady realist arguments about the convergence of scientific inquiry on the best representation of reality. On one view there are many more standards of rationality than dreamed of in our philosophy. On the other, all inquiry is seen to progress toward one rational scheme. On the one view the notion that reason demands the convergence of beliefs and values on a single conceptual scheme is dogmatic and totalitarian; against this, rational pluralism is thought to yield a kind of exhilarating liberation. On the other view, rational pluralism is perniciously relativistic and nihilistic, yielding the conclusion that any beliefs, values, or theories are as good as any other.

In the first part of this chapter I shall sketch two sorts of issues that have made reason problematic for recent philosophy. The first has to do with "the new philosophy of science" following from Kuhn's work which has given certain traditional epistemological controversies new interest and urgency. The second grows out of increasing criticism of the tendency among many Western social scientists to apply our own standards of rational inquiry to the interpretation of alien beliefs and practices. These two sources of concern about reason, however, pull in different directions, and I shall suggest that the tension between the epistemologists' and the social scientists' concern with reason can be viewed as a conflict between different notions of rationality. One takes rationality to be tied to objectivity, truth, and correct representation of reality, whereas the other takes it to be connected with such things as judgment, the openness of the practice of inquiry, and the intelligibility and success of beliefs in coping with the world and with social and moral conflicts. Against this background I shall be concerned to support the latter view, not by defending it as a theory of rationality but by undermining the dogmatism-relativism dichotomy that has structured these recent controversies and has cast the former notion of rationality as the only alternative to relativism. My claim will be that the implications of arguments by Thomas Kuhn, Donald Davidson, and Charles Taylor undercut that dichotomy with the result that confidence in the rationality of our own beliefs and practices of inquiry is restored as the only base from which criticism can take place. It is this result that places the recent controversy over the nature of rationality within the context of the Pyrrhonian challenge.

I shall argue initially that the view that rationality must be understood in terms of objectivity, truth, realism, and the like will seem to be the necessary alternative to relativism if we take a certain sort of skeptical challenge seriously. Furthermore, I shall suggest, the dichotomy that that sort of skeptical challenge is playing off—either "rationality as objective truth" or relativism—is intelligible only if what Davidson has called the third and final dogma of empiricism—the dualism of scheme and content—is intelligible. Applying Davidsonian arguments that conceptual relativism is incoherent, suggestions of Kuhn about the sense in which theory choice in science is objective, and Taylor's argument that a pluralistic conception of rationality is compatible with evaluating incommensurable cultural practices, I shall argue that we can resist dogmatism in our beliefs and values without lapsing into a pernicious relativism.

## I

Apart from specific philosophical controversies and intellectual crises, the challenge to justify the rationality of our beliefs rather than merely assume it, the demand to defend rather than accept and expect that we are rational, the attempt to construct theories of rationality rather than attribute it automatically to any coherent and sustaining system of belief would all seem fairly sterile. In either the domain of ethics, science, or social theory, it is implausible to think that one could be an intuitive relativist. The idea that there is no nonarbitrary basis for evaluating alternative values, theories, or cultures, or its companion idea that our confidence in our own values and beliefs is unjustifiably dogmatic, is an *outcome* rather than an initial intuition. It is only when placed in the space of controversies between, say, skeptics and dogmatists, or truths of heart and head, or science and pseudo-science, or ours and alien cultures that challenges to the rationality of one's beliefs have any urgency at all. This is just to say that reason is neither initially nor chronically and continually in need of defense and justification against skeptical challenges.

Removed from particular controversies, the very idea of justifying rationality smacks of a contrived circularity, since justification itself is at home only in the context of reason. One form of the challenge to rationality—what W. W. Bartley calls the *tu quoque* argument against reason [1]—claims that any attempt to justify rationality is destined to fail either because of an infinite regress of justification or because of an inevitable circularity. The irrationalist can be thought of as saying: "A commitment to rationality is, at bottom, arbitrary and irrational. *Tu quoque.* One leap of faith is no better or worse off than another." Put in this way the *tu quoque* argument appears anything but a fallacy. It has seemed to some that one must simply admit the argument and try to mitigate its force by asserting that a self-consciously irrational commitment is preferrable to an unconscious one, and that a commitment that is self-critical is at least better than one that is not; that is, *critical* rationality is better than dogmatic commitment. This has been the tack taken, for example, by Karl Popper and his followers.[2]

In a similar way, the challenge to justify rational commitment, when removed from particular controversies, has a certain self-defeating ring about it. By demanding a justification for one's basic commitments, this shows at least minimally that the skeptical challenger takes justification to be something one ought to be able to provide. This skeptic is saying something like "you *ought* to be able to justify a commitment to reason but you can't." If, on the other hand, the skeptic is viewed as agreeing that a certain commitment was rational but is asking why we should be rational, this would be rather like someone agreeing that a certain action was our duty while demanding an additional argument that we should do our duty. The former demand is as out of place as the latter. If, furthermore, this skeptical challenge is taken to be a question about justifying *that* we are rational, I think there is something right about Joseph Agassi's[3] suggestion that the very ability to ask "Should I be rational?" already shows that we are rational, at least to some degree. Devoid of context, a demand for justification for rationality—as if we had some choice in the matter, as if we really might not be rational—is entirely artificial. The *tu quoque* argument would lack any bite at all if there were not already other forces at work undermining rational commitment.

The primary crisis that has made rationality problematic for our generation of philosophers is the loss of faith in science as the exemplification of rationality at its best and the measure by which all systems of beliefs and people are to be judged. Quine's attack on the dogmas of empiricism, Sellars's attack on the givenness of experience, Feyerabend's attack on the theory-observation distinction, Kuhn's attack on the Hempelian view of the nature of scientific change, Rorty's attack on epistemological foundationalism, Winch's attack on those who interpret alien cultures on the basis of Western scientific rationality, and Habermas's attack on the positivist image of science divorced from knowledge-constitutive human interests have all forced a reevaluation of the nature of scientific inquiry. The ideal of science as objective and value free and of changes in science as progressively enlarging the scope and universality of theories and laws in conformity with the a priori standards of rationality has been dismantled, and in its place we get charges of subjectivism and relativism; accounts of science changing through crisis and revolution or through social domination; and calls for epistemological anarchism and methodological nihilism. If the nature of scientific rationality has become suspect and problematic, how much more so the nature of rationality generally, since modern science is the model for the Enlightenment ideal of reason we have inherited.

This internal collapse of the Enlightenment image of rationality modeled on science has been joined by an indictment of science as an institution. According to some critics, when the image of scientific methodology as the standard for what is rational is coupled with the realization that the development of the scientific enterprise is increasingly institutionalized—where research programs are at the mercy of government grants and professional-society politics, for example—the Enlightenment view of rational inquiry understood within an environment of free and open exchange is replaced by a view of reason that is subordinate to relations of power and of rational standards that prescribe and prohibit the growth of knowledge rather than foster it. From the point of view of this sort of criticism, the Enlightenment ideal has degenerated into rigidity, sterility, conservatism, conformity, and dogmatism. Where once science was seen as liberating humankind from dogma, authority, and superstition, it is increasingly being thought of as ideological—in the neo-Marxist sense of the term—and therefore as itself dogmatic.[4]

The Enlightenment had envisioned the conquest of myth, superstition, and dogma by bringing everything equally before the bar of reason. The method of scientific inquiry as the model of rationality and the best defense against prejudice was the model for that ideal. One result of a more relaxed, post-positivist, Kuhnian, or Popperian attitude about scientific change is a new form of romantic reaction against positivist excess in the name of this Enlightenment ideal. Within the positivist framework, for example, we could draw easy contrasts between the scientific and the pseudo-scientific or between the scientific and the prescientific, and apply those dichotomies to the interpretation of alien cultures. With the demise of positivism, however, primitive, alien, and unorthodox beliefs have gained a new respectability in the name of rational pluralism.

As Hans-Georg Gadamer has pointed out with respect to the older reaction, some of this new romantic reaction is simply the counterimage of the Enlightenment ideal it opposes and is therefore inevitably wedded to that ideal. Gadamer put the point about the older form of reaction this way: "The reversal of the Enlightenment presuppositions results in the paradoxical tendency to restoration, i.e., the tendency to reconstruct the old because it is old, and conscious return to the unconscious, culminating in the recognition of the superior wisdom of the primeval age." But, he continues, "Primeval wisdom is only the counter-image of primeval stupidity'."[5] The same categories of thought that once made us think of alien beliefs as primitive now swing in the other direction so we can think of them as wise, as if we can recover our lost wisdom by overcoming our Western tradition. It is not just that this sort of reaction against the positivist conception of scientific rationality tends toward a new romanticism, but it is played out on the stage set by excessive claims for scientific reason and thus is of a piece with what it is opposing. It opposes the Enlightenment conception of rationality by merely reversing it.

Within this current crisis in the scientific image, the relativist sees our Enlightenment confidence in science and reason as just Whiggish self-justification and concludes that once we see science as a historical phenomenon developing in discontinuous fashion, then we must see that all our beliefs and values are historical and revisable in principle. The dogmatist reasserts the rationality of our beliefs and values against alternatives, demanding in the name of reason the convergence of all inquiry on a single conceptual scheme. The skeptic plays our pluralist intuitions off against our Enlightenment intuitions about scientific rationality, thus forcing the issue between relativism and dogmatism.

I shall suggest later that failure to appreciate that these alternatives are of a piece leads to the hopeless view that reason must forever swing between dogmatism and relativism. In an especially illuminating book, Richard Bernstein has structured certain contemporary debates in terms of the contrast between objectivity and relativism, and the point he draws from that contrast is the one I will draw in different ways. According to Bernstein,

One reason why these controversies seem to generate more heat than light is that the entire discussion is still infected with the legacy of the Cartesian Either/Or; many of the participants in these disputes argue as if we must choose between the alternatives of objectivism (e.g., scientific realism) or relativism. But this way of framing the key issues is misleading. We gain a better insight into the positive achievement of the postempiricist philosophy and history of science when we appreciate that what is really going on is that the whole framework of thinking that poses issues with reference to these and related dichotomies is being called into question.[6]

What I intend to show is how the relativism/dogmatism dichotomy has been undercut recently, and how that brings us back to the beliefs and practices of current inquiry in the way the Pyrrhonian opposition to philosophy aimed at restoring the appearances, customs, and traditions of common life.

Entering the dialectical space left by various attacks on the received view of science, friends of rationality have a double burden. They must join hands with the opponents of conformity and dogmatism without slipping into a new romanticism or reckless relativism. The "new rationalist" must abandon old notions of the objectivity, universality, and necessity of current practices without embracing the view that any beliefs and practices are as good as any other. One reason, then, that it has seemed that rationality stands in serious need of justification is the need to steer between an unduly restrictive image of rationality—or an unjustifiably rigid demarcation of science and nonscience—and no image at all.

Against this background old controversies take on new importance, and it should not surprise us that the *tu quoque* argument should lose some of its artificiality. It should not surprise us either that skepticism about rationality should find new supporters. The result is that there is a new generation of philosophers who see the threat and stand ready to take up the challenge. On the one hand we find philosophers such as Peter Unger arguing not only that no one ever knows anything but that no one is ever reasonable about anything either. On the other hand we find philosophers such as John Kekes who understand that this is not merely an idle epistemological issue but an issue that has moral significance. As Kekes has put it, skepticism about rationality results in "the impossibility of settling conflicts in a civilized manner. It encourages an appeal to prejudice and the use of force, propaganda, and dogmatism. It is an attack on what is finest in the Western tradition."[7] In this sense, the attack on the rationality of science or on the rationality of Western beliefs and values or on the foundational task of philosophy is a contemporary version of the Pyrrhonian challenge—a challenge that eliminates the possibility of a framework for rational criticism and results either in uncritical acquiescence in the authority of our own beliefs and values simply because they are traditional and customary, or—what is just the other side of that coin—a challenge that implies that we are cut off from tradition as the source of beliefs and values since they are ungrounded and, to that extent, optional.

The attempt to meet the challenge by developing theories of rationality which offer criteria for scientific theory choice or for evaluating alternative beliefs and practices has led to problems of another sort, however, that put the epistemological requirements of rationality at odds with the requirements of social theory. A theory of rationality must be rigorous in its demands if it is to meet the skeptic's challenge. However, a theory of rationality that is *too* limiting runs the risk of becoming simply a parochial apologetic for one's own favorite epistemological practices. Even with more relaxed attitudes about scientific change, Western science is still taken as the model for a theory of rationality. The reason is that scientific rationality is still taken to be the best example of a self-regulating, self-correcting activity which aims at objectivity, truth, and reality. But this view of rationality creates special problems when we are confronting systems of beliefs different from our own. Jarvie and Agassi, among others,[8] have been especially critical of anthropologists who interpret the rationality of other cultures on the basis of epistemological criteria drawn from Western science. In criticizing Beattie's view that magic represents symbolic activity as contrasted with the systematic, analytic thinking of science, they charge that "this is the parochialism of the twentieth century in its worst manifestation: science is always right, science is rational, *ergo* rationality leads to the avoidance of error. . . . Embedded here is the incredible idea that there exists something like a rational or scientific thought process which leads to the discovery of truth."[9]

This tension between the epistemological concern with rationality and the social scientist's concern to avoid ethnocentrism can be approached at a slightly different angle. According to Kekes, one must avoid two approaches in developing a theory of rationality:

> One is to treat rationality as a character trait possessed by people who have a disposition to make decisions and accept beliefs by weighing reasons. To develop a theory of rationality based on this assumption is a psychological task and can, perhaps be discharged by empirical psychologists. But having a psychological theory of rationality will not silence the sceptic. . . . The other temptation is to account for rationality entirely in formal terms.[10]

What is telling about this way of structuring the problem is that Kekes takes the formal approach to be very close to what a philosophical account should be. One must avoid being *entirely* formal, but a psychological approach—that is, a theory of *natural* rationality—is to be avoided altogether since it will not silence the skeptic. This concern to defeat the skeptic rather than to treat rationality as a disposition of people or constitutive of a system of beliefs, however, seriously effects our understanding of alien cultures.

Barry Barnes draws attention to the problem by considering what happens in the social sciences when one fails to recognize the difference between what he calls an evaluative concept of rationality—he has Popperian criteria in mind but he uses the term to cover *any* set of epistemological criteria—and a theory of natural rationality:

> The distinction between natural rationality and an evaluative concept based on culturally accepted conventions is not . . . recognized in the work of most social scientists. They tend to pick their favorite epistemology and consider how far cultures embody it. And then, without even showing why on earth that epistemology *should* be embedded in a particular culture, they become puzzled when it is not found and offer causes of irrationality. . . . Such a conflation of evaluation and naturalistic investigation inevitably impedes any attempt to increase our understanding of human activity.[11]

For Barnes, only a theory that treats rationality as a natural propensity of peoples and cultures will be sufficiently tolerant to be of use to the social scientist.

The dilemma then is this: the epistemologists' attempt to refute the skeptic and avoid relativism by developing a theory of rationality tends to result in criteria of rationality that are problematic when social scientists confront practices and beliefs that are different from their own. However, any account of rationality that is tolerant enough to count beliefs in God, magic, poison oracles, cargo cults, alchemy, phlogiston, and astrology as rational stands little chance of defeating the skeptic. This dilemma grows out of a need to mediate conflicting intuitions. On the one hand we favor the avoidance of dogmatism in interpreting the beliefs and practices of alien cultures, and tolerance and pluralism can be preserved only if we embrace, at most, a minimal view of rationality. On the other hand, we wish to combat skepticism and avoid a pernicious relativism through a conception of rationality that allows us to judge some beliefs and values as more rational, better, or more likely to be right than others; and this seems possible only if we adopt a more stringent and, therefore, less tolerant view.

The problem of rationality, then, has become located between extremes. In the philosophical literature one can see Feyerabend—and Kuhn and Rorty on a rather common interpretation[12]—at one end, and defenders of scientific rationality and realism such as Popper, Roger

Trigg, or Hilary Putnam[13] at the other. In the social science literature, the pendulum swings between Benjamin Whorf or Winch, and someone such as Evans-Pritchard or Beattie. And once the problem of rationality becomes located between these extremes it is tempting to split the difference between the two in the manner of a Steven Lukes[14] or a John Kekes. But it is equally tempting to extend Feyerabend's criticism of Lakatos to all such middle-position attempts: theories of rationality that prohibit nothing are mere embroideries, anarchism in disguise.[15] I shall argue that it is not the middle course that is wanted but rather the dogmatism-relativism nexus that defines the problem and structures the possible solutions that must be overcome.

## II

This swing between dogmatic and relativist intuitions comes about from the conflation of distinct notions of rationality. The confusion is between rationality viewed as constitutive of any coherent and sustaining system of beliefs and rationality identified with a mode of inquiry leading to objectivity, truth, and reality. The broad contrast is between the view that rationality is a feature of our practices and the view that it is a property of the relation between knower and known or between theory and the world. For convenience I shall refer to the former as rationality$_1$ and the latter as rationality$_2$.[16] It is important not to assimilate this distinction to what Jarvie and Agassi—and following them, Evan Fales—have distinguished as a weak and strong sense of rationality. Fales characterizes weak rationality in the following way: "[a] belief in a social ideology which fails to accommodate the preponderant evidence concerning the nature of the world (social and/or natural) but which nevertheless 'works' in the sense that belief in it produces appropriately socialized behavior is *weakly rational* belief."[17] By contrast, a strongly rational belief is one that accommodates the preponderant evidence. There are two reasons why I wish to avoid this way of distinguishing senses of rationality. First, weak rationality is characterized negatively on the basis of an assumption about "full-blooded" rationality, whereas what I wish to suggest is that rationality$_1$ is itself full-blooded. Second, it is tempting to think that weak rationality and strong rationality are continuous notions such that increasing rationalization by a process of self-criticism or self-correction of one's beliefs will eventually yield strongly rational beliefs, whereas what I intend by the distinction is that rationality$_1$ and rationality$_2$ are competing notions. Rationality$_2$ entails the idea that self-criticism and self-correction will yield ultimate convergence on the objective, true, correct representation of reality. It is consistent with rational$_1$ beliefs, however, that significantly different sets of beliefs could be the outcome of inquiry without the implicit assumption that further inquiry will decide between them. This is not to be taken as a remark about the proliferation of theories in the manner of Feyerabend. Rather it is to say that inquiry can be as self-critical or self-correcting as one likes in confronting the world, but that nothing about being self-critical or self-correcting necessitates the way criticism or new phenomena will be accommodated or necessitates ultimate commensurability of all frameworks of inquiry.

What makes a commitment to rationality$_2$ appealing—apart from its rather long history—is the observation that it is the tendency in any system of beliefs or competing alternative solutions to problems to converge on agreement. Since a successful solution to problems confronting a system of beliefs is necessary for the system's survival, convergence on agreement has survival value for systems of beliefs. This observation, however, is neutral between the two notions of rationality. Yet defenders of rationality$_2$ extend this observation to show that agreement and success are symptoms of objectivity, truth, and correct representations of reality. They see the world as independent of any system of beliefs, skepticism as a genuine threat to the possibility of accurately representing the world, and rationality$_2$ as assuring that at the end of inquiry, reality will be accurately represented. The world leads rational$_2$ inquiry, through its confrontation with new phenomena, to itself.[18] It is the teleology of truth—to use Foucault's phrase—that directs rational$_2$ inquiry. It is only in terms of this conception of rationality that one would be inclined to agree with Roger Trigg that a commitment to reason *must* include a commitment to objective truth; or to say with Sheldon Richard's gloss on Trigg that "the possibility of rationality depends on the truth of realism."[19] What I want to suggest in the next section is that it is only if one thinks that skepticism about rationality must be defeated or else relativism embraced that the controversy is taken to be about rationality$_2$.

## III

I shall begin to undermine the relativism-dogmatism nexus by considering Peter Unger's skepticism about reason,[20] which is the most comprehensive skepticism to come out of the intellectual scene I have been sketching. Unger's skepticism about reason is a consequence of two skeptical arguments about knowledge. The first is a fancier version of Descartes' evil deceiver. On Unger's view, certainty is a necessary condition for knowledge, and for anyone to be certain of anything we must be certain that there is not an evil scientist cleverly inducing all of our beliefs—including the belief that there is not an evil scientist—by manipulating our brains. The second argument—what Unger calls the Argument for Universal Ignorance—says that if someone knows something, it is alright to have an attitude of *absolute certainty* about it, but since it is never alright to have an attitude of absolute certainty, then no one ever knows anything. The skeptical argument about reason—the Basis in Knowledge Argument—follows from this. According to Unger, if anyone is reasonable about anything there must be something that one knows which is the reason, thus no one is ever reasonable.

The general line of his argument can be illustrated in one of his examples. If seeing that Fred's hat is wet is Ralph's reason for thinking that it is raining, then Ralph must know that the hat was wet since it would be inconsistent to say "Ralph's reason was that Fred's hat was wet but he wasn't absolutely certain that it was." The point the example is intended to make rests on two different arguments. The first is straightforwardly epistemological: if reason must have a basis in knowledge and knowledge is impossible, reason is impossible as well. The second is normative: to be rational requires an attitude of absolute certainty, but such an attitude is always dogmatic and it is never right to be dogmatic. The charge of dogmatism is the underlying theme of Unger's book and, I am inclined to think, its most interesting but least developed feature. I shall return to it shortly.

As a first attempt at undermining Unger's Basis in Knowledge Argument, consider the following extension of his example. Suppose from my interior office I notice students passing my door dripping wet, removing raincoats, shaking umbrellas, and the like. Suppose also, that Fred walks by and it appears as if he has a wet hat. I'm not absolutely certain that Fred's hat is wet or that the coats or umbrellas are, for that matter. For all I know, it may be an elaborate deception staged by an especially evil student of epistemology to lead me to believe mistakenly that his hat was wet. I suppress my claim to absolute certainty yet I wish to go out, so I take my umbrella. The reason I take my umbrella is, among other things, that Fred's hat was wet. In addition, I remember such things as the morning weather report, and the fact that the children went off with raincoats. I am also aware that generally my students are not sufficiently clever or enterprising enough to cook up such a hoax, and so on. Now the point of this extension is not just that there seems to be an intuition behind the example which suggests that absolute certainty is too strong for reason; rather, the example suggests that the reasonableness of a particular belief or practice is found in its connection with a whole pattern of beliefs and practices; ultimately if you like, with a whole "form of life." Unger, however, treats beliefs in isolation, as if to argue that since no individual belief is reasonable, the enumerated whole could not be either. But if Unger's argument is to have any bite, it must be directed toward the dogmatic character of a whole system of beliefs. I shall return to this point shortly.

One way of defeating Unger's skepticism about rationality would be to defeat his skepticism about knowledge. His so-called "theory of absolute terms" and the "syntacto-semantic evidence" notwithstanding, this might be done by offering a theory of knowledge without certainty. Keith Lehrer,[21] for example, and any number of other "foundations-without-certainty" epistemologists could agree with Unger that reason must have a basis in knowledge yet they would claim that absolute certainty is much too strong a condition for knowing. On Lehrer's account, a belief in a statement is completely justified if, on comparison with the possibility of alternative statements, the expected value of believing the statement is positive; that is, if there is a better chance of it being true than there is of the strongest competitor being true. On this view someone is reasonable so long as he has justified beliefs, but justification does not rest on certainty. My point in mentioning Lehrer is only to suggest that it is not obvious that certainty is the criterion for knowledge, thus it is not obvious that skeptical objections to certainty theories of knowledge undermine the reasonableness of belief. Unger's serious challenge to the reasonableness of belief must lie elsewhere.

Even if certainty is too strong a condition for knowledge—as I think it is—and even if a program of knowledge without certainty were to be successful, this could undercut the epistemological form of Unger's argument but not the normative form. The antidogmatism argument—which I think is the serious challenge—rests on an attitude about a belief that serves as a reason, not on the certainty of the belief. That is, even if I am not absolutely certain that a particular belief is true, this is consistent with my having an attitude of certainty about it, and on Unger's view it would be bad faith for a particular belief to serve as my reason if I seriously entertain the possibility that I am mistaken about it. If to be reasonable I must at least have an attitude of certainty, then Unger's second argument is set. He puts the case for the normative argument in the following way:

> to be absolutely certain of something is, owing to a certain feature of personal certainty, to be *dogmatic* in the matter that the thing is so. It is because of this dogmatic feature that there is always something wrong with being absolutely certain. . . . It's the attitude that *no* new information, evidence, or experience will now be seriously considered by one to be at all relevant to any possible change in how certain one should be in the matter. (*Ignorance,* p. 105).

One thing that such an attitude excludes is the possibility that I am the target of an evil scientist and, according to Unger, any undogmatic attitude must take that into account. Any number of philosophers—not the least of whom are Peirce, Wittgenstein, and Austin—have made us rightly suspicious of that sort of universal-deception worry, yet even if we can dismiss Descartes' evil genius, there is still Unger's point that an attitude of absolute certainty excludes the possibility that new information or evidence could change my attitude. And such an attitude would indeed be unjustifiably dogmatic. If I avoid dogmatism by thinking that new information could change my attitude or thinking that I might be mistaken, then Unger's point is that there would be a contradiction in saying "I am convinced that X (that is, I have an attitude of certainty), yet I may be mistaken."

I want to enlarge Unger's view somewhat since the contradiction he claims to exist if I adopt an undogmatic attitude toward a belief that can serve as my reason seems far more problematic when applied to our beliefs as a whole. What makes his case for universal skepticism troubling is not so much his analysis of rationality in terms of certainty as it is the larger context of his normative argument. If it were just that analysis, then even the most modest holistic attitude toward knowledge or foundations-without-certainty theory of justification would show it to be worth little serious worry for rationality. What is indeed a worry is that it points up a general malaise about our attitude toward our current beliefs and practices—our acting dogmatically as if we are at the end of inquiry while knowing full well that we are not. His formulation of the normative argument catches us between dogmatism and bad faith.

Put another way, while it may not seem initially convincing to think that I would be dogmatic in any serious and problematic sense, given the contradiction Unger addresses about my belief about Fred's hat, it is far more troubling with respect to our knowledge as a whole and its place in historical development. On the one hand we have confidence in our theories, our solutions to problems, our justified beliefs; yet insofar as we have any sense of history at all we realize their fallibility. The dogmatist elevates our confidence by laying a track through history leading necessarily to the truth of our own system of beliefs, with the conclusion that the truth of our views removes them from the play of time and social practice. This form of dogmatism—the dogmatism that my extension of Unger opposes—is, of course, not the sort of dogmatism the Enlightenment had opposed. Nor even is it the ordinary dogmatism of people who refuse to justify their views or who refuse to consider as relevant evidence what everyone else considers relevant. Rather it is identical with the specifically philosophical sense of rationality$_2$ that we got from the Enlightenment. In this sense, the normative thrust of this expanded version of Unger's skepticism is tied to the Pyrrhonian strategy against philosophical dogma, even though Unger does not draw the moral point of Pyrrhonism.

What is wrong with certainty theories of knowledge besides, the impossibility of certainty is that they take our beliefs as true for time and eternity, and *that* is a dogmatic attitude. Against the dogmatist, the relativist exploits our historicity and our fallibility, extending the same view that we have of our relation to the past to the way our beliefs and practices will look in the eyes of our descendants. Suddenly nothing is excluded from the possibility of error, change, and revision. Unger's skepticism can be seen, then, as working one side of this dogmatism-relativism nexus against the other. Cast in these terms, the way to get at Unger's skepticism about reason is to understand something about this apparently contradictory attitude. In the remainder of this section I will suggest that there is nothing seriously wrong with the conflicting attitude—that is, I want to suggest that it is not really contradictory. In the next section I shall try to give weight to the suggestion by showing how the dogmatism-relativism dichotomy itself can be undermined along Davidsonian lines.

Arthur Danto has provided a useful way of casting the source of the problem I am interested in. He has pointed out that we can be relativist about everything except ourselves. This is not because of some natural dogmatic impulse but because we cannot, without bad faith, think of ourselves as having beliefs *about* the world or as living in *a* world at all. Danto puts the point this way:

> The beliefs of others are part of the reality we have to deal with when we explain their conduct in the world. We can speak of *their* world meaning only their beliefs about the world. We cannot in the same sense speak of "our world." For us, our world is: *the world*. . . . Our beliefs, because we regard them as true are not thought of as *our* beliefs. . . . What is curious is that in our own case, the distance between ourselves and the world which the concept of truth requires is automatically closed . . . because we do not think of the representation of the world, to which truth properly applies, but to *what* is represented, namely the world.[22]

While I think Danto is right that we cannot seriously be relativist about ourselves we do have a second-level view of ourselves in the flux of history which brings with it the realization that perhaps our descendants will stand to us as we stand to sixteenth-century medicine or seventeenth-century attitudes toward slavery. At one level, our relation to the past and to the future is asymmetrical since we cannot even imagine what it would be like for our descendants to find out that we were mistaken in the large part of our beliefs. Yet at the other level of reflection we do realize the possibility of differences between ourselves and our descendants since we see the difference between ourselves and our ancestors. But Danto's point is that no genuine symmetry can exist here. I will support the point in the next section in terms of the notion of alternative conceptual schemes, and in the final chapter I will consider a similar point of Rorty's; but for now it is enough to suggest that the apparent contradiction and the conflict between dogmatism and relativism is a result of mixing these different levels of reflection about ourselves.

In terms of this difference the dogmatist can be seen to extend the confidence we have in our own views by virtue of their being ours and by virtue of our being unable to think of them as beliefs about the world that could in general be false, to some claim that we are at the end of inquiry. The relativist is engaging in bad faith by thinking that there is a genuine symmetry between past and future and thus that there is something in principle optional or arbitrary about current beliefs, theories, and values.

To return to Unger, then, the dogmatism that he says is always wrong is just this attitude that we are at the end of inquiry writ small; that is, he is attacking the view that to have knowledge is to be in possession of truths that are not subject to new information, new experience, future revision. The little contradiction, "I know that X, but I am not absolutely certain that X," trades on the larger mixing of first- and second-level reflection about our beliefs as a whole. If it were just the little contradiction itself that was at issue, it would be enough to show that it dissolves once rationality or knowledge is seen to be connected with a whole system of beliefs and practices. If Unger's argument has any force at all, it is because of the dogmatic character of the whole of our beliefs. At the level of our entire system of beliefs and practices we seem forced into dogmatism since we cannot imagine what to make of the charge that they may all be wrong, yet we seem forced in the other direction toward bad faith when we imagine that we can look at our own beliefs in the way they will appear to future generations.

## IV

I have been concerned so far only with setting the problem of rationality in various ways between the threats of relativism and dogmatism. I now turn to the issue that underwrites this dichotomy in its various forms in recent philosophy: the possibility of alternative and incommensurable conceptual schemes. This is the issue that makes problematic the relation between competing scientific theories, between ourselves and alien cultures, and between ourselves and other epochs. I will not detail the arguments since they are well known. I wish only to recast them in order to indicate how they depend on what Donald Davidson has called "the third and last dogma of empiricism."[23]

Toward the end of "Two Dogmas of Empiricism" Quine summed up his opposition to the dogmas of analyticity and reductionism:

> it is misleading to speak of the empirical content of an individual statement—especially if it is a statement at all remote from the experiential periphery of the field. Furthermore it becomes folly to seek a boundary between synthetic statements, which hold contingently on experience, and analytic statements, which hold come what may. Any statement can be held true come what may, if we make drastic enough adjustments elsewhere in the system. . . . Conversely, by the same token, no statement is immune to revision.[24]

The problem of analyticity, against which this holistic alternative is suggested, was the problem of making sense of the notion of synonomy necessary for the view that some propositions are "true in virtue of meaning alone" and that others, by contrast, are true in virtue of the world.

Translation from one language to another provides another source for the same problem since it is tempting to think of translation as giving a sentence in one language that has the same meaning as a sentence in the other language. While translational synonomy poses the same sort of problems about synonomy that is at issue with analyticity, the case of radical translation—translating the language of an alien culture—raises an even more serious issue. For Quine, one cannot speak of the translation of a single sentence from one language to another any more than one can speak of the empirical content of a single sentence apart from the whole of a scientific theory. Translation of a single sentence requires a general scheme of translation. Such a scheme might not pose too much of a problem for translation of French to English—because of a shared background of practices, values, and traditions—but there could be an inevitable indeterminacy in cases of "radical translation," since it seems possible that for an alien language there could be incompatible translation manuals that were nonetheless each consistent with the aliens' behavior.[25]

In addressing the problem of radical translation, Quine's work has the same relativist consequences found in Benjamin Whorf's studies of the Hopi as well as in Kuhn's study of theory change in the history of science and Feyerabend's argument against meaning invariance across alternative scientific theories. Kuhn has put the concern with the distance between translations or cultures or historical epochs or theoretical vocabularies into what has become the slogan for conceptual relativism. In the Postscript to the *Structure of Scientific Revolutions* Kuhn had said that "two groups, the members of which have systematically different sensations on receipt of the same stimuli, do *in some sense* live in different worlds."[26]

The notion of conceptual relativism that follows from Quine, Kuhn, and Feyerabend, and the rearguard arguments for realism and rationality$_2$ depend, according to Davidson, on a third dogma of empiricism—the dualism of scheme and content or of organizing system and something waiting to be organized. While this is indeed a dogma of empiricism, the contrast between scheme and content is at once the source and fundamental dichotomy of modern philosophy. Heidegger, for example, in "The Age of the World Picture," found the essence of the modern age in the related distinction between the world as an object—the world as a view or picture—and ourselves who are the subject or ground for the possibility of knowledge of the world.[27] Since Descartes it has seemed as if we could hold the world at arm's length and test the accuracy of our representations of it. It is this large dualism between ourselves as subject and the world as object; between the knower and the known; between that which organizes the world and the world waiting to be organized that has provided the problematic for modern philosophy. This brings us not only to the idea of the world as a view but to the possibility of alternative views, and it tempts us to think of different scientific theories as different worlds, of different cultures as incommensurable world-views, and to imagine our own views as optional or mistaken when measured against the future.

In "The Very Idea of a Conceptual Scheme," Davidson opposes the relativist implications of Quine, Kuhn, and Feyerabend and the more fundamental duality of scheme and content which gives plausibility to conceptual relativism. The consequence of Davidson's view is that we would not even be in a position to judge that there are systems of beliefs radically different from our own. His argument turns on the claim that "translation into a familiar tongue is a criterion of languagehood." This argument depends in part on the larger Davidsonian project,[28] but a sketch of certain features of the project will do for my purpose.

According to Davidson, it is a condition for any theory of translation that for any sentence S in some language L, a theorem of the following form is provable:

The sentence S in L is true if and only if *p*

where *p,* in our case, is a sentence in English. And further, for every sentence *p,* there is a Tarski sentence of the form

*p* is true if and only if p.

For example, if "Il pleut" is the sentence in L, then

(1) The French sentence "Il pleut" is true if and only if "It is raining" is true; and,
(2) "It is raining" is true if and only if it is raining.

Now, of course, this truth-preserving requirement in translating from French to English does not address the situation that concerns Quine since we have enough cultural affinity with the French to warrant the usual assumptions we make about the truth of their beliefs when we pair them with our own. The problem arises in the case of radical translation, where the assumptions we make about the truth of alien beliefs cannot be warranted in terms of shared background. In radical translation, the truth-preserving requirement of translation must be supported by what has been called—following N. C. Wilson—the "principle of charity." The principle of charity requires that even in cases of radical translation we must consider the bulk of an alien culture's beliefs as true. Davidson argues for the principle in the following ways:

> We can take it as given that *most* beliefs are correct. The reason for this is that a belief is identified by its location in a pattern of beliefs; it is this pattern that determines the subject matter of the belief. . . . Before some object in, or aspect of the world can become part of the subject matter of belief (true or false) there must be endless true beliefs about the subject matter. False belief tends to undermine the identification of the subject matter; to undermine, therefore, the validity of a description of the belief as being about the subject; and so, in turn, false beliefs undermine the claim that a connected belief is false. . . . What makes interpretation possible, then, is that we can dismiss *a priori* the chance of massive error. A theory of interpretation cannot be correct that makes a man assent to very many false sentences.[29]

If we attribute beliefs to the aliens at all, then just as we must assume that the bulk of our beliefs are true, we must extend that assumption to theirs. Not to do so would be to deny the attribution that theirs are beliefs after all. The principle of charity, then, is not merely some chauvinistic injunction of benevolence toward alien cultures. If it were, it would deserve Ian Hacking's sneer to the effect that the principle is just our latest missionary vanguard and that "Our 'natives' may be wondering whether philosophical B52s and strategic hamlets are in the offing if he won't sit up and speak like the English."[30] What the principle emphasizes is not benevolence or linguistic imperialism, but a recognition of what a system of beliefs is, the way the truth of a particular belief must figure in a whole pattern of true beliefs, and a recognition of the fact that even in the confrontation between theories or cultures or historical epochs, the vast majority of home truths go unquestioned and unchanged.

These points become obscured when we think of beliefs as *theories*—as views about the world—and when we think of alien cultures and historical epochs on the model of competing theories. Indeterminacy of translation, for example, gains plausibility by raising the possibility of alternative observation predicates and thus alternative translation manuals. Incommensurability gains plausibility by viewing beliefs on the model of alternative theoretical vocabularies in science. Maximizing agreement in translation, then, is not so much an act of charity toward others or to the past as it is a way of showing how misleading it is to think of the process of inquiry or the confrontation between cultures or our knowledge of the past on the model of theory change in science. When we apply the principle of charity to alien cultures, not only does indeterminacy of translation and radical incommensurability of frameworks lose their plausibility, the relativism that has come in the wake of the problem of incommensurability becomes implausible as well.

One must avoid the temptation, however, of thinking that this Davidsonian strategy results in a vindication of our own beliefs and values against alternatives or of the realist conviction that there will ultimately be a single conceptual scheme secure against conceptual relativism. According to Davidson it is "wrong to announce the glorious news that all mankind—all speakers of language, at least—share a common scheme and ontology. For if we cannot intelligibly say that schemes are different, neither can we intelligibly say that they are one" ("The Very Idea," p. 20). If we drew that conclusion, we would simply succumb yet again to the dogmatism side of the dichtomy. The moral of the argument is that relativism is not rendered implausible by vindicating the view that ours is the only rational framework, or that we have correctly represented reality. Not only do those who declare rationality relative require the scheme-content duality in order to make plausible the possibility of alternative schemes, those who think relativism can be defeated only by a defense of rationality$_2$, objective truth, and realism, require the duality as well since they require that at the end of inquiry we will be in possession of the *one true* scheme.

Davidson sees the result of his argument as "reestablishing unmediated touch with the familiar objects whose antics make our sentences and opinions true or false" ("The Very Idea," p. 20), but one must be cautious of making too much of this conclusion. It possesses a certain rhetorical advantage over Richard Rorty's conclusion, drawn from the same sorts of arguments, that we may, with relief, realize "the world well lost,"[31] but the difference is no more than a difference between one who is optimistic and one who is pessimistic about the future of philosophy. Davidson gives no more aid and comfort to the realist conceptions of rationality than Rorty. By undermining the scheme-content dichotomy that structured the debate between relativists and realists, he has rendered the rationality of our entire system of beliefs unproblematic, since he has removed the basis for thinking that, in the confrontation with alternative beliefs, ours might turn out to be irrational or radically false.

In the preceding sections I have attempted to set the philosophical space in which the problem of rationality is situated. Briefly, the structure of that space is the skeptical challenge which plays off our fears of relativism against our conviction that dogmatism is a bad thing. In attempting to put Unger's skepticism about rationality in its place, I have suggested that we have nothing to fear from the skeptic who says that no one is ever rational about *anything*. While particular beliefs and practices may be irrational, the possibility of large-scale irrationality is unintelligible. But we are rational not because we are able to discover about our beliefs that they conform to standards of rationality; nor do we have the beliefs we have because we are assured of their rationality. Not to put too fine a Wittgensteinian point on the matter, our "form of life" is rational not because it conforms to certain criteria or exhibits certain properties; rather it is rational because our doing as we do is just what being rational amounts to. It is no more, nor is it any less.

## V

Finally, what we require is an understanding of rationality that is tolerant without being relativist; one that allows for enough slack to avoid dogmatism by taking seriously the possibility that cultural perspectives or moral systems or scientific theories might be incommensurable—though for Davidsonian reasons not radically so—yet one that does not yield the reckless relativist result of any culture, system of values or beliefs being as good as any other. I want to move toward such a conception—what I have loosely called rationality$_1$—in two ways. First, I want to turn to the notion of objectivity and its relation to rationality. Second, I will consider an argument of Charles Taylor's in which he shows that incommensurability is compatible with a nonrelativist conception of rationality, that incommensurability does not rule out comparative judgments about competing beliefs, values, or theories.

In the first phase of the "new philosophy of science" it was standard to make Kuhn into Everyman's relativist because he had claimed that there were no neutral or independent criteria of theory-choice, no algorithmic decision-procedure guaranteeing objectivity that one could appeal to in favoring one paradigm over another. According to his critics, he had stripped the history of science of rational development and reduced theory-choice to individual preferences or mob psychology.[32] Though Kuhn has responded to the charges of relativism and subjectivism many times and in several different ways, the most illuminating was offered in "Objectivity, Value Judgment, and Theory Choice," in his collection *The Essential Tension.* In a quite traditional-sounding list, he enumerated and endorsed several characteristics of a good scientific theory—accuracy, consistency, scope, simplicity and fruitfulness—but he urged that these criteria of choice "function not as rules, which determine choice, but as values, which influence it."[33] Drawing from this the conclusion that there are both subjective and objective elements in theory-choice, Kuhn turned to the charge of subjectivism by explaining how he was using the terms. "'Subjective' is a term with several established uses: in one of these it is opposed to 'objective,' in another to 'judgmental.' When my critics describe the idiosyncratic features to which I appeal as subjective, they resort, erroneously I think, to the second of these senses. When they complain that I deprive science of objectivity, they conflate the second sense of subjective with the first" (*Essential Tension,* p. 336).

The point of this rejoinder is that the use of criteria as values is a matter of judgment, not a matter of individual bias, taste, or personal preference. If it was merely a matter of taste, then differences of theory-choice would turn out to be indiscussible in much the way that noncognitivist ethical theorists used to claim that disagreement over moral values was, in an important sense, indiscussible since the disagreement represented conflicting attitudes rather than conflicting beliefs. Kuhn argues, however, that while there is no algorithmic decision-procedure for theory-choice—although criteria of theory-choice function as values—nonetheless such judgments are indeed discussible. Scientists must be in a position to exhibit the basis of their choices, give reasons for them, and open them to reflection and criticism. It is in that sense that criteria for theory-choice are not merely preferential. Though they function as values that influence decisions, the decisions are a part of the practices of inquiry and judgment that open up choices between theories for discussion and criticism.

Having distinguished the notion of preference from judgment, Kuhn suggests that perhaps the significance of his discussion of theory-choice was not so much to set limitations of objectivity, but that "it may be the meaning rather than the limits of objectivity that my argument shows" (*Essential Tension,* p. 338). If we use this suggestion to rephrase his earlier remarks, to make them consistent with it, it would be better to state that what he has shown is not two meanings of subjective but, instead, two meanings of objective. The traditional understanding of objectivity ties it to notions of exactitude, externality, impartiality and detachment, independence from consciousness and therefore from subjective influences, certainty, accuracy of representational fit, and so on. Kuhn's suggestion, however, is that theory-choice in science is objective in the sense of its being a matter of judgment. In terms of this second notion, objectivity characterizes certain sorts of practices. It does not refer to properties of that which is known or features of the relation between the knower and the known or between theories and the world.[34]

Max Deutscher has recently argued against treating objectivity as some static property conveyed by the abstract noun, and instead has suggested that we understand it as a process or attitude conveyed by the term "objecting"[35]—a process that is inevitably interested and involved, having more to do with notions of openness or fairness than with exactitude, detachment, and value neutrality. While one may question the lengths to which this suggestion is taken by Deutscher, there is certainly something right about his insight that ties it to Kuhn's notion of objectivity as a matter of judgment.

I want to amplify this point from a slightly different angle. The traditional notion of objectivity emerged in the Enlightenment and in positivism from a particular view of the natural sciences and the notion of rationality proper to it, and this natural scientific paradigm was extended to our understanding of social reality. That paradigm has been called into question recently in the debate over the relation between the natural and human sciences. As I indicated in the previous chapter, certain opponents of the positivist reduction of the human sciences to the natural sciences have argued that they are different both ontologically and methodologically. It is argued, for example, that because human beings are self-interpreting and atoms are not, the objects of inquiry in the human sciences are fundamentally different, entailing a difference in the proper mode of inquiry. Furthermore, it is argued that because the aim of the human sciences is understanding and emancipation, not explanation and control, the methods of the human sciences must be entirely different. This "hermeneutic turn" in the human sciences conceives of understanding on the model of communication and interpretation rather than of explanation. It is to this sort of model that Kuhn turns—though only implicitly at first[36]—for illustrating his notion of objectivity in theory-choice. Characterizing both the model and its problems, he writes:

> Proponents of different theories are . . . like native speakers of different languages. Communication between them goes on by translation, and it raises

all translations' familiar difficulties. . . . I simply assert the existence of significant limits to what the proponents of different theories can communicate to one another. . . . Nevertheless, despite the incompleteness of their communications, proponents of different theories can exhibit to each other, not always easily, the concrete technical results achievable by those who practice within each theory. (*Essential Tension,* pp. 338–39).

The significance of this shift in models is that instead of our thinking about the judgments between different systems of beliefs, values, or cultures on the model of the relation between alternative scientific theories, Kuhn has suggested that it should be the other way around. Theory-choice should be modeled on interpreting different languages. But has not this reduction of the problem of objectivity of theory-choice to translation between speakers of different languages just grafted one difficult issue on to a more intractable one? After all, part of the motivation for relativist notions of rationality arose from the problem of radical translation and the possibility that alien cultures might have significantly different standards of rationality. By turning to an argument of Charles Taylor, I want to suggest why this move has not simply shifted the locus of the problem.

In brief, the dilemma about incommensurability has been this: if we deny the possibility that theories, or cultural values, or systems of beliefs could be incommensurable, we become subject to the charges of dogmatism that Winch, Agassi, Feyerabend, et al. have brought; yet if we agree that incommensurable frameworks are possible, we seem driven to a relativist view about rationality which is problematic because it eliminates the possibility of meaningful judgments between alternatives. One way of summing up my argument so far is that we seem caught in this untenable dilemma because we have taken rationality to be bound up with the Enlightenment-cum-positivist notion of objectivity. Taylor, however, argues that a pluralist conception of rationality *is* consistent with incommensurable cultural frameworks since incommensurability is precisely what makes meaningful judgments possible.[37] Taylor's argument will serve to illuminate what I have called rationality$_1$.

Much of the recent social science literature on rationality has been initiated by Peter Winch's Wittgensteinian critique of ethnocentrism in anthropology. In "Understanding a Primitive Society,"[38] for example, Winch had opposed Evans-Pritchard's conclusion, drawn from the comparison of Azande witchcraft to scientific inquiry, that Azande witchcraft practices were irrational. Winch argued that the sort of ethnocentrism displayed by Evans-Pritchard resulted from his attempt to assimilate the foreign practices of witchcraft to familiar practices of our own, with the result that the Azande were judged on the basis of standards derived from our practices. He argued that one must avoid this sort of ethnocentricity in the social sciences by attempting to understand the meaning Azande practices have for the Azande, not the meaning they might have in terms of our own practices. Winch concluded that because Azande practices are different from our own, they must be understood as involving different standards of rationality. If that is the case, there is no warrant for judging their practices inferior to ours.

Taylor enters the issue of rationality by way of Winch's opposition to Evans-Pritchard and the pluralism about standards of rationality that follows from it. Taylor thinks that while there is something right about Winch's response, nevertheless it does not provide a basis for a sufficiently radical critique of ethnocentrism on the one hand, and it does not support the conclusion that incommensurable practices cannot be judged in terms of superiority on the other. By declaring that we and the Azande are engaged in different sorts of practices, Winch merely sidestepped the issue.

Taylor's departure from Winch turns on the difference between claiming that alien cultures are engaging in different practices and claiming that alien practices and ours are incommensurable. If cultural practices are incommensurable, they are not merely different, they are genuinely incompatible—that is, they are competitor practices. Deciding when to plant the crops and how to worship the gods are different sorts of activities and it makes no sense to compare one against the other precisely because they are different. But if that is what the issue of the incommensurability of alien beliefs comes to, it is devoid of philosophical interest. Consulting the meteorologist and consulting the poison oracle to decide when to plant the crops are incommensurable because they are incompatible, alternative, competitor practices. This philosophically interesting incommensurability, however, does not eliminate the possibility of comparative judgements. It is precisely what makes comparative judgements possible. Taylor summarizes his departure from Winch this way:

> In a sense, I entirely agree that we must speak of a plurality of standards. The discourse in which matters are articulated in different societies can be very different. . . . The standards are different, because they belong to incommensurable activities. But where I disagree with Winch is in claiming that plurality does not rule out judgements of superiority. I think the kind of plurality we have here, between the incommensurable, precisely opens the door to such judgements. ("Rationality," p. 151)

Though it is incommensurability that makes value judgments between alternative practices possible, this does not imply that there must be framework-independent criteria to which we and alien cultures are agreed. It means only that the incommensurability of certain practices opens up the possibility of real disagreement, discussion, and argument. The result of Taylor's view is, I think, the same sort of thing Kuhn has in mind when he writes that theory-choice in science is a matter of judgment rather than the application of an algorithmic decision-procedure. On both accounts, incommensurability does not result in a pernicious relativism—that is, in the impossibility of communication and understanding or the impossibility of comparative judgment. Nor does the recognition that judgments of superiority are possible imply dogmatism. We undercut the disjunction "relativism or dogmatism" by realizing that the incommensurability of beliefs, values, or theories places real differences in the space of reasons.

## VI

I suggested earlier that rationality is not chronically and continually in need of defense and justification. Rather, confidence in the rationality of one's beliefs is eroded as a result of intellectual crises which force one either toward dogmatism or relativism. In our day the primary crisis that has undermined our confidence and rendered rationality problematic results from issues in the philosophy of natural and social sciences that cast relativism as the consequence of opposition to objectivity or dogmatism. That formulation of the issues has made skeptical challenges to rationality urgent for us. What I have attempted to do is put these challenges in their place; that is, to locate the threat of relativism in the countermovement against dogmatic implications of certain claims in the philosophy of the natural and social sciences, and to see skepticism as working one countermovement against the other. Relativism and dogmatism are made for each other in a way that requires that they be undermined together, otherwise any antidogmatic or antirelativist attempt will simply set the pendulum swinging again and will remain necessarily tied to what it opposes.

What the Davidsonian account shows us is that the relativism that theories of critical rationality opposed and the dogmatism that Unger opposes have a single source, namely, the duality between scheme and content which gives plausibility to conceptual relativism and against which realists must react. Exposing this source as a dogma in the way that Davidson does results in undermining the motivation for both relativism and dogmatism equally. What Kuhn's work suggests is a conception of objectivity in science and an understanding of theory-choice modeled on communication and interpretation between alternative cultures rather than the other way around. What Taylor shows is the compatibility of a pluralist conception of rationality and of value judgments with incommensurability, providing enough slack to avoid dogmatism without sliding into the view that rational pluralism allows no basis for judging between alternative beliefs, values, or theories.

There is a lesson in this for my claim that while we cannot say of our beliefs that they are $rational_2$ they are, nonetheless, $rational_1$. Earlier I distinguished the latter as constitutive of any sustaining system of beliefs and I characterized it in terms of the practice of inquiry and of the success of a system of beliefs in resolving conflicts and solving problems. It is tempting to think that we might or should go on to say how it is that our beliefs happen to be successful in coping with the world by identifying properties or deriving criteria—albeit pragmatic rather than necessary and sufficient ones—to explain our success. But to do so would be to fall victim to the same difficulty that I see with theories of critical rationality. It is to attempt a middle course between dogmatism and relativism and thus it would remain caught up in the dichotomy that has been set aside.

The upshot of undermining the relativism-dogmatism nexus is that rationality is rendered unproblematic. What I have termed $rationality_1$, is not then a *theory* of rationality but the result of restored confidence in our system of beliefs once the dual threats of dogmatism and relativism are put in their place. Our beliefs *are* rational insofar as, and only insofar as they are successful in coping with the world, since removed from the threats of dogmatism and relativism we cannot imagine what it would mean to think that we were successful but not rational. Saying so, though, does not justify particular beliefs and values of ours nor does it vindicate or legitimize specific practices and social institutions. That can only come from within, since there is no standpoint outside from which to judge.

We should worry about the legitimacy of particular practices, values, and institutions but that is possible only against the background of the unproblematical character of our beliefs as a whole. We are rational for the most part most of the time, but to make this claim outside of the threats of relativism and dogmatism or the challenge of skepticism is not—to paraphrase Davidson—to announce the glorious news that our beliefs and values are justified after all. It is simply a statement of our condition. The problem we face is not the rationality of our beliefs as a whole, but the possibility of criticizing particular beliefs, values, and institutions, given that there are no foundations, system-independent criteria, or meta-frameworks on which to rest rational critique. In the next chapter I will turn to the way this problem arises in the context of Rorty's opposition to epistemology-centered philosophy. His view has been influenced, in part, by the developments in recent philosophy of science that I have sketched, and I shall interpret him as attempting to reject the traditional conception of philosophy and the notions of reason, objectivity, truth, and reality proper to it without abandoning the possibility of meaningful criticism of current practices of inquiry or of current social values and institutions.

# 6 Edification and the End of Philosophy

In December of 1972, Richard Rorty read a paper to the American Philosophical Association provocatively and polemically titled "The World Well Lost." In that paper, Rorty extended views of Quine about the fact-language distinction, views of Sellars about the "myth of the empirically given," and views of Davidson about the coherence of conceptual relativism in a way that served to undermine the philosophical notion of the world independent of thought and the correspondence theory of truth proper to it. His aim was to *trivialize* the current debate, growing out of referential theories of language and recent philosophy of science, over realism and idealism. He concluded the paper by claiming that "if we can come to see both the coherence and correspondence theories as noncompeting trivialities, then we may finally move beyond realism and idealism and to the point at which, in Wittgenstein's words, we are capable of stopping doing philosophy when we want to."[1] The sense of horror experienced by analytic philosophers in the audience over the fact that one of their own should side with Hegel over Kant and turn analytic developments against the significance of a favored controversy was only matched by the pleasure and anticipation experienced by Continentally oriented philosophers, who sensed that they had gained an ally from the opposing camp.

In retrospect it is clear that the paper not only signaled a turning point in philosophical discussion in America, it announced what was to come in Rorty's far more comprehensive critique of the philosophical tradition in *Philosophy and the Mirror of Nature.*[2] In that work, he attacked what he termed "epistemology-centered" philosophy in order to undermine the whole philosophical enterprise since Plato. Thus what had initially appeared as a rather local critique of developments in the analytic tradition could be extended to the phenomenological tradition as well, and Rorty joined hands with the later Heidegger and more recent "postmodern" writers such as Derrida whose aim is the end of philosophy.

One must be careful with the slogan "the end of philosophy," however. It has served more as a rallying cry than a phrase of common principles, and though Rorty occasionally identifies himself too closely with other attempts to overcome or deconstruct the philosophical tradition, his stand toward philosophy is quite different. For Heidegger, for example, the end of philosophy does not mean the termination of the metaphysical tradition. Instead, the end of philosophy is its limit—its extreme possibility—and the purpose of his account of the end of philosophy was to reveal that at the limit of philosophy there was left a more original task that Heidegger referred to as thinking—a non-philosophical mode of relation to Being that remained when metaphysics had reached its limit. For Derrida, the end of philosophy is its closure, and his various deconstructive strategies aim not at eliminating philosophy but at preventing it from achieving closure and, therefore, at keeping philosophy going by opening it up to a play of interpretations. Rorty, however, means something both more radical and more troubling, since he seeks to trivialize philosophy and its place in culture in order that we can quit doing philosophy whenever we like.

## I

The traditional view of philosophy is that it is an inquiry in which its participants seek agreement on the solutions to a common stock of fundamental problems. On this view, the problems of philosophy are fundamental in at least two senses. First, they arise for those who begin to reflect about themselves, their relation to others, the nature of the good life, the difference between themselves and the brutes, why there is something rather than nothing, their place in nature, and so on. Connected with this, it is thought that deeply imbedded in reflective consciousness are a series of intuitive dichotomies or binary opposites—between consciousness and matter, self and other, values and facts, reality and appearance, truth and fiction, suprasensible and sensory—that structure any possible reflective outcome on these issues. Second, because the binary oppositions that structure reflection are thought to be so deeply imbedded, the solutions to these fundamental problems of philosophy are necessary for securing the rest of inquiry and for settling the conflicting claims of the rest of culture. The task of philosophy, then, is to discover a neutral, ahistorical framework of criteria for judging the correctness of solutions to problems fundamental to the possibility of inquiry in order to guarantee that the solutions achieved are the truth about ourselves and reality. This foundational inquiry is carried out by philosophers whose self-understanding is formed in terms of these problems and whose roles in the ongoing inquiry are fixed by the sides they take on which solutions are the correct ones. On this view, Plato, Augustine, Aquinas, Descartes, Kant, Wittgenstein, Heidegger, Kripke, and ourselves are joined in the inquiry by a common set of problems, and the history of the inquiry is written in terms of progress toward agreement on their solutions.

For Rorty, however, philosophy is not a set of fundamental and eternal problems. Instead, he sees it as an ongoing conversation, and our participation in the conversation is not so much as overseers or under-laborers of inquiry but as informed dilettantes and cultural kibitzers. Insofar as philosophy has a unique role in the conversation, it is not to secure the foundations of inquiry for the rest of culture or to serve as a tribunal of reason before which the rest of inquiry is to be judged. Its role is merely to prevent the partners of the conversation from the self-deception of thinking that momentary agreement is the whole truth for time and eternity. The end of philosophy is not to achieve the truth about ourselves and reality but to keep the conversation going by constantly calling current agreement into question and sending the conversation off in new directions. What unites conversational partners in the culture of the West is not fundamental problems but common texts. The philosopher is not the one who has solutions to fundamental problems but the one who—in a phrase from Wilfred Sellars that Rorty fondly cites—is interested in how things in the largest sense hang together in the largest sense.

Rorty has drawn the contrast between these two notions of philosophy in different ways at different times. Sometimes it is the difference between pure and impure philosophy, sometimes between professionalized philosophy and cultural criticism, sometimes between philosophy that is constructive and philosophy that is destructive, sometimes between capitalized Philosophy and uncapitalized philosophy.[3] In *Philosophy and The Mirror of Nature,* the more usual contrasts are between systematic philosophy and edification and between epistemology-centered philosophy and hermeneutics—contrasts between those who seek theories as solutions to fundamental problems and those who debunk the idea of seeking theories because they reject the idea of fundamental problems.

Against this traditional view of the philosophical enterprise, however, Rorty's notion of edification or abnormal discourse or hermeneutics should not be thought of as alternative conceptions of what philosophy ought to be, in the way, for example, that Heidegger's attack on the philosophical tradition offered an alternative task—a task that Heidegger called "thinking" in order to distinguish its more fundamental mode of relation to Being from metaphysics. Rorty's critique is entirely reactive and parasitic on the traditional conception of philosophy as an ahistorical, foundational discipline and tribunal of reason for the rest of culture. In that sense, it is intentionally marginal. "The mainstream philosophers are the philosophers I shall call 'systematic,' and the peripheral ones are those I shall call 'edifying.' The peripheral, pragmatic philosophers are skeptical primarily *about systematic philoso-*

*phy,* about the whole project of universal commensuration" (*Mirror of Nature,* pp. 367–68). Whereas Rousseau had marginalized the critical function of intellect as much because of his own circumstances and psychology as by design, Rorty's edifying thinker is self-consciously marginal since the task of edification is defined by its reaction to systematic philosophy.

The contrast between systematic philosophy and edification, then, is not a contrast between two conceptions within traditional philosophy. Its entire point and force must be understood as a reaction to the traditional philosophical desire to escape the finitude and contingency of our condition by grounding inquiry in the ahistorical and by demanding that all inquiry be commensurable. In the Introduction to *Consequences of Pragmatism,* Rorty referred to the Platonic urge to escape the finitude of one's time and place as "the impossible attempt to step outside our skins—the traditions, linguistic and other, within which we do our thinking and self-criticism" (*Consequences,* p. xix). What he alternately calls edification or abnormal discourse or hermeneutics reacts against this philosophical urge to escape and it is a reaction with therapeutic intent. In much the way that Hume's critique of false philosophy's attempt to achieve autonomy from the world of appearance brought us back to the beliefs and customs of common life, the end of philosophy on Rorty's view brings us back to notions of inquiry, truth, and social criticism as normal results of normal discourse and thus subject to all the fallibility and contingency of our circumstances and conditions. This is a point I will come back to at the end since it is this that connects Rorty to the tradition of opposition to philosophy that I have traced to the Pyrrhonian skeptics.

## II

Each of the ways in which Rorty has phrased the contrast between the traditional conception of philosophy and his reaction to it can be brought under the general contrast between philosophy with mirrors and philosophy without mirrors. In commenting on the title of his book, *Philosophy and the Mirror of Nature,* Rorty writes:

> It is pictures rather than propositions, metaphors rather than statements, which determine most of our philosophical convictions. The picture which holds traditional philosophy captive is that of mind as a great mirror containing various representations—some accurate, some not—and capable of being studied by pure, nonempirical methods. Without the notion of mind as mirror, the notion of knowledge as accuracy of representation would not have suggested itself. Without this latter notion, the strategy common to Descartes and Kant—getting more accurate representations by inspecting,

repairing, and polishing the mirror, so to speak—would not have made sense. Without this strategy in mind, recent claims that philosophy consists of "conceptual analysis" or "phenomenological analysis" or "explication of meaning" or of "explicating the logic of our language" or "the structure of the constituting activity of consciousness" would not make sense. (*Mirror of Nature,* p. 12)

He has traced the source of the traditional conception of philosophy to the metaphor of mind as a mirror of nature and knowledge as accurate representations; thus his opposition to the traditional conception will turn on a critique of representation. Though the book focuses its attack on recent developments in the analytic tradition—in the philosophy of mind, epistemology, and philosophy of language—its point cuts deep to the heart of philosophy generally, turning against a conception of philosophy practiced on both sides of the Atlantic.

Rorty is conscious of the fact that the metaphor of mind as the mirror of nature and the view of philosophy it embodies could be traced at least to Plato. A Heideggerian analysis would locate this view of philosophy in the transition from truth as *aletheia*—unconcealedness—to truth as correctness of representation, for example. But the primary source for his concern is that conception of philosophy as it has come to us through Descartes, Locke, and Kant; Descartes because of his notion of mind as separate, Locke because he based the theory of knowledge on an understanding of mental processes, and Kant for the notion of philosophy as "a tribunal of pure reason, upholding and denying the claims of the rest of culture" (*Mirror of Nature,* p. 3). In the Descartes-Locke-Kant conception, the task of philosophy is to ground inquiry in the relation between the mind and the world it mirrors—in the difference between mind and matter and the idea that the foundations of knowledge are to be discovered in a privileged relation between the knower's mind, or its contents, and the objects it represents. It is this Descartes-Locke-Kant conception that captures what he means by foundationalism, and his opposition to epistemology-centered philosophy is not an opposition to an interest in knowing but to foundationalism so understood.

The assumption that governs Rorty's critique of this conception of philosophy is the Wittgensteinian insight that there is nothing intuitive or necessary about this conception. Our thought that the conception *is* somehow intuitive is merely our readiness to fall in with a particular philosophical language-game. "In my Wittgensteinian view, an intuition is never anything more or less than familiarity with a language-game, so to discover the source of our intuitions is to relive the history of the philosophical language-game we find ourselves playing" (*Mirror of Nature,* p. 35). We can find the source of our intuitions about mind and knowledge and the notion of philosophy proper to them by reliving the history of the metaphor of mirroring.[4] The result will be the realization that there is something optional about the way philosophy has understood itself since Descartes, Locke, and Kant. If there is something optional about the metaphor of mirroring, then the various controversies that arise within the metaphor—that is, within epistemology-centered philosophy—lose their interest, and the dichotomies that have structured philosophy will turn out to be the binary equivalents of Wittgenstein's idle wheel. This is the sense in which Rorty seeks to trivialize philosophy.

## III

Rorty's strategy against the metaphor of mirroring does not seek to offer new solutions to perennial philosophical problems or even new projects for philosophical inquiry. Rather, he aims to defuse the entire concern about minds and knowledge that underwrites the traditional conception of philosophy. Such a strategy, however, frustrates interpretation since the outcome of Rorty's critique of post-Cartesian philosophy of mind and epistemology is a behavioristic and holistic approach to knowing, an approach that he claims is not a "theory of knowledge" and a materialism that he claims is not a "theory of mind." His is not another view about perennial philosophical problems; he says, rather, that edifying philosophers "decry the very notion of having a view" (*Mirror of Nature,* p. 371).

One line of critical concern about Rorty's attack on philosophy has turned on the question whether—or how—it is possible to defuse a concern about minds or knowledge without it simply being an indirect way of offering new solutions or offering something else for philosophy to do.[5] Rorty has characterized what he calls the abnormal discourse of edifying thinkers as merely reactive: "abnormal and existential discourse is always parasitic upon normal discourse. . . . the possibility of hermeneutics is always parasitic upon the possibility (and perhaps upon the actuality) of epistemology. . . . edification always employs materials provided by the culture of the day" (*Mirror of Nature,* pp. 365–66). But is it possible for a critique of philosophy to be merely reactive in this way? Rorty has certainly read Heidegger, Wittgenstein, and Dewey—his heroes of edification—as if they were only reactive, edifying thinkers rather than constructive or systematic ones,[6] but this reading has motivated a number of critics to rescue Heidegger, Wittgenstein, and Dewey from Rorty's admiring attempt to read out of them anything constructive and programmatic.[7] The issue raised by Rorty's work is not just the accuracy of his interpretation of his heroes. It raises, in addition, a quite general question about the very possibility of a postmodern strategy against philosophy, and it also poses an interpretive question about the consistency of Rorty's own work.

The general form of the issue posed against Rorty is similar to that already raised about the coherence of the Pyrrhonian skeptics' opposition to philosophical dogma and their desire to live without beliefs: how could they oppose claims to know without themselves being committed to beliefs of some sort? The recent version of this question turns on whether it is possible to overcome or end philosophy without simply being one more contributor to it—merely a fellow traveler with a different view. Heidegger, for example, had argued that Nietzsche's attempt to overcome the Western metaphysical tradition was just its countermovement and, therefore, simply the extreme possibility of metaphysics and inevitably entangled in it. Heidegger even came to see that his own early attempts to overcome metaphysics were a part of metaphysics and that finally he should cease all overcoming.[8]

Rorty is keenly aware of this problem. He sees the attempt to overcome the tradition as caught up in a dilemma, either horn of which is paradoxical. In his account of Derrida's attempt to deconstruct the metaphysical tradition by "writing at the margins of the metaphysical text," or through "the play of différance" and so on, he writes that Derrida "is caught in a dilemma. He can either forget about philosophy as the liberated slave forgets his master, demonstrating his forgetfulness by his own uncaring spontaneous activity, or he can insist on his rights over the master, on the dialectical dependence of the text of philosophy on its margins."[9] And he also sees this dilemma in his own pragmatic opposition to philosophy. In the Introduction to *Consequences of Pragmatism,* he writes that "pragmatists keep trying to find ways of making antiphilosophical points in nonphilosophical language. For they face a dilemma: if their language is too unphilosophical, too 'literary,' they will be accused of changing the subject; if it is too philosophical it will embody Platonic assumptions which will make it impossible for the pragmatist to state the conclusion he wants to reach" (*Consequences,* p. xiv).

To generalize the criticism of Derrida and the dilemma for pragmatism, if the opposition to philosophy grasps the first horn, if it is too literary, then it loses all contact with its subject and thus it is not really saying anything about philosophy after all. It is not so much a challenge to philosophy as it is merely turning its back and changing the subject. If it grasps the second horn by expressing opposition in philosophical terms, then it is just a continuation of the philosophical tradition, attempting to beat philosophy in its own terms, at its own game. Is it possible for Rorty—or for edifying thinkers generally—to decry the philosophical tradition without becoming forever entangled in it? I intend to return to that question later by setting Rorty's opposition to the philosophical tradition against Heidegger's and Derrida's.

The interpretive question for the consistency of Rorty's work arises because Rorty is increasingly writing with a new tone of voice. Whereas the work leading up to and including *Philosophy and the Mirror of Nature* and his collection of essays in *Consequences of Pragmatism* is destructive of the traditional conception of philosophy as a foundational discipline, more recent work has criticized various postmodern attacks—especially those of Heidegger, Foucault, and Lyotard—and has championed instead quite substantive commitments to the very liberal democratic values, Enlightenment faith in progress, and hope for technology that have been so much the subject of postmodernist criticism.[10] At best this recent work appears at odds with the purely destructive conception of edifying discourse. At worst, it appears to yield apparently contradictory conceptions of the end of philosophy and of our relation to tradition, as well as a more substantive inconsistency between Rorty's existential conception of the uniqueness of the self in *Philosophy and the Mirror of Nature* and his more recent calls for social solidarity and a Deweyean sense of community. Charles Guignon, for example, has argued that "Rorty's deconstruction of philosophy effectively undermines any prospects for maintaining the kind of *apologia* for democratic and Christian ideals that crops up in his writings. . . . [and] by his own criteria, Rorty can be neither a 'pragmatist' nor a 'humanist' as these labels are ordinarily understood" because his Sartrean version of humanism is at odds with his postmodernism.[11]

This inconsistency can be illuminated through two lines of criticism—one trading on his descriptive pluralism and the notion of the self that follows from it, the other on the notion of knowledge as social practice and its implications for social criticism. The criticisms themselves are no mere rejection of Rorty's attack on epistemology-centered philosophy. They arise from deep, sensitive, and sympathetic readings. Each develops by restoring to significance what is lost by Rorty's appropriation of the merely destructive features of his exemplars of edification—Martin Heidegger and John Dewey. One line emphasizes the Sartrean strand in Rorty's thought—the part of his argument that aims to liberate us from the "freezing over of culture" which results from the philosophical demand that all inquiry be commensurable and that supposes the end of inquiry to be a single true description of ourselves and the world. The other emphasizes the Deweyean strand which opposes the philosophical notion that our practices and values require a culture-neutral and ahistorical grounding, urging instead that loyalty to ourselves—recognition of ourselves as members of a community—is justification enough for rational inquiry, social responsibility, and social hope.

John Caputo has offered a compelling version of the first objection. He casts it in terms of Rorty's appropriation of Heidegger and Gadamer.

> Rorty takes not only the name of Heidegger but also of Gadamerian hermeneutics in vain. Hermeneutics for Rorty is the open-endedness of this discourse, a resolve not to close off innovative redescriptions of ourselves which are fresh and interesting. . . . But hermeneutics for Heidegger is our openness to the messages of the gods, listening to the silent address of Being. And in Gadamer, in whom this dark Heideggerian saying takes on more manageable proportions, hermeneutics bears the full weight of our historical situatedness in the world. . . . [T]he language we speak has been handed down to us by the tradition. We do not inventively devise language games, but we are historically rooted speakers whose speaking is anchored in the world, speaking which bears ontological and historical weight. Rorty's language games are weightless creatures and his hermeneutics a mechanics of weightlessness. There can be no hermeneutic situation, no bond of thought to Being, to the world, to history ("Thought of Being and the Conversation of Mankind," pp. 678–79).

Whereas Caputo's objection turns on the way Rorty's descriptive pluralism cuts us loose from our tradition and its values, Richard Bernstein's objection—which is the reverse of the coin—contrasts Rorty and Dewey, pointing out the way Rorty's identification of knowledge with social practice so much accommodates us to current practices that he provides no basis for criticism of traditional values or for decision between competing practices.

> Dewey would certainly agree with Rorty that all justification involves reference to existing social practices and that philosophy is not a discipline that has any special knowledge of knowing or access to more fundamental foundations. But for Dewey this is where the real problem begins. What are the social practices to which we should appeal? How do we discriminate the better from the worse? Which ones need to be discarded, criticized and restructured. . . . Rorty never quite gets around to asking these and related questions. ("Philosophy in the Conversation of Mankind," p. 768)

John Dunn has recently expressed similar concerns about the social implications of the Wittgensteinian aspects of Rorty's view.

> [His] Wittgensteinian emphasis on practices and forms of life as the reality beyond which no human appeal can be made is certainly bracing to the imagination and may well be simply philosophically valid. What remains

elusive, however, is just what positive implications it would have, if it were indeed valid, for ethical, social and political values. Rorty's own view of this question seems as yet a little unsteady, stretching from the somewhat fideist orientation towards existing practices offered by a conservative philosopher like Michael Oakeshott to the decidedly more intrepid (if perhaps equally vague) approach of the American pragmatist John Dewey. Since the question of whether an existing assemblage of human practices is essentially appropriate as it stands or whether it requires drastic and systematic reconstitution is at the core of social and political theory, a simple appeal to the authority of practice has no determinate content and is necessarily either evasive, insidious or vacuous.[12]

For similar reasons, Richard Eldridge has framed the problem of the possibility of social criticism—given Rorty's identification of knowledge with social practice—as a dilemma: "Either Rorty means, however sketchily, to argue in favor of a criterion for settling [cases of conflicting social practices], a criterion which involves attention to something besides the simple succession of cultural facts, attention, say, to facts about human nature and the nature of value. In that case Rorty would abandon his version of pragmatism. Or he does not mean to argue for such criterion. In that case he would lapse into irrationalism and skepticism about culture generally."[13]

By working out the connection between the two aspects of Rorty's thought that motivate these criticisms, I will suggest how he attempts to have a basis for social criticism without epistemology-centered philosophy; how his is a strategy against philosophy, much like the Pyrrhonian challenge, that seeks to return us to the contingent, finite, and fallible critical practices of normal discourse. The general form of my argument will take seriously *both* sides of Rorty's distinction between abnormal and normal discourse. That distinction generalized Kuhn's distinction between normal and revolutionary science. According to his extension of Kuhn, "normal discourse is that which is conducted within an agreed-upon set of conventions about what counts as a relevant contribution, what counts as answering a question, what counts as having a good argument for that answer or a good criticism of it. Abnormal discourse is what happens when someone joins in the discourse who is ignorant of these conventions or who sets them aside" (*Mirror of Nature,* p. 320). Most commentators have focused on the abnormal or reactive side of Rorty's call for the end of epistemology-centered philosophy and have charged him with relativism and the abandonment of objective truth. Yet the result of Rorty's reactive side is his claim that objective truth is the normal outcome of normal discourse and that no one can be a relativist about alternative theories in the course of normal inquiry. Abnormal or edifying discourse is dialectically tied to normal practices of inquiry and criticism in the sense that the opposition to epistemology-centered philosophy results in the realization that the practices of normal inquiry do not require grounding outside themselves. The Deweyean themes of community, liberal democratic values, and social hope in Rorty's recent work are urged within the values and practices of normal discourse.

I will center the interpretation initially on his criticism of the Cartesian conception of mind because I want to focus the connection between Cartesian consciousness and personhood in order to suggest how the results of Rorty's criticism of the Cartesian conception of the mental—while not a "theory" of mind—is nonetheless substantive for moral life. Next, I will turn to his antifoundationalism and the idea of knowledge as social practice in order to understand his notion of community and our connection to tradition. In this context, I will return to Caputo's and Bernstein's objections to Rorty, objections that expose a deep tension in his work between two strands in his thought: the Nietzschean-Sartrean strand based on descriptive pluralism which understands the autonomy of the self reactively as the impossibility of a single commensurable description for conveying the whole truth about ourselves; and the Deweyean strand that emphasizes social solidarity and understands the self in terms of tradition and membership in a community. The Nietzschean-Sartrean theme is the most obvious outcome of opposition to the Cartesian tradition. The Deweyean theme has become more pronounced in Rorty's criticism of Foucault because Foucault's analysis of modern forms of power cannot support a notion of social solidarity[14] and in Rorty's more recent rejection of a Kantian basis for liberalism and his alternative claim that "loyalty to itself is morality enough [for society] and . . . such loyalty no longer needs an ahistorical backup."[15] In the end I will claim that this tension and the criticisms that turn on it can be resolved in terms of the dialectical relation between abnormal and normal discourse.

My purpose, then, is to show that there is a substantive moral result of Rorty's opposition to philosophy, in much the same way that there was a substantive moral result of Pyrrhonian skepticism, and to claim that the end of philosophy is not the end of meaningful social criticism since the abnormal and reactive side of Rorty's work serves to situate social criticism within the norms and values of our tradition. I will return to this point at the end in order to connect Rorty's opposition to philosophy with the Pyrrhonian tradition.

## IV

It has been common since the early 1960s to pose the mind-body problem in the form of the question: Is consciousness a brain process? It is often assumed that there is something obvious about this formulation because it is also assumed that there is an intuitive difference between mind and body which turns on consciousness, and that in the absence of this difference not only would we be unable to distinguish ourselves from the brutes, we would be unable to understand our own uniqueness as human beings and as individuals. Rorty's claim, however, is that our intuitions about consciousness and the mental are simply a result of the specific language-game we have been playing since Descartes. The first part of *Philosophy and the Mirror of Nature* exposes this language-game by working out the history of mind from Plato and Aristotle through the seventeenth century. His purpose is to show how ancient worries about how we can have knowledge of the unchanging and how we differ from the brutes became entangled with the specifically modern problem of the relation between states of consciousness and states of our brains.

In the course of tracing the transition from the ancient view of "mind as the ability to grasp universals" to the Cartesian view of "mind as inner arena of consciousness" Rorty distinguishes three sorts of problems that were run together in the transition: the problem of reason, the problem of personhood, and the problem of consciousness. In sum, "the problem of consciousness centers around the brain, raw feels, and bodily motions. The problem of reason centers around the topics of knowledge, language and intelligence—all of our 'higher powers.' The problem of personhood centers around attributions of freedom and moral responsibility" (*Mirror of Nature,* p. 35). Rorty's thesis is that these distinct problems become confused in the modern discussion of the mind-body problem, and that once they are disentangled, we can see how the post-Cartesian problem of consciousness—and the foundational epistemology that underwrites it—swings entirely free of questions about human freedom, the uniqueness of the self, and moral agency.[16] Once we see this, the controversy over the relation between consciousness and brain processes loses its philosophical interest, since nothing about autonomy, uniqueness, and personhood turns on it.

This thesis is developed in two ways. First he argues that, for Descartes, the distinction between the mental and the material ultimately turned on the incorrigibility of mental representations rather than on the nonspatiality of the mental or the ability of the mental to exist in separation from the material.[17] Once incorrigibility became the mark of the mental, the problem of consciousness—which supposedly had something to do with the nature of reason and our personhood—turned out to be the epistemological problem of our privileged relation to our own inner representations. Second, in an extremely witty and densely argued science-fiction story, he draws the metaphilosophical conclusion that once we realize that "the purportedly metaphysical 'problem of consciousness' is no more and no less than the epistemological 'problem of privileged access'. . . . questions about dualism versus materialism lose their interest" (*Mirror of Nature,* p. 69).

The science-fiction story begins this way: "Far away, on the other side of our galaxy, there was a planet on which lived beings like ourselves—featherless bipeds who built houses and bombs, and wrote poems and computer programs. These beings did not know that they had minds" (*Mirror of Nature,* p. 70). To anticipate a bit, the point of reliving the history of the concept of mind from Plato through Descartes and of telling science-fiction stories about persons without minds is to realize that there is something entirely contingent and optional—and therefore not deeply imbedded—about the identification of the problems of consciousness, reason, and personhood. I will fill out this point in terms of the science-fiction story.

It seems that on this planet at the other side of our galaxy, biochemistry and neurophysiology were the first sciences to make major advances. One result of this was that inhabitants of the planet came to refer to their inner lives in physiological terms—in terms of C-fiber firings, neurological states, and so forth. One day the planet was visited by an expedition from Earth. The expedition included philosophers who dubbed the inhabitants Antipodeans, "in reference to an almost forgotten school of philosophers, centering in Australia and New Zealand, who in the previous century had attempted one of many futile revolts against Cartesian dualism" (*Mirror of Nature,* p. 72). The philosophers became interested in determining whether the Antipodeans, in addition to experiencing brain-processes, were conscious, that is, whether they also experienced sensations. After many inconclusive experiments, the issue finally came down to whether there was anything they could claim to report incorrigibly about their inner lives which would finally settle the dispute over whether, in addition to brain processes, they experienced "raw feels." This science fiction not only provides a wonderful way of retelling contemporary philosophy of mind from Ryle and Smart to Kripke, but, more important for my purpose, it locates Rorty's place in the story.

The disagreement about whether there is anything the Antipodeans report incorrigibly became roughly the same as the disagreement between behaviorists, identity-theorists, and skeptics about minds. It turned on whether it is essential to incorrigible reports of inner experiences that what is experienced are raw feels. According to Rorty, this issue finally comes down to a choice between three views about the Antipodeans:

> (a) that the Antipodean language, just by virtue of containing some incorrigible reports, is about raw feels, or (b) that we shall never know whether the Antipodeans speak a language just because we shall never know whether they have raw feels or (c) that the whole issue about raw feels is a fake because the example of the Antipodeans shows that we never have any raw feels ourselves. (*Mirror of Nature,* p. 95)

One would expect as a result of Rorty's early papers on the "disappearance theory of mind" that he would side with (c), and in fact his disappearance theory has often been interpreted this way.[18] Instead, however, he suggests that we abandon the very notion that incorrigible knowledge is possessed in virtue of our special relation to raw feels, and as a result that we become neither behaviorists, skeptics, nor identity-theorists. We should simply set aside the Cartesian conception of mind and our view about a privileged relation to our inner experiences that has made these the possible solutions to the question whether the Antipodeans have sensations. Instead of siding with one of the alternatives, he adopts a "don't care" attitude toward the question because nothing interesting turns on it.

I have sketched the general line of Rorty's account of the recent debate in the philosophy of mind in order to suggest that there is more involved here than just a metaphilosophy of boredom. It has substantive results for notions of personhood and our uniqueness. To say why, it is necessary to suggest something more general about the recent controversy in the philosophy of mind. I think that the hidden agenda of much of the antimaterialism side of the recent debate about mind-brain identity turned less on questions of the logic of contingent identity claims, reductionism, or descriptive and explanatory adequacy, and more on implicit existential worries. Within the Cartesian framework, our uniqueness was thought to consist in our privileged relation to our own inner representations, and thus the background concern of many opponents of various forms of the identity theory was that if the inner life is not Cartesian, human beings would be turned into mere objects.

This worry has been made explicit in a fascinating and controversial article by Thomas Nagel titled "What Is It Like To Be A Bat?" in which he opposed materialism by claiming that a materialist description of ourselves will inevitably fail to capture the essential subjectivity of conscious experience. Nagel takes the problem of consciousness to be what makes the mind-body problem so intractable and he understands consciousness as a uniquely subjective point of view. In formulating the problem of consciousness by considering what it is like for a bat to be a bat, Nagel joins this notion of the subjective character of conscious experience with an antiverificationist claim that bats are conscious—that is, they have a unique point of view insofar as there is something it is like to be a bat—even though it would be impossible for us to know what it is like to be a bat. According to Nagel, "reflection on what it is like to be a bat seems to lead us to the conclusion that there are facts that do not consist in the truth of propositions expressible in human language. . . . [and] If the facts of experience—facts about what it is like *for* the experiencing organism—are accessible only from one point of view, then it is a mystery how the true character of experience could be revealed in the physical operation of the organism."[19]

Rorty agrees with Nagel's existential point about the uniqueness of the "I" but he disagrees that it rests on anything interesting about consciousness; if it did, our uniqueness would be a matter of our privileged relation to our own inner episodes.[20] In contrast to the sort of position Nagel defends, Rorty cryptically suggests that "our uniqueness lies in our poetic ability to say unique and obscure things, not in our ability to say obvious things to ourselves alone" (*Mirror of Nature,* p. 123). Less obscurely, he claims toward the end of the book that "the complete set of laws which enable prediction . . . plus complete descriptions (in atoms-and-the-void terms) of all human beings, would not yet be the whole 'objective truth' about human beings, nor the whole set of true predictions about them. There would remain as many other distinct sets of objective truths . . . as there were incommensurable vocabularies within which normal inquiry about human beings could be conducted" (*Mirror of Nature,* p. 338). It is the plurality and incommensurability of possible descriptions of ourselves, not the subjective character of conscious experience, that constitutes our uniqueness and which prevents us from becoming mere objects of science. And it is this view that sums up what I have referred to as the Nietzschean-Sartrean strand of this thought.

This last point raises, it seems to me, the most important theme of Rorty's book, the theme that connects his opposition to epistemology-centered philosophy with this Nietzschean-Sartrean view of the self. Within the metaphor of mind as the mirror of nature, we are seen essentially as knowers, and knowing is, on the one hand, understood to build out of our privileged relation to inner representations and, on the other, to be guided by the reduction of a plurality of possible vocabularies about ourselves and the world to a single vocabulary. "The dominating notion of epistemology," Rorty writes, "is that to be rational, to be fully human, to do what we ought, we need to find agreement with other human beings" (*Mirror of Nature,* p. 316). But for the edifying thinker, the notion that there is a single true description of ourselves and that all inquiry should converge in agreement results in the "freezing over of culture [and the] dehumanization of human beings" (*Mirror of Nature,* p. 377). Rorty, like Paul Feyerabend,[21] sees pluralism about vocabularies for describing ourselves as essential to our humanization. The reverse of the coin is that once the issue of consciousness inherited from Descartes is separated from the problem of personhood, we realize how unimportant, since the seventeenth century, the inner-life story is to the uniqueness of the "I." In that sense, Rorty has not taken a position on the mind-body problem. Instead, he has attempted to trivialize it because, if he is right, we now see that nothing interesting about ourselves turns on the relation between consciousness and privileged representations. And this is the sense in which he can deny a view without its becoming a view.

The point of working through Rorty's analysis of the recent debate of mind-body identity is to set the stage for developing two sorts of issues. The first has to do with the autonomy of the self and personhood. So far, I have only considered one aspect of Rorty's notion—the purely reactive and thin conception of the self that understands our uniqueness in terms of a pluralism about possible descriptions. It is merely reactive in the sense of being a protest against the view common to both Descartes and materialism that there is a single vocabulary for capturing the truth about the self. Personhood, however is more substantive. Early in *Philosophy and the Mirror of Nature,* Rorty suggests that once one separates out issues of consciousness and reason, "personhood can be seen for what I claim it is—a matter of decision rather than knowledge, an acceptance of another being into fellowship rather than a recognition of a common essence" (*Mirror of Nature,* p. 38). This idea of personhood as fellowship with other beings or as membership in an ethical community—an idea he gets from Wilfrid Sellars[22] as much as from Dewey—will be considered in Section VII below. The second issue has to do with the end of philosophy—the sense, for Rorty, that trivializing philosophical issues allows us to quit doing philosophy whenever we like. I turn to that issue now.

## V

Rorty does not always give exactly the same reason why he opposes the traditional philosophical attempt to escape our contingency by securing inquiry in the essential or the ahistorical or transcendental. Sometimes the claim is that the foundational project of epistemology-centered philosophy is an impossible one. Sometimes the claim is that several hundred years of attempts to ground inquiry or to establish reason as a tribunal have been unsuccessful and prospects for future success are not encouraging. Sometimes it is the claim that nothing very interesting turns on the success or failure of the Platonic tradition. The last reason, it seems to me, is the most important since it distinguishes his opposition to philosophy from other postmodern strategies. In the Introduction to *Consequences of Pragmatism,* for example, Rorty writes: "Pragmatists think that the history of attempts to isolate the True or the Good, or to define the word 'true' or 'good,' support their suspicion that there is no interesting work to be done in this area. . . . So pragmatists see the Platonic tradition as having outlived its usefulness" (*Consequences,* p. xiv). It is this last claim—what I have called a metaphilosophy of boredom—that needs to be filled out.

In a recent paper, Rorty criticized the attempts by Heidegger and Derrida to "overcome" metaphysics in a way that clearly distinguishes his stand toward the philosophical tradition from their more familiar "end of philosophy" views that he is sometimes identified with. The central claim of the paper is that "The big esoteric problem common to Heidegger and Derrida of how to 'overcome' or escape from the onto-theological tradition is an artificial one and needs to be replaced by lots of little pragmatic questions about which bits of that tradition might be used for some current purpose" ("Deconstruction," p. 3).

This claim rests on two arguments. First, the attempt to overcome the tradition is caught on the horns of a dilemma: either one is liberated from philosophy and thus one loses contact with the subject; or one is dialectically tied to philosophy and merely continues it. He rejects Derrida's attempt to "twine the horns together" rather than steer between them because Derrida takes the abstract problem of escape from the metaphysical tradition as real and central to culture; because he—like Heidegger—thinks that the metaphysical tradition and its binary oppositions are at the heart of culture and, for that reason, they require overcoming or deconstructing. In assuming, however, that the dichotomies of the metaphysical tradition are imbedded in our language and our culture, Heidegger and Derrida ironically join hands with traditional philosophers about the centrality of philosophical dichotomies to reflection on ourselves and culture. They merely take different stands toward them. Whereas the philosophical tradition takes the view that the imbeddedness of the binary oppositions that structure the metaphysical tradition is a sign of the importance of philosophy for the rest of culture, the deconstructionists take it as an indication of why we must be constantly vigilant—always on guard against the pull of metaphysics, always resistant to the philosophical urge for closure. I have suggested in the first chapter the similarity between Derrida and the Pyrrhonian skeptics who thought that they maintained mental health only by being constantly ready to oppose the latest dogmatic claims with their bag of tropes. But Rorty departs from the deconstructionists and from the Pyrrhonians, because he does not think that the metaphysical tradition *is* so fundamental to culture. He would not write, as Heidegger had, "metaphysics, our language," and he does not think, as Derrida does, that metaphysical limits are always at work and that there is no "landing beyond" metaphysics.

And this leads to his second argument. His Wittgensteinian, therapeutic approach aims at trivializing the binary oppositions that structure epistemology-centered philosophy so we can quit doing philosophy whenever we like. In regard to the common denominator of the philosophical tradition, and in contrast to those who would overcome it, he suggests that, as a matter of fact, philosophy or metaphysics has not been so central to high culture as its opponents have thought and thus the project of deconstruction is not all that urgent. "There is not an urgent task called 'deconstructing metaphysics' which needs to be performed before we can get to work on the rest of culture" ("Deconstruction," p. 20). The danger that Heidegger and Derrida see is artificial: "The discourse of high culture has, particularly in the last two hundred years, been considerably more fluid and chatty and playful than one would guess from reading either Heidegger or Derrida" ("Deconstruction," p. 15).

The irony of the attempt to overcome metaphysics is that, in seeing it at the heart of language or culture, the attempt reinstates the traditional notion of the fundamental problems of philosophy by implying that the binary oppositions of metaphysics are deeply imbedded; so Heidegger and Derrida end up joining hands with traditional philosophers. Rorty's Wittgensteinian and pragmatic line aims to show that these oppositions are not "deep"; it aims to trivialize them. The end of philosophy is not its extreme possibility or its closure. The end of philosophy is the realization that we can quit doing it whenever we like.

## VI

A good deal of recent analytic epistemology has centered on attacks and alternatives to the Cartesian demand that inquiry must rest on indubitable foundations. This foundational project is motivated by the skeptical argument that the requirement that knowledge be justified generates an infinite regress of justificatory claims, and post-Cartesian epistemology has developed in terms of Descartes' foundational metaphor. Typically, antifoundationalist attacks on the Cartesian project have generated two sorts of nonskeptical response to the problems of foundational epistemology. On the one hand, it is argued that one can have a foundational theory of justification without being committed to a "certainty theory" about the foundations. On the other hand, it is argued that some successor subject—naturalized epistemology, referential theories of language, hermeneutics, or some such—can succeed in securing inquiry where foundational epistemology has failed. It is tempting to think that Rorty's antifoundationalist attack moves in one or the other of these directions since he characterizes the results of his opposition to foundationalism as "epistemological behaviorism" and he sides with hermeneutics against epistemology. It is clear, however, that the holistic, behavioristic result about knowledge that he thinks follows from Quine, Sellars, and Davidson is not one among possible alternative theories in the recent debate in analytic epistemology. He writes, for example, that "a holistic approach to knowledge is not a matter of antifoundationalist polemic, but a distrust of the whole epistemological enterprise" (*Mirror of Nature,* p. 181). Furthermore—and this has produced consternation among some Continental philosophers, much as his antifoundationalism produced it among analytic philosophers—it is clear that he does not take hermeneutics to be the successor method to epistemology. Instead, he claims that "'hermeneutics' is not the name for a discipline, nor for a method of achieving the sort of results which epistemology failed to achieve, nor for a program of research. On the contrary, hermeneutics is an expression of the hope that the cultural space left by the demise of epistemology will not be filled" (*Mirror of Nature,* p. 315).

The point of his antifoundationalism is that once we realize that there is something optional about the metaphor of mirroring and the idea of accurate representation proper to it, then we realize that knowledge is not the sort of thing that presents a problem that a theory of knowledge must solve. Knowledge is simply "successful coping," or "what society allows us to get away with saying," or "what inquiry, for the moment, is leaving alone." Knowledge is not a relation between the mind or a theory or true propositions and what they represent. It is the normal result of normal discourse.

It is this result of his opposition to epistemology-centered philosophy that has generated the frequent charges of epistemological relativism, and the less frequent but more problematic concerns about the social implications of his antifoundationalism. Rorty anticipated the relativism charge by claiming that relativism in any problematic sense only makes sense within a conception of philosophy as epistemology-centered.

> To say that the True and the Right are matters of social practice may seem to condemn us to a relativism which, all by itself, is a *reductio* of a behavioristic approach to either knowledge or morals. . . . Here I shall simply remark that only the image of a discipline—philosophy—which will pick out a given set of scientific or moral views as more "rational" than the alternatives by appeal to something which forms a permanent neutral matrix for all inquiry and all history, makes it possible to think that such relativism must automatically rule out coherence theories of intellectual and practical justification. (*Mirror of Nature,* pp. 178–79)

Part of the backup for this rejoinder to the relativism charge is his interpretation of the Davidsonian argument that the controversy between realism and conceptual relativism makes sense only within the scheme-content dogma of empiricism and his defense of Kuhn against the same sort of relativism charge. Since I have considered this rejoinder in the context of relativist conceptions of rationality in the previous chapter, I will not return to those conceptions here. It is necessary, however, to set this response in the context of Rorty's metaphilosophical claim, and to draw out its social implications.

In his presidential address to the American Philosophical Association, Rorty suggests that the identification of his brand of pragmatism with relativism "is a result of a confusion between the pragmatist's attitude toward *philosophical* theories with his attitude towards *real* theories" (*Consequences,* p. 167). If relativism is the view that there is no way of deciding between alternative beliefs and values and that any view is as good as any other, he claims that no one is a relativist about real theories. It is only with respect to philosophical theories that Rorty is a relativist, since the whole point of abnormal or edifying discourse is to show that nothing interesting turns on which side one takes in philosophical controversies. "Real" theories, however, are the normal outcomes of normal discourse and to think that he is relativist about them is to think that real theories are dependent on philosophical theories—that is, to think that normal inquiry must be backed-up or grounded in something other than itself. He puts the point this way: "objectivity should be seen as conformity to the norms of justification (for assertions and for actions) we find about us. Such conformity becomes dubious and self-deceptive only when seen as something more than this—namely, as a way of obtaining access to something which 'grounds' current practices of justification in something else" (*Mirror of Nature,* p. 361).

Rorty's claim is that choices between real theories can be made only within the norms and values of current practice. The philosophical attempt to ground our choices is the attempt to get behind those practices and legitimize them in terms of the nature of reason itself, or ground them on claims of objectivity and truth. In the end, the realization that there is something optional about epistemology-centered philosophy—that knowledge need not be understood as accuracy of representation and that normal inquiry is not in need of foundations—not only undermines foundationalist epistemology, it undermines the original Platonic demand that we must be liberated from our condition and escape the Cave if we are to lead a good life; and it restores the idea of knowing as one among various social practices, with as much contingency, fallibility and finitude as the rest of life. Ultimately, the object of Rorty's attack, then, is not recent, local views about knowledge and language but the motivating urge of philosophy to liberate us from our contingency and fallibility by thinking that knowledge must be something more than "successful coping."[23] In the Introduction to *Consequences of Pragmatism,* in a passage I have cited before, he makes this point directly: "[Philosophy] is the impossible attempt to step outside our skins—the traditions, linguistic and other, within which we do our thinking and self-criticism—and compare ourselves with something absolute. . . . [the] Platonic urge to escape from the finitude of one's time and place, the 'merely conventional' and contingent aspects of one's life" (*Consequences,* p. xix).

The attempt to escape our condition is no merely abstract urge. Since Plato's allegory, it has been thought that liberation or escape from the contingent to the eternal is the realization of our true nature, and for that reason, it is necessary for our moral and social lives. In undermining the philosophical urge to escape, Rorty—like the Pyrrhonian skeptics, Montaigne, and Rousseau—is disconnecting philosophy and the good life. He certainly appreciates the concern of those who oppose his loose, holistic, behavioristic notion of knowing since it not only undercuts the attempt to escape but also appears to eliminate a place for rational criticism of moral and social values. "One reason why professional philosophers recoil from the claim that knowledge may not have foundations, or rights and duties an ontological ground, is that the kind of behaviorism which dispenses with foundations is in a fair way toward dispensing with philosophy. For the view that there is no permanent neutral matrix within which the dramas of inquiry and history are enacted has a corollary that criticism of one's culture can only be piecemeal and partial—never 'by reference to eternal standards'" (*Mirror of Nature,* p. 179). The threat of the end of philosophy is that social criticism will lack foundations, that it will be impossible to call current practices into question, to resolve disagreement, or to achieve consensus. This brings us to the social implications of Rorty's opposition to epistemology-centered philosophy.

He has positioned his pragmatism in terms of a fundamental choice, a choice "between accepting the contingent character of starting-points, and attempting to evade this contingency. To accept the contingency of starting-points," he tells us, "is to accept our inheritance from, and our conversation with, our fellow-humans as our only source of guidance. . . . If we give up [hope of evading contingency], we shall lose what Nietzsche called 'metaphysical comfort,' but we may gain a renewed sense of community" (*Consequences,* p. 166). The problem is whether—in the restoration of a sense of community and in the return to the normal practices of normal inquiry—we are driven to a pernicious conservatism that merely accommodates us uncritically to our current practices and values or whether it is possible to support nonarbitrary social criticism.

There is another problem, however, that is not just the risk that criticism is ungrounded and arbitrary, though certainly that is problem enough. If our culture and its beliefs, institutions, and values are ungrounded, it is not just the Platonic or Descartes-Locke-Kant image of philosophy that is optional; there also seems to be something optional about current practices and our tradition as well, and the result is that they no longer appear to have legitimate claims on our assent or on our loyalty. If they are ungrounded, then we can take them or leave them alone.

## VII

In his critique of the image of philosophy that has dominated Western thinking, Rorty appears to end up, then, with a view about our relation to the practices and values of our culture and its tradition that is, at best, ambiguous. The fact that our practices are ungrounded seems to entail that they are optional and arbitrary, and the abnormal thrust of Rorty's opposition to epistemology-centered philosophy has this result. Yet Rorty wants to claim that normal practices of discourse are ground enough for ongoing inquiry and social criticism and that loyalty to these practices are ground enough for a sense of our belonging, or community. If abnormal discourse is in the service of restoring confidence in normal inquiry by opposing the urge to ground what we do in something other that itself, as I have suggested, then does not this just accommodate us in a conformist way to our current practices and values—to merely reaffirm the normalcy of the normal?[24] Either aspect of this ambiguity is traded on in the two apparently opposite lines of criticism of Caputo and Bernstein that nevertheless reflect a common theme of concern over the social implications of Rorty's critique of the philosophical tradition.

I have already suggested how the first of these criticisms exploits the abnormal, reactive Nietzschean-Sartrean aspect of Rorty's thought that offers a voluntarist conception of the self in terms of a plurality of possible self-descriptions. A conception of the self that frees us from the dehumanizing effects of the demand that all inquiry be commensurable also cuts us free from the constraints of tradition and its values since we are free to let a thousand vocabularies bloom. The second concerns itself with the normal and Deweyan side that understands personhood as membership in a community. But the attempt to have Sartrean freedom as well as Deweyan belonging seems to present an irresolvable tension at the heart of Rorty's work, a tension which is Guignon's chief concern. What I will now argue is that, far from being ambiguous or inconsistent, it is the very maintenance of this tension between the normal and abnormal that is essential for the resolution of the problem of our critical relation to current practices.

This same issue and the connection between both aspects of Rorty's view can be approached from a slightly different angle. On the face of it, it appears that Rorty is caught in the same sort of dilemma critics of liberal political theory have found at the heart of that tradition from Locke and Kant through Rawls. Rorty wants a conception of the autonomous self—the self free of any privileged self-description and independent of the constraints of culture—and he wants a strong sense of community and an understanding of personhood and moral agency in terms of community membership and community values. But is he in any better position than traditional liberal philosophers to have it both ways? I think this question can be sharpened by way of an especially acute criticism of liberal political philosophy by Michael Sandel.[25]

Sandel argues against Rawls's theory of justice and against liberalism generally, in part because the theory requires a strong sense of community to sustain its social vision of justice yet its individualistic account of the self—the antecedent individuation of the subject—cannot sustain this sense of community and thus cannot sustain the social values it wishes to support. Developing Rawls's distinction between two accounts of community, Sandel distinguishes three: an instrumental account in which "the subjects of co-operation are assumed to be governed by self-interested motivations alone, and the good of community consists solely in the advantages individuals derive from co-operating in pursuit of their egoistic ends (*Limits of Justice,* p. 148)"—this is the view Rousseau criticized and that Rawls also finds inadequate; the Kant/

Rawls view which Sandel dubs the sentimental conception because it involves benevolent feelings toward others as well as selfish ones; and a strong or constitutive sense of community which is not individualistic in that it does not antecedently identify the subject but, instead, conceives of community as part of self-understanding, and thus partly constitutive of the agent's identity. Sandel contrasts the strong sense with the others by suggesting that with community derived from the antecedent individuation of the subject "'association' and 'co-operation' typically presuppose the antecedent plurality of those who join together to associate or co-operate, [but] 'community' and 'participation' may describe a form of life in which the members find themselves commonly situated 'to begin with,' their commonality consisting less in relationships they have entered than in attachments they have found" (*Limits of Justice,* pp. 151–52).[25]

This is very suggestive, I think, for structuring the attempt to pull together in a coherent way the two strands of Rorty's view. Initially it seems that he wants both a Nietzschean-Sartrean sense of the self and Dewey's notion of the "great community," or what Sandel calls the strong or constitutive sense of community; and that just as Sandel has written of the liberal conception of justice, Rorty can't have it both ways—for reasons similar to those I offered against Foucault, it seems that he cannot derive a sense of social solidarity from his view of autonomy. I think, however, that Rorty's work suggests a complete separation of the question of autonomy from the question of personhood and community in a way that avoids this line of criticism. Most modern moral and political theorists have attempted to understand autonomy and moral agency in terms of each other—either freedom as moral agency, with Kant, or moral agency as freedom, with Mill—and have developed social relations as the association and cooperation of autonomous agents. Rorty, however, has separated the issue of autonomy from moral agency. Autonomy is a purely reactive notion, understood as the resistance of the self to capture by any single or privileged description. Though this is a conception of the self as a plenitude of possible self-descriptions in much the way that Foucault's is, it is nonetheless a completely thin self, because the self is understood in a way that is entirely reactive and parasitic on the notion of the Cartesian subject. It is not so much a conception of the self or a view about autonomy as it is an abnormal thinker's protest against philosophical attempts to have a theory of autonomy grounded in some notion of the truth about ourselves or our essence or fundamental nature. Personhood or moral agency, however, is not to be found in nor does it develop out of the Nietzschean-Sartrean self of abnormal or edifying therapy.

Rather, personhood is a matter of belonging—of a sense of community that we make rather than discover through philosophical reflection on the nature of the self. "Our identification with our community—our society, our political tradition, our intellectual heritage—is heightened when we see this community as *ours* rather than *nature's, shaped* rather than *found,* one among many which men have made. In the end, the pragmatists tell us, what matters is our loyalty to other human beings clinging together against the dark, not our hope of getting things right" (*Consequences,* p. 166). In Sandel's terms community is constitutive of the self-understanding of the moral agent. The therapeutic or reactive or abnormal side of Rorty that opposes the epistemological demand for commensurable discourses, the idea of common human nature, and the attempt to ground community or traditional values in terms of something "higher" aims to restore a strong sense of community by realizing that "loyalty to itself is morality enough [for society], and that such loyalty no longer needs an ahistorical backup" ("Postmodernist Bourgeois Liberalism," p. 585). This way of structuring Rorty's view, however, does not mean that I think he has succeeded in achieving a strong sense of community by restoring the practices and values of common life. The only point I want to suggest now is that when we separate the notions of autonomy and personhood along the lines of the results of abnormal and normal discourse, and understand that abnormal discourse is dialectically tied to and gets its force from reacting against the normal, our critical relation to our community and its values must be a result of maintaining the tension between autonomy and personhood.

Rorty has rather carelessly written of personhood as a matter of being "one of us," as if it was like picking members for the country club rather than a feature of our self-understanding *constituted* by our tradition. As a result, he has been criticized for the implications of reducing community to a kind of clubbiness.[26] The consistent view, however, must be more like Wittgenstein's notion of our relation to our form of life: we are "one of us" not because we have chosen the traditions and values of our moral community and convinced ourselves of their correctness, but because we are born into them. It is not obvious, however, that this relatively modest Wittgensteinian notion of belonging can support the strong sense of community central to Dewey or Sandel. What Rorty's view seems to suggest is that the sense in which our community is ours is not because we form it like forming a club or even because we are born into it, but because our realization that our form of life is ungrounded transforms the fact that we are born into it into a reflective, critical self-understanding. The serious problem this view must face, then, is this: if personhood and moral agency are a matter of thinking of ourselves as "one of us" and the legitimacy of our community or our traditional values is not to rest on ahistorical foundations, can we escape either dogmatism or conservatism with respect to our own values and institutions on the one hand, or arbitrariness of social criticism on the other? The first issue needs to be approached in terms of what Rorty has referred to as his "mild ethnocentrism" and the second in terms of the unique way his descriptive pluralism has reaffirmed a liberal commitment to toleration.

In his exchange with Lyotard over the question whether, outside of a Kantian conception of humanity and the rhetoric of emancipation, we can still understand human events in terms of a universal history with cosmopolitan intent, he sides with Dewey in thinking that we can praise Western liberal values and write an uplifting narrative of progress without grounding it in a meta-narrative and without thinking of history as the emancipation of human nature; it follows that only within the context and against the background of "our" values is criticism of ourselves and comparison with other values possible. In anticipation of the charge of dogmatism about our Western liberal democratic values, Rorty suggests—for primarily Wittgensteinian and Davidsonian reasons—that "mild ethnocentrism is . . . inevitable and unobjectionable; it amounts to no more than the claim that we can only rationally change some of our beliefs by holding most of our beliefs constant" ("Cosmopolitisme," p. 570).[27] In much the way that Kuhn has claimed that standards of normal scientific inquiry constitute values that guide inquiry rather than criteria that determine it, Rorty's mild ethnocentrism with respect to beliefs that we hold constant amounts to the realization that we can engage in criticism only on the basis of the values from our tradition that guide inquiry.[28] This suggests, however, an ambiguity in the notion of community that reinforces my concern that Rorty cannot derive a strong sense of community from his Wittgensteinianism. On the one hand, he seems to want a sense of community in the sense of belonging or social solidarity, yet on the other, community seems to be no more than the recognition that we can only begin criticism from our own beliefs and values. The more modest view does not entail the stronger.

Rorty thinks that the possibility of reform is not eliminated when we reject the notion of moral agency understood in terms of essential human nature and drop the rhetoric of emancipation: "the pragmatist wants narratives of increasing cosmopolitanism which are not narratives of emancipation. He thinks there was nothing to emancipate—no human nature which was once in chains. Rather, humanity has been making up a nature for itself as it has gone along, through ever larger and richer 'blends of opposing values'. . . . The pragmatist drops the revolutionary rhetoric of emancipation and unmasking . . . in favor of a reformist rhetoric about increased tolerance and decreased suffering" ("Cosmopolitisme," p. 571). Recognizing that we can only begin from confidence in our own beliefs, that we cannot call all of our beliefs into question at once, and that we cannot justify the whole of our beliefs and values to the whole of humanity, we avoid a dangerous dogmatism only in the hope that with increased tolerance the conversation of humankind will be one of interpretation, persuasion, and compromise rather than dogmatism and force.

Rorty's pluralism, then, and his notion of conversation and community, seem much like Hannah Arendt's notion of the polis or common world—the world in which differences can be brought into the public sphere—and he can say with Arendt that "the end of the common world has come when it is seen only under one aspect and is permitted to present itself in only one perspective."[29] Within epistemology-centered philosophy, the common world was thought to be assured by the demand that inquiry be commensurable and, by extension, community was understood in terms of our increasing agreement with other human beings. But for Rorty, the world is held in common and we understand ourselves in terms of community not because inquiry is commensurable or because agreement is guaranteed by the nature of reason or by an ahistorical standpoint but because we are conversational partners.

In his reconciliation of loyalty to our community and its values with descriptive pluralism, he joins hands, I believe, with Montaigne's own use of Pyrrhonian arguments to return self-consciously and critically to our customary and traditional values and to Hume's mitigated skepticism, which allowed a tranquil but not uncritical return to common life. For each, the effect of skepticism is that we return to the customary and traditional with a sort of bifocal vision that allows us to see that criticism can take place only within the values of common life but also allows us to see that none of those values are philosophically fixed and immune from revision. In the first chapter, above, I quoted a passage from Jean Starobinski's book *Montaigne in Motion* in order to anticipate this ironic relation to the traditional and customary. I now quote another because I think that Starobinski's sensitive reading of Montaigne, which captures the paradox and richness of skepticism, also captures the importance of the tension that I think must exist between the abnormal and the normal for Rorty.

What Montaigne has brought to light is a "duty of humankind," a "mutual obligation" that applies to all who share the same experience of the senses, even though it is impossible to state any positive law that is not open to debate and controversy: the sense of felt *similarity* justifies the repudiation of violence. The apparent paradox is that *acquiescence* in the inherited order is based, for the enlightened mind, on the infinite *variety* of usages and customs, among which no criterion of superiority enables one to choose: no criterion, that is, except for that of public tranquillity and the survival of the community. Yet the convention to which the war-weary skeptical mind rallies is unlike the convention it earlier denounced: it is the same appearance but henceforth deprived of the foundation it once claimed, and which guaranteed it a timeless, not to say transcendental, authority. What has been the object of attack and criticism, and what continues to be held suspect, is the "mystical" authority that the civil and religious order had claimed. What is finally recognized is the *usage* (the living moral order) that *appears* to best serve the general welfare. A loyalism becomes possible.[30]

In a similar way, Hume had found benefit even in the excessive Pyrrhonism he criticized when that Pyrrhonism was tempered by nature and common sense. Simply to live ignorantly or unreflectively according to custom or nature renders "the greater part of mankind . . . naturally apt to be affirmative and dogmatical in their opinions,"[31] but "a small tinture of Pyrrhonism" might instill "a degree of doubt, and caution, and modesty which, in all kinds of scrutiny and decision, ought for ever to accompany a just reasoner" (*Enquiries,* pp. 161–62). Mitigated skepticism was not a praise of ignorance, a support for indifference, an acquiescent conservatism, or an abandonment of inquiry; it was the realization that "philosophical decisions are nothing but the reflections of common life, methodized and corrected [and one] will never be tempted to go beyond common life, so long as they consider the imperfection of those faculties which they employ, their narrow reach, and their inaccurate operations" (*Enquiries,* p. 162). Mitigated skepticism is beneficial in that it enables us to be at home with the limitations and contingencies of common life and to achieve a balance with respect to them.

This stand toward practices and values of common life—an ironic stand that both works within them and remains skeptical and at their margin—is possible in Rorty's view, I think, only by retaining the tension between normal and abnormal discourse. While the result of Rorty's opposition to philosophy is that we can quit doing it whenever we like, the edifying thinker cannot quit the margins and quit being abnormal. To do so would be to lapse into a wooden conformism and conservatism. But to be simply abnormal and marginal is to alienate us from the traditions and customs which not only provide the framework for the possibility of normal discourse but also the basis for our sense of belonging.

Now within the framework of normal discourse, Rorty's conclusion that knowledge is only a matter of the state of current inquiry, that social criticism must always be piecemeal and from within, and that legitimacy is only a matter of loyalty to ourselves can be expressed in differing tones of voice. One is resigned—"This is the best we can hope for given the impossibility of discovering the foundations of knowledge and the independent legitimization of current practice." Another is diagnostic—"The attempt to escape our conventions and contingencies to something foundational, neutral, and ahistorical will inevitably alienate us from our traditions and lead to nihilism." Another is more positive—"The normal practices of justification are justification enough for inquiry and community." It is the last voice that Rorty is increasingly using. In the end, while Rorty is very pessimistic about the future of philosophy, he is optimistic—or at least not pessimistic—about the future of normal inquiry, and especially about the future of liberal democratic society. In his exchange with Lyotard, he writes that "The pragmatist hopes, but has no metaphysical justification for believing, that the further universal histories of humanity will describe us twentieth-century Western social democrats in favorable terms. But he has to grant that we have no very clear idea what those terms will be. He would only insist that, if these new terms are adopted as a result of persuasion rather than force, they will be better than the ones we are presently using" ("Cosmopolitisme," p. 578.). Though Rorty has no metaphysical support for his apology for liberal democratic values, he has, quite surprisingly, given them a conservative rationale. The reactive aspect of Rorty's view has forced us back to the values of normal discourse as the only basis for inquiry and criticism, and our current practices of inquiry happen to take place precisely against the backdrop of those liberal values of toleration, progress, and optimism that Rorty praises. Now it is easy to think that his optimism about Western social values is a form of Western chauvinism or cultural imperialism, but the temptation to become dogmatic about Western liberal values is resisted by the marginal or abnormal critic, much the way Hume's mitigated skepticism served to avoid a dogmatic conformity with nature and the practices of common life. Finally, an edifying thinker like Rorty is not just a reactive, abnormal thinker, nor is he simply an apologist for Western liberal values. Instead, he is one who opposes dogmatic attempts to close off conversation at the same time that he expresses optimism that within the framework of toleration and normal inquiry the conversation of humankind will be one of increasing hope.

## VIII

I now must return to where I began. The organizing theme of these essays has been the Platonic notion that we can realize our true selves and achieve the good life only by the philosophical project of escape from the contingent and finite into the necessary and eternal, and the Pyrrhonian challenge to that notion which aims to break the connection between knowledge and virtue and return us to the appearances and values of the customary and traditional. This Pyrrhonian challenge has survived, not in the epistemological opposition to the skeptical attack on the possibility of knowledge, but in the aftermath of the failure of the Enlightenment attempt to meet this challenge by connecting reason, freedom, and community. I have situated recent discussions around the themes of power, reason, and legitimacy within the context of a Pyrrhonian opposition to philosophy as it has emerged out of controversies over Enlightenment values, and I have provided a way of reading Rorty in terms of the Pyrrhonian opposition that not only makes sense of otherwise incompatible strands of his thought but gives voice to the moral thrust of the Pyrrhonian tradition. I have interpreted Rorty's opposition to epistemology-centered philosophy as an attempt to retain an Enlightenment hope and its commitment to social criticism, community, and progress without Enlightenment pretensions about the centrality of reason as a tribunal or philosophy as foundational. While I have attempted to suggest how his view can respond to certain lines of criticism, I do not intend to suggest that he has resolved what is deeply troubling about the outcome of Pyrrhonism.

I am tempted to ask of Rorty whether we can expect that his pluralism and plea for toleration can bear the weight of social criticism and social hope any better than ahistorical foundations, the nature of reason, or a teleology of history. To pose this question to Rorty, though, is to require that his optimism for the future of democratic liberal values be *more* than an expression of hope. His is a philosophy of limits that does not try to turn the contingency of our traditions, the fallibility of our inquiry, the finitude of our condition, or the confused quality of our lives into something more. Given that this Enlightenment hope has been so much under attack in twentieth-century thought, it is natural to expect some justification for his optimism as opposed, say, to the despair of Heidegger or Foucault about the modern age—and maintaining a critical tension between the normal and the abnormal seems neutral between hope and despair. At this most basic level of reflection about our circumstances and our future, we expect that there is something more to persuade us to side with Dewey against Heidegger. But at the end of philosophy, there is nothing more to be said. What is finally so disturbing about Rorty and his version of the Pyrrhonian challenge to philosophy, and why the challenge is alive for us, is that we can no longer seek security from the contingencies of common life in the quest for certainty; with Rorty, we run the risk that, in the end, the conversation of humankind may become merely an exchange of attitudes toward our current condition. Given the fact that so many recent events appear to confirm the success of narcissism over belonging, dogmatism over toleration, and terror over reason, we expect a more satisfying answer to the question of why we should share his optimism.

# Notes

Introduction

1. Plato, *Republic,* Book VII, 514 a–b, *Collected Dialogues of Plato,* ed. Edith Hamilton and Huntington Cairns (Princeton: Princeton University Press, 1963), p. 747.

2. Richard Rorty, *Consequences of Pragmatism* (Minneapolis: University of Minnesota Press, 1982), p. xix.

3. Richard Rorty, "Mind-Body Identity, Privacy, and Categories," *Review of Metaphysics* (1965); and "Incorrigibility as the Mark of the Mental," *Journal of Philosophy* (1970).

4. See my "Is Eliminative Materialism Materialistic?" *Philosophy and Phenomenological Research* (1978); and "The Disappearance Theory and the Denotation Argument," *Philosophical Studies* (1980).

5. Thomas Nagel, "What Is It Like to Be a Bat?" *Philosophical Review* (1974).

6. See my "Materialism and the Inner Life," *The Southern Journal of Philosophy* (1978).

Chapter One

1. Peter Unger, *Ignorance: A Case for Universal Scepticism* (Oxford: Clarendon Press, 1975).

2. Barry Stroud, *The Significance of Philosophical Scepticism* (Oxford: Clarendon Press, 1984).

3. Malcolm Schofield, Myles Burnyeat, and Jonathan Barnes, eds., *Doubt and Dogmatism: Studies in Hellenistic Epistemology* (Oxford: Clarendon Press, 1980).

4. Myles Burnyeat, ed., *The Skeptical Tradition* (Berkeley: University of California Press, 1984).

5. Oliver A. Johnson, *Skepticism and Cognitivism* (Berkeley: University of California Press, 1978), chap. 4; and Arne Naess, *Scepticism* (London: Routledge and Kegan Paul, 1968), chaps. 1–3.

6. Benson Mates, "On Refuting the Skeptic," *Proceedings and Addresses of The American Philosophical Association* 58 (September 1984).

7. See David Sedley's introduction to Schofield et al., *Doubt and Dogmatism: Studies in Hellenistic Epistemology* (Oxford: Clarendon Press, 1980); Mary Mills Patrick, *The Greek Sceptics* (New York: Columbia University Press, 1929), pt. 1; and Charlotte L. Stough, *Greek Skepticism: A Study in Epistemology* (Berkeley: University of California Press, 1969).

8. Sextus Empiricus, *Outlines of Pyrrhonism,* trans. R. G. Bury (Cambridge: Harvard University Press, 1933), p. 19.

9. David Sedley, "The Motivation of Greek Skepticism," in *The Skeptical Tradition,* p. 10.

10. I think Arne Naess is wrong when he interprets the skeptic as "a seeker because he has not found truth and he leaves open the possibility of finding it." *Scepticism,* p. 27.

11. Sedley, "The Motivation of Skepticism," p. 21.

12. Michael Frede, "Stoics and Skeptics on Clear and Distinct Impressions," in *The Skeptical Tradition.*

13. Jonathan Barnes, "The Beliefs of a Pyrrhonist," *Elenchos* 4 (1983): 5.

14. See David Sedley's introduction to Schofield et al., *Doubt and Dogmatism.*

15. Jacques Derrida, "Différance," in *Margins of Philosophy* (Chicago: University of Chicago Press, 1982), p. 7.

16. Jacques Derrida, *Positions* (Chicago: University of Chicago Press, 1981), p. 12.

17. Richard Rorty, *Philosophy and the Mirror of Nature* (Princeton: Princeton University Press, 1979), pp. 377–78.

18. Arne Naess has provided a careful account of the skeptic's "way of announcing," surveying the variety of terms Sextus used in contrasting the skeptic with the dogmatist. See his *Scepticism,* pp. 7ff.

19. Myles Burnyeat, "Can the Sceptic Live His Scepticism?" in Schofield et al., *Doubt and Dogmatism,* p. 52.

20. Roderick Chisholm, "Sextus Empiricus and Modern Empiricism," *Philosophy of Science* 8 (1941).

21. In *Greek Skepticism: A Study in Epistemology,* Charlotte Stough argues that Sextus's skepticism *follows* from his empiricism.

22. Avner Cohen, "Sextus Empiricus: Skepticism as a Therapy," *The Philosophical Forum* 15 (1984): 413.

23. Frede, "Stoics and Skeptics on Clear and Distinct Impressions," p. 67.

24. Richard Popkin, *The History of Scepticism from Erasmus to Spinoza* (Berkeley: University of California Press, 1979), p. 47.

25. Michel de Montaigne, "Apology for Raymond Sebond," in *The Complete Essays of Montaigne,* trans. Donald M. Frame (Stanford: Stanford University Press, 1965).

26. Popkin, *The History of Scepticism,* pp. 44–45.

27. Craig B. Brush, *Montaigne and Bayle: Variations on the Theme of Skepticism* (The Hague: Martinus Nijhoff, 1966).

28. Pierre Charron, *Of Wisdom,* (New York: Da Capo Press, 1971), III, xiii, pp. 469–470. For a further discussion of Charron, see Maryanne Cline Horowitz, "Pierre Charron's View of the Source of Wisdom," *Journal of the History of Philosophy* 9 (1971).

29. Jean Starobinski, *Montaigne in Motion* (Chicago: University of Chicago Press, 1985), pp. 251–52.

30. Francis Bacon, "The Masculine Birth of Time," in *The Philosophy of Francis Bacon,* trans. Benjamin Farrington (Chicago: University of Chicago Press, 1964), p. 71.

31. The extent to which Descartes was really motivated by Pyrrhonism is a subject of dispute. E. M. Curley believes that the influence of Pyrrhonism has not been taken sufficiently seriously by most commentators. Margaret Wilson, on the other hand, acknowledges Descartes' concern with skepticism but considers the concern less connected with defeating Pyrrhonism than with clearing the way for the new science. See Curley's *Descartes Against the Skeptics* (Cambridge: Harvard University Press, 1978); and Wilson's *Descartes* (London: Routledge and Kegan Paul, 1978).

32. René Descartes, "Objections and Replies," in *Philosophical Works of Descartes,* vol. 2, trans. Elizabeth S. Haldane and G. R. T. Ross (Cambridge: Cambridge University Press, 1972), p. 31.

33. Richard Popkin, "David Hume: His Pyrrhonism and His Critique of Pyrrhonism," *The High Road to Pyrrhonism* (San Diego: Austin Hill Press, 1980).

34. Donald W. Livingston, *Hume's Philosophy of Common Life* (Chicago: University of Chicago Press, 1984).

35. See Richard Popkin, "David Hume and the Pyrrhonian Controversy," *The High Road to Pyrrhonism.*

36. Blaise Pascal, *Pensées,* trans. A. J. Krailsheimer (Baltimore: Penguin Books, 1966), no. 131, p. 64.

37. David Hume, *Enquiries Concerning Human Understanding and Concerning Principles of Morals,* ed. L. A. Selby-Bigge (Oxford: The Clarendon Press, 1963), p. 151.

38. David Hume, *A Treatise of Human Nature,* ed. L. A. Selby-Bigge (Oxford: Clarendon Press, 1963), p. 183.

39. Barry Stroud, *Hume* (London: Routledge and Kegan Paul, 1977), p. 75.

40. See Livingston's illuminating discussion in Chapter 8 of *Hume's Philosophy of Common Life.*

41. David Fate Norton, "History and Philosophy in Hume's Thought," in David Fate Norton and Richard Popkin, eds., *David Hume: Philosophical Historian* (New York: Bobbs-Merrill, 1965), p. xxxviii.

42. Popkin, "Hume's Pyrrhonism and His Critique of Pyrrhonism," *The High Road to Pyrrhonism,* p. 128.

43. Barnes, "The Beliefs of a Pyrrhonist," p. 42.

44. See Sheldon Wolin, "Hume and Conservatism," in *Hume: A Re-Evaluation,* ed. Donald W. Livingston and James T. King (New York: Fordham University Press, 1976), p. 254.

45. Livingston, *Hume's Philosophy of Common Life,* p. 308.

46. Jean-François Lyotard, *The Postmodern Condition: A Report on Knowledge* (Minneapolis: University of Minnesota Press, 1984), pp. xxiv–xxv.

47. Charles Taylor, "Foucault on Freedom and Truth." *Philosophical Papers, 2: Philosophy and the Human Sciences* (Cambridge: Cambridge University Press, 1985), p. 178. See also, Jürgen Habermas, "The Entwinement of Myth and Enlightenment," *New German Critique* (1982).

Chapter Two

1. Louis-René de Caradeus de la Chalotais, *Essay on National Education or Plan of Studies for Young Persons,* in F. de La Fontainerie, trans. and ed., *French Liberalism and Education in the Eighteenth Century* (1932; reprint, New York: Burt Franklin, 1971), pp. 41–42.

2. See Anne-Robert-Jacques Turgot, *The Manner of Preparing Individuals and Families to Participate Properly in Good Social Organization,* and Marie-Jean-Antoine-Nichoas de Condorcet, *Report on the General Organization of Public Instruction,* both in La Fontainerie, *French Liberalism and Education in the Eighteenth Century.* For a full discussion of Condorcet's educational theory and its relation to progress, see J. Salwyn Schapiro, *Condorcet and the Rise of Liberalism* (New York: Harcourt, Brace, 1934) chaps. 11 and 12; and Manuela Albertone, "Enlightenment and Revolution: The Evolution of Condorcet's Ideas on Education," in Leonora Cohen Rosenfield, ed., *Condorcet Studies 1,* (Atlantic Highlands: Humanities Press, 1984).

3. Jean-Jacques Rousseau, *Emile, or On Education,* trans. Alan Bloom (New York: Basic Books, 1979), p. 41.

4. Apparently not all educational reformers were convinced that education should be extended to everyone. Harvey Chisick has concluded in a recent and persuasive book that the great majority of the enlightened community in the eighteenth century thought only the most rudimentary education should be provided to lower classes, and this for purely economic reasons. See his *The Limits of Reform in the Enlightenment: Attitudes Toward Education of the Lower Classes in Eighteenth-Century France* (Princeton: Princeton University Press, 1981).

5. In the introduction to his critical edition of Locke's work on education, James Axtell notes that since the epistemological principles of the *Essay* are universal for human understanding and since *Some Thoughts Concerning Education* can be seen as an application of those principles, Locke's views on education should also be universally applicable; however, he states that "it simply never occurred to Locke that all children should be educated, or that those who should should be educated alike." *The Educational Writings of John Locke,* ed. James L. Axtell (Cambridge: Cambridge University Press, 1968), p. 51. For an interesting account of Locke's views of the relation between education and virtue, see John W. Yolton, *Locke: An Introduction* (Oxford: Basil Blackwell, 1985), especially chapter 2.

6. Antoine-Nicolas de Condorcet, *Sketch for a Historical Picture of the Progress of the Human Mind,* trans. June Barraclough (London: Weidenfeld and Nicolson, 1955), p. 61.

7. Immanuel Kant, "An Answer to the Question: What Is Enlightenment?" in *Perpetual Peace and Other Essays,* trans. Ted Humphrey (Indianapolis: Hackett Publishing Company, 1983), p. 33.

8. J. B. Bury, *The Idea of Progress: An Inquiry into Its Origins and Growth* (New York: Macmillan, 1932), p. 5.

9. Robert Nisbet, *History of the Idea of Progress* (New York: Basic Books, 1980), p. 11.

10. Immanuel Kant, "Idea for a Universal History with a Cosmopolitan Intent," in *Perpetual Peace and Other Essays,* p. 39.

11. It has been common to interpret the belief in progress as simply secularized religious belief in divine Providence. For a significant argument against this interpretation of the Enlightenment, see Hans Blumenberg, *The Legitimacy of the Modern Age,* trans. Robert M. Wallace (Cambridge: MIT Press, 1983).

12. Charles Frankel has suggested that the new element in the Enlightenment conception of progress grew out of the appearance of modern mathematico-experimental methods and the institutionalization of inquiry, and that "ideas of progress emerged in the attempt to understand the social implications of this event." *The Faith of Reason: The Idea of Progress in the French Enlightenment* (New York: King's Crown Press, 1948), p. 3.

13. Jürgen Habermas has characterized the eighteenth century in terms of a view of humanity "that produces itself. . . . thus the realization of the good, happy, and rational life has been stretched out along the vertical axis of world-history; praxis has been extended to cover stages of emancipation." *Theory and Practice* (Boston: Beacon Press, 1974), p. 253.

14. Immanuel Kant, "Lecture-Notes on Pedagogy," in *The Educational Theory of Immanuel Kant,* trans. Edward Franklin Buchner (Philadelphia: J. B. Lippincott, 1904), p. 114.

15. Ira O. Wade, *The Intellectual Origins of the French Enlightenment* (Princeton: Princeton University Press, 1971), p. 24.

16. David Hume, *A Treatise of Human Nature,* ed. L. A. Selby-Bigge (Oxford: Clarendon Press, 1963), p. xix.

17. See also Heidegger's argument that with modernity the world is turned into a picture, and that at the same time that the world is projected as an object for representation, we cast ourselves in the fundamental position as the foundation or ground for the possibility of representation. "The Age of the World Picture," in *The Question Concerning Technology and Other Essays* (New York: Harper and Row, 1977).

18. Alasdair MacIntyre, *After Virtue* (Notre Dame: The University of Notre Dame Press, 1981), p. 52.

19. Charles Coulston Gillispie, *The Edge of Objectivity: An Essay in the History of Scientific Ideas* (Princeton: Princeton University Press, 1960), p. 76.

20. Frederick Lange was even less charitable. In a footnote indebted to Friedrich Ueberweg's *History of Philosophy,* he commented: "[T]he facts are too forcible. The most frivolous dilettantism in his own scientific experiments, the degradation of science to hypocritical courtliness, ignorance or misapprehension of the great scientific achievements of a Copernicus, a Kepler, a Galileo . . . these are points enough to display Bacon's scientific character in as unfavourable a light as his political and personal character." *The History of Materialism* (London: Routledge and Kegan Paul, 1957), p. 237n.

21. I owe the distinction between "understanding" and "attunement" to Charles Taylor. In a discussion of the early seventeenth-century controversy over Galileo's discovery of the moons of Jupiter meant to illuminate the

problem of assessing the rationality of alien cultures, Taylor observes that "the breaking of the connection between understanding and attunement was an essential part of the modern revolution in science." Charles Taylor, "Rationality," *Philosophical Papers, 2: Philosophy and the Human Sciences* (Cambridge: Cambridge University Press, 1985), p. 143.

22. For an unusually careful account of Bacon's epistemology of science, see Mary Hesse, "Francis Bacon's Philosophy of Science," in *Essential Articles for the Study of Francis Bacon,* ed. Brian Vickers (Hamden, Conn: Archon Books, 1968).

23. Francis Bacon, *The New Organon,* in *Francis Bacon: A Selection of His Works,* ed. Sidney Warhaft (New York: The Odyssey Press, 1965), p. 360.

24. Benjamin Farrington, *Francis Bacon: Philosopher of Industrial Science* (London: Lawrence and Wishart, 1951), p. 3.

25. In his essay accompanying his translations of various early texts of Bacon, Farrington emphasized the connection between the religious and social aspect of Bacon's thought and the scientific aspect. "He found in the Bible a world-outlook in which his new conception of science could take root and grow. For the new science consisted primarily of a new goal and only secondarily and incidentally of a new method." *The Philosophy of Francis Bacon* (Chicago: University of Chicago Press, 1964), p. 26.

26. Francis Bacon, "The Masculine Birth of Time," in *The Philosophy of Francis Bacon,* p. 64.

27. Francis Bacon, *The Great Instauration,* in *Francis Bacon: A Selection of His Works,* p. 310.

28. Bacon, *The New Organon,* p. 370.

29. Francis Bacon, *Wisdom of the Ancients,* in *Essays and Historical Works of Lord Bacon* (London: George Bell and Sons, 1871), pp. 258–60.

30. Francis Bacon, *The Proficience and Advancement of Learning,* in *Francis Bacon: A Selection of His Works,* p. 235.

31. Francis Bacon, "Thoughts and Conclusions," in *The Philosophy of Francis Bacon,* pp. 78–79.

32. Paolo Rossi, *Philosophy, Technology and the Arts in the Early Modern Era* (New York: Harper and Row, 1970), p. 81.

33. Locke's influence came down to the following ideas, each connected in one way or another with the rejection of innate ideas and acceptance of the *tabula rasa* conception of the mind: acceptance of Locke's sensationalist psychology as extended by Condillac; development by la Mettrie and d'Holbach of Locke's remarks about the possibility of "matter which thinks" into a full-blown materialism; an interpretation of Locke's rejection of the rationalist doctrine of innate ideas which undermined religious orthodoxy and supported either Deism or religious skepticism; and an acceptance of Locke's view of the nature of man which provided the basis for arguing for the perfectibility of man. See Ira O. Wade, *The Structure and Form of the Enlightenment* (Princeton: Princeton University Press, 1977), especially vol. 1, pt. 1.

34. John Locke, *Essay Concerning Human Understanding,* ed. Alexander Campbell Fraser (New York: Dover, 1959), vol. 1, p. 28.

35. See *Essay Concerning Human Understanding,* vol. 2, bk. 4, iii, pp. 213ff.

36. Steven Seidman has observed that "the philosophes . . . saw in modern rationalism a disposition towards intellectual closure and dogmatism, not unlike that of dogmatic religion. Science, with its empirical, fallibilist, and therefore 'open' character, was interpreted as inherently critical and resonant with liberal values." *Liberalism and the Origin of European Social Theory* (Berkeley: University of California Press, 1983), p. 35.

37. Max Horkheimer, *Eclipse of Reason* (New York: Seabury Press, 1974), p. 18.

38. See also Geoffrey Harrison, "Relativism and Toleration," *Ethics* 89 (1976); and Paul Feyerabend, *Against Method* (London: New Left Books, 1975). In Feyerabend's work, toleration and theoretical pluralism are defended not as a method to assure truth, as was the case with Mill, but as ends in themselves for essentially relativist reasons.

39. See for example, Robert Paul Wolff et al., *A Critique of Pure Tolerance* (Boston: Beacon Press, 1965).

40. Keith Baker, in his excellent book on Condorcet, has summed up the dialectic of power and science this way: "Princes and powers are led to favor the advancement of sciences for their utility. Once regarded as an essential part of education, knowledge of the physical sciences forms in the people the habit of accurate, methodical, critical reasoning. . . . Thus Condorcet not only posited a relationship between scientific advance and social welfare. He also insisted that scientific progress necessarily entailed the rationalization of the whole social order." *Condorcet: From Natural Philosophy to Social Mathematics* (Chicago: The University of Chicago Press, 1975), p. 75.

41. See, for example, Jürgen Habermas, "Technology and Science as 'Ideology'," *Toward a Rational Society* (Boston: Beacon Press, 1970).

42. In the beginning of the essay, Cassirer quotes the passage from Kant's fragments: "I am myself by inclination a seeker after truth . . . and I despised the common man who knows nothing. Rousseau set me right. This blind prejudice vanished; I learned to respect human nature." Ernst Cassirer, *Rousseau, Kant and Goethe* (Princeton: Princeton University Press, 1945), p. 1. (Though Cassirer refers to his own edition of Kant's works, the passage is found in *Gesammelte Schriften,* Prussian Academy, 20:44.) See also Hannah Arendt, *Lectures on Kant's Political Philosophy* (Chicago: University of Chicago Press, 1982), pp. 28–29, where she also cites the passage in the course of developing Kant's view of the relation between philosophy and human affairs. On the influence of Rousseau on Kant, in addition to Cassirer, see Charles Taylor, "Kant's Theory of Freedom," *Philosophical Papers, 2: Philosophy and the Human Sciences* (Cambridge: Cambridge University Press, 1985); and Warren E. Steinkraus, "Kant and Rousseau on Humanity," *The Southern Journal of Philosophy* (1974).

43. Immanuel Kant, *Groundwork of the Metaphysics of Morals,* trans. H. J. Paton (New York: Harper and Row, 1964), p. 114.

44. See Sidney Axinn, "Rousseau *Versus* Kant on the Concept of Man," *The Philosophical Forum* (1981).

45. Lewis White Beck, "Kant as Educator," *Essays on Kant and Hume* (New Haven: Yale University Press, 1978), p. 203.

46. Arendt, *Lectures on Kant's Political Philosophy.*

47. Ernst Cassirer, *Kant's Life and Thought,* trans. James Haden (New Haven: Yale University Press, 1981), p. 225.

48. Immanuel Kant, *Religion Within The Limits of Reason Alone,* trans. Theodore M. Greene and Hoyt H. Hudson (New York: Harper and Brothers, 1960), p. 89.

49. For an alternative account not dependent upon Kant's philosophy of history, see Charles Taylor's "Kant's Theory of Freedom," *Philosophical Papers, 2: Philosophy and the Human Sciences,* where he provides a plausible analysis of the way the transition from moral to political community constitutes the moral agent in terms of civil society.

50. William Sullivan has summed up the general problem facing post-seventeenth-century liberal political philosophy in its attempt to reconcile autonomy and community, and the problem applies especially to the Kantian view in the absence of his philosophy of history: "The inadequacies of liberal political discourse chiefly revolve around its inability convincingly to connect an assertion of the intrinsic dignity of the human self with its own premises about the nature of the world and the capacities of human reason. . . . This difficulty reveals the center of philosophic liberalism as a highly utopian teaching masquerading as common sense. This is the notion that social solidarity, reciprocity, and mutual aid can and should result exclusively from contractual relationships of self-interest or individual moral decision." *Reconstructing Public Philosophy* (Berkeley: University of California Press, 1982), p. 15.

51. Robert Paul Wolff, *The Poverty of Liberalism* (Boston: Beacon Press, 1968), p. 162.

52. Michael J. Sandel, *Liberalism and the Limits of Justice* (Cambridge: Cambridge University Press, 1982), pp. 147ff.

53. Max Horkheimer and Theodor W. Adorno, *Dialectic of Enlightenment* (New York: Herder and Herder, 1972).

54. Martin Heidegger, *The Question Concerning Technology and Other Essays.*

55. Hans-Georg Gadamer, *Truth and Method* (New York: The Seabury Press, 1975).

56. Michel Foucault, *Discipline and Punish: The Birth of the Prison* (New York: Vintage Books, 1979).

57. See MacIntyre's *After Virtue.*

58. See especially, Richard Rorty, "Postmodernist Bourgeois Liberalism," *Journal of Philosophy* (1983); and "Le Cosmopolitisme Sans Emancipation," *Critique* (1985).

Chapter Three

1. Morton White, "Reflections on Anti-intellectualism," *Daedalus* (Summer 1962): 457.

2. Leszek Kolakowski, "Intellectuals Against Intellect," *Daedalus* (Summer 1972): 5f.

3. Voltaire, "Letter to Jean-Jacques Rousseau, August 1755," in Voltaire: *Selected Letters,* trans. and ed. Theodore Besterman (London: Thomas Nelson and Sons, 1963), pp. 148–49. For a comprehensive account of Voltaire's reaction to the second *Discourse* and other works of Rousseau, see George R. Havens, *Voltaire's Marginalia on the Pages of Rousseau,* (Columbus: The Ohio University Press, 1933).

4. Jean-Jacques Rousseau, *The Confessions,* trans. J. M. Cohen (Baltimore: Penguin Books, 1954), p. 327.

5. Jean-Jacques Rousseau, *The First and Second Discourses,* trans. Roger D. and Judith R. Masters (New York: St. Martins Press, 1964), p. 32.

6. Ernst Cassirer, *The Question of Jean-Jacques Rousseau,* trans. Peter Gay (Bloomington: Indiana University Press, 1963), p. 48.

7. Noting that the uproar caused by the first *Discourse* made Rousseau's reputation, he suggests that "Diderot, who was all too familiar with the social machinations of the world of letters, knew that his friend could only profit by proposing a paradoxical answer to the question posed by the Academy of Dijon." Bronislaw Baczko, "Rousseau and Social Marginality," *Daedalus* (Summer 1978), p. 33.

8. Robert Wokler, "The 'Discours sur les sciences et les arts' and Its Offspring: Rousseau in Reply to His Critics," in *Reappraisals of Rousseau,* ed. Simon Harvey (New York: Barnes and Noble, 1980), p. 251. Wokler provides a useful survey of the critical reaction to the essay by Rousseau's contemporaries and Rousseau's responses.

9. Hannah Arendt, *The Human Condition* (Chicago: University of Chicago Press, 1958), p. 38.

10. See Michel Foucault, *Discipline and Punish* trans. Alan Sheridan (New York: Vintage Books, 1979); *Power/Knowledge,* ed. Colin Gordon (New York: Pantheon, 1980); and *The History of Sexuality,* vol. 1, trans. Robert Hurley (New York: Vintage Books, 1980).

11. Richard Rorty, *Philosophy and the Mirror of Nature* (Princeton: Princeton University Press, 1979); and "Postmodern Bourgeois Liberalism," *Journal of Philosophy,* (1984).

12. Jean-Jacques Rousseau, "A Preface to 'Narcisse: or the Lover of Himself'," trans. Benjamin R. Barber and Janis Forman, *Political Theory* (November 1978): 549. *Narcisse,* one of seven plays written by Rousseau, concerned a young man who had to be cured of his narcissism before he could wed. His sister had a portrait of him retouched to make him look like a woman. He fell in love with the "woman" in the portrait, but finally that love was overcome by the woman he was to wed, and he was thus cured of self-love. Rousseau wrote the play when he was eighteen but it was not performed until some years later. The Preface was added at that time in order to respond to charges that the fact that he wrote plays and music contradicted his arguments against the sciences and arts. Though he offered several defenses against the charge, he finally concluded that the arts and sciences may serve some purpose in a corrupt age:

"I would esteem myself more than happy to have a play hissed every day if I were able, at this price, to contain for even two hours the malicious designs of a single spectator, and thereby save the honor of the daughter or wife of his friend, the secret of his confidant, or the fortune of his creditor" ("Preface," p. 552).

13. Michael J. Sandel, *Liberalism and the Limits of Justice* (Cambridge: Cambridge University Press, 1982), p. 148.

14. In an especially illuminating discussion of Kant and the modern conception of freedom, Charles Taylor credits Rousseau with rehabilitating the distinction between vice and virtue and with making the will once more relevant in ethics. Of Rousseau he writes: "virtue and vice themselves are given a new interpretation in terms of freedom. For the key to vice is other-dependency, a failure to be determined by one's own internal purposes; and virtue is nothing other than the recovery of this self-determination." Charles Taylor, "Kant's Theory of Freedom," *Philosophical Papers, 2: Philosophy and the Human Sciences* (Cambridge: Cambridge University Press, 1985), p. 320.

15. Ronald Grimsley, *The Philosophy of Rousseau* (Oxford: Oxford University Press, 1973), p. 19.

16. See Nannerl O. Keohane, "'The Masterpiece of Policy of Our Century': Rousseau on the Morality of the Enlightenment," *Political Theory* (November 1978), pp. 457–84, for an examination of themes in Rousseau to be found in Montaigne and the Jansenists.

17. Jean-Jacques Rousseau, *The Reveries of the Solitary Walker,* trans. Charles E. Butterworth (New York: Harper Colophon Books, 1982), p. 1.

18. See Baczko's "Rousseau and Social Marginality."

19. Jean-Jacques Rousseau, "Letter to M. d'Alembert on the Theatre," in *Politics and the Arts,* trans. Allan Bloom (New York: Cornell University Press, 1968), p. 37.

20. Jean Perkins has observed that "the first area of alarm, as far as Rousseau was concerned, is that of reconciling the individual 'I' with a steadily deteriorating society. . . . His problem was to fit himself into this system, and to that end he had to recreate society in such a way that his integration with it would become possible." *The Concept of the Self in the French Enlightenment* (Geneva: Libraire Droz, 1969), p. 100.

21. Jean-Jacques Rousseau, *Emile: or On Education,* trans. Allan Bloom (New York: Basic Books, 1979), p. 266.

22. Immanuel Kant, *Critique of Pure Reason,* trans. by Norman Kemp Smith (London: Macmillan, 1956), p. 9, n.a.

23. In a letter of 22 January 1763, to Comtesse de Boufflers who had asked Hume's opinion of *Emile,* Hume wrote that it shared the defect of Rousseau's other writings: "with this domineering force of genius there is always intermingled some degree of extravagance. . . . were it not for his frequent and earnest protestations to the contrary, one would be apt to suspect that he chooses his topics less from persuasion, than from the pleasure of showing his invention, and surprizing the reader by his paradoxes." David Hume, *The Letters of David Hume,* vol. 1, ed. J. Y. T. Greig, (Oxford: Clarendon Press, 1969), p. 373.

24. See, for example, Wolker, "The 'Discours sur les sciences et les arts' and Its Offspring: Rousseau's Reply to His Critics," pp. 255f.

25. Toward the end of the "Fourth Stage" of the *Progress of the Human Mind,* Condorcet had criticized those who make the "general mistake of identifying the natural man with the product of the existing state of civilization," but he also opposed Rousseau, claiming that "we shall prove that the eloquent declamations made against the arts and sciences are founded upon a mistaken application of history." Antoine-Nicolas de Condorcet, *Sketch for a Historical Picture of the Progress of the Human Mind,* trans. by June Barraclough (London: Weidenfeld and Nicolson, 1955), pp. 55–54.

26. Allan Bloom has observed that what critics often call a tension in Rousseau's thought is not a flaw in Rousseau but a reflection of our condition. "[The paradoxical tone of Rousseau's thought as a whole] is not a result of his own complications but of those of human life itself." See Bloom's introduction to Jean-Jacques Rousseau, "Letter to M. D'Alembert on the Theatre," *Politics and the Arts,* p. xxvii.

27. John Charvet has summed up the project of *Emile* and *The Social Contract:* "the new social whole involves no division and opposition between self and other; rather the individual, although only a part of a larger whole, is yet not limited by this limitation, but enters into the other parts and is the whole; a whole made up of many people yet without division." "Rousseau and the Ideal of Community," *History of Political Thought* (1980): 69.

28. The occasion for the letter was a remark d'Alembert had made in passing in his article on Geneva in the *Encyclopédie.* He had recommended a theater for Geneva. Rousseau responded that such a recommendation had been made without considering whether the theater was good or bad, and whether it was consistent with the virtue of a free and austere people. The purpose of the letter was to take up that issue.

29. On the issue of the relation between intellectuals and tradition, see S. N. Eisenstadt, "Intellectuals and Tradition," *Daedalus* (Spring 1972).

Chapter Four

1. David Hume, *Enquiries Concerning Human Understanding and Concerning Principles of Morals,* ed. L. A. Selby-Bigge (Oxford: Clarendon Press, 1963), p. 5.

2. Charles Taylor, "Interpretation and the Sciences of Man," *The Review of Metaphysics* 25 (1971); and "Understanding in the Human Sciences," *The Review of Metaphysics* 34 (1980). Hubert Dreyfus has defended a similar view in "Holism and Hermeneutics," *The Review of Metaphysics* 34 (1980), though in a recent piece, "Why Current Studies of Human Capacities Can Never Be Scientific," *Berkeley Cognitive Science Reports* (1983), he has modified his position.

3. Mary Hesse, *Revolution and Reconstruction in the Philosophy of Science* (Brighton: Harvester Press, 1980), especially chap. 7.

4. Richard Rorty, *Philosophy and the Mirror of Nature* (Princeton: Princeton University Press, 1979), pp. 350ff.

5. See Max Horkheimer and Theodor W. Adorno, *Dialectic of Enlightenment* (New York: Herder and Herder, 1972); and Jürgen Habermas, *Knowledge and Human Interest* (Boston: Beacon Press, 1971).

6. Michel Foucault, "What Is Enlightenment," *The Foucault Reader,* ed. Paul Rabinow (New York: Pantheon Books, 1984).

7. Jürgen Habermas, "Taking Aim at the Heart of the Present," *University Publishing* 13 (Summer 1984): 5.

8. Jürgen Habermas, "The Entwinement of Myth and Enlightenment: Re-Reading *Dialectic of Enlightenment, New German Critique,* no. 26 (1982).

9. Jürgen Habermas, "Modernity versus Postmodernity," *New German Critique,* no. 22 (1981).

10. Nancy Fraser, "Foucault on Modern Power: Empirical Insights and Normative Confusions," *Praxis International* 1 (1981).

11. Charles Taylor, "Foucault on Freedom and Truth," *Political Theory* 12 (1984).

12. Richard Rorty, "Habermas and Lyotard on Postmodernity, *Praxis International* 4 (1984); and "Method, Social Science, and Social Hope," *Consequences of Pragmatism* (Minneapolis: University of Minnesota Press, 1982).

13. Michel Foucault, *Discipline and Punish: The Birth of the Prison* (New York: Vintage Books, 1979), p. 31.

14. Some interpreters have suggested that the methodological shift was because of a fundamental shift in Foucault's thought, much in the way commentators have attempted to separate out an early and late Heidegger or early and late Wittgenstein. However, it is clear from the essay on Kant's "What Is Enlightenment?" that he conceived of the archaeology and genealogy as parts of a single project rather than an intellectual break between earlier and later method.

15. Michel Foucault, *The Birth of the Clinic: An Archaeology of Medical Perception* (New York: Pantheon Books, 1973), p. xv.

16. Michel Foucault, *The Order of Things: An Archaeology of the Human Sciences* (New York: Pantheon Books, 1970), pp. 384–87.

17. Michael Roth, "Foucault's 'History of the Present'," *History and Theory* 20 (1981): 43.

18. Alan Sheridan, *Michel Foucault: The Will To Truth* (London: Tavistock Publications, 1980), p. 195.

19. Michel Foucault, "Intellectuals and Power," in *Power/Knowledge: Selected Interviews & Other Writings,* ed. Colin Gordon (New York: Pantheon Books, 1980), p. 210.

20. Horkheimer and Adorno, *Dialectic of Enlightenment,* p. 9.

21. Though Habermas includes Heidegger in the group of young conservatives, Heidegger was certainly conscious of the risk of merely negating an age. See the concluding paragraphs of "The Age of the World Picture," in *The Question Concerning Technology and Other Essays* (New York: Harper and Row, 1977), p. 136.

22. There is, of course, more to Heidegger's analysis than this, turning on his view of science and technology as the completion of metaphysics and his view of Nietzsche, through the will to power, as the philosopher of technology. See, "The End of Philosophy and the Task for Thinking," in *Basic Writings,* ed. David Krell (New York: Harper and Row, 1977); and *Nietzsche,* vol. 4 (Harper and Row, 1982).

23. There is a third issue that concerns Taylor and is connected with Foucault's account of modern power as "strategies without strategists." An answer to that objection could be developed in terms of what I have already said about Foucault's account of the relation between subjectivity and power and about the way power/knowledge functions in his work as a field of struggle that "structures the actions of actors."

24. Jürgen Habermas, "Dogmatism, Reason, and Decision: On Theory and Praxis in Our Scientific Civilization," *Theory and Practice* (Boston: Beacon Press, 1974).

25. See Charles Taylor, "Interpretation and the Sciences of Man," and his exchange with Hubert Dreyfus and Richard Rorty, "Understanding in the Human Sciences."

26. Charles Baudelaire, "The Painter of Modern Life," in *My Heart Laid Bare and Other Prose Writings,* trans. Norman Cameron (New York: Haskell House Publishers, 1975), pp. 36–37.

27. Michel Foucault, "The Subject and Power," in *Michel Foucault: Beyond Structuralism and Hermeneutics,* 2d ed., by Hubert L. Dreyfus and Paul Rabinow (Chicago: University of Chicago Press, 1983), p. 208.

28. Karlis Racevskis's recent book, *Michel Foucault and the Subversion of Intellect* (Ithaca: Cornell University Press, 1983), chap. 1, exploits the influence of Lacan in setting the problematic for Foucault. See also Charles C. Lemert and Garth Gillan, *Michel Foucault: Social Theory and Transgression* (New York: Columbia University Press, 1982), pp. 100ff., where they distinguish Foucault's history of the subject from Lacan's and Kristeva's.

29. There are important similarities between this and Heidegger's analysis of the modern epoch in which the world both becomes a picture and man "gets into the picture" as the setting in which what can appear is made possible. See "Age of the World Picture," in *The Question Concerning Technology,* pp. 131f.

30. See Dreyfus and Rabinow, *Beyond Structuralism,* chap. 2, for an excellent discussion of the "doubles."

31. Michel Foucault, *The History of Sexuality,* vol. 1 (New York: Vintage Books, 1980), p. 139.

32. Foucault, *Discipline and Punish,* pp. 136f. See also "Two Lectures," *Power/Knowledge,* pp. 107f.

33. See *Discipline and Punish,* pp. 26–27, and pp. 176–77; *History of Sexuality,* pp. 93–94; *Power/Knowledge,* pp. 96–101.

34. There are at least three levels to Foucault's analysis of Power: power/knowledge as a general notion involving the idea that power and knowledge co-constitute the field of struggle that structures possible actions; biopower, which is the distinctively modern form of power/knowledge; and the way power is exercised in contemporary society through the juxtaposition of juridical-sovereign power and biopower. See my "Foucault's Analysis of Power: Political Engagement without Liberal Hope or Comfort," *Praxis International* 4 (1984).

35. Foucault, *Power/Knowledge,* pp. 105f.

36. Michel Foucault, "Preface to Transgression," in *Language, Counter-Memory, Practice,* ed. Donald F. Bouchard (Ithaca: Cornell University Press,

1977), p. 34. This essay was originally published in 1963, the same year as the publication of *The Birth of the Clinic.* In the introduction to that book Foucault had said that he was able to write the archaeology of the clinic because we were at the edge of an impending rupture in medical experience which made possible an understanding of the old experience; thus archaeology as effective history was both at the limit of medical experience and transgressed it, making our present experience past. There is a similar theme in the final sections of *The Order of Things* in terms of the demise of the age of man.

37. Jacques Derrida, *Positions,* trans. Alan Bass (Chicago: University of Chicago Press, 1981), p. 12.

38. Rorty has made a similar claim for the liberating effect of what he calls edifying philosophy in the final section of *Philosophy and the Mirror of Nature.* The same theme of connecting opposition to epistemological closure with liberty occurs in Feyerabend's methodological anarchism and his attack on empiricism as totalitarian. See his *Against Method* (London: New Left Books, 1975), pp. 20f; and "How to Be a Good Empiricist—A Plea for Tolerance in Matters Epistemological," *Philosophy of Science, The Delaware Seminar,* vol. 2, (New York: Interscience Publishers, 1963).

39. Dreyfus and Rabinow, *Beyond Structuralism and Hermeneutics,* p. 231.

40. Michel Foucault, *The Use of Pleasure: The History of Sexuality,* vol. 2 (New York: Pantheon Books, 1985), p. 9.

41. Charles Baudelaire, *Intimate Journals,* trans. Charles Isherwood (Westport, Conn.: Hyperion Press, 1957), p. 82.

42. Rorty, "Habermas and Lyotard on Postmodernity": 40–1. See also his "Method, Social Science,and Social Hope," in *Consequences of Pragmatism.*

43. Michel Foucault, "Intellectuals and Power," in *Language, Counter-Memory, Practices,* p. 207.

44. Michel Foucault, "Revolutionary Action: Until Now," in *Language, Counter-Memory, Practice,* p. 233.

Chapter Five

1. W. W. Bartley, *The Retreat to Commitment* (London: Chatto and Windus, 1962).

2. See Karl R. Popper, *The Open Society and Its Enemies* (London: Routledge and Kegan Paul, 1966); and *Conjectures and Refutations: The Growth of Scientific Knowledge* (London: Routledge and Kegan Paul, 1972).

3. Joseph Agassi, "Rationality and the *Tu Quoque* Argument," *Inquiry* 16 (1973).

4. See Jürgen Habermas, "Technology and Science as 'Ideology'," *Toward a Rational Society* (Boston: Beacon Press, 1970).

5. Hans-Georg Gadamer, *Truth and Method* (New York: Seabury Press, 1975), pp. 242–43.

6. Richard Bernstein, *Beyond Objectivism and Relativism: Science, Hermeneutics, and Praxis* (Philadelphia: University of Pennsylvania Press, 1983), p. 23.

7. John Kekes, *A Justification of Rationality* (Albany: State University of New York Press, 1976), p. 256.

8. See, for example, the essays by Peter Winch, Robin Horton, and Steven Lukes in Bryan R. Wilson, ed., *Rationality* (Oxford: Basil Blackwell, 1970).

9. I. C. Jarvie and Joseph Agassi, "The Problem of the Rationality of Magic," *British Journal of Sociology* 18 (1967): 67.

10. Kekes, *A Justification of Rationality,* p. 116.

11. S. B. Barnes, "Natural Rationality: A Neglected Concept," *Philosophy of Social Science* 6 (1976): 118; see also his *Scientific Knowledge and Sociological Theory* (London: Routledge and Kegan Paul, 1974), chap. 2.

12. Stephen Toulmin, for example, interprets Kuhn this way: "the merits of intellectual 'revolutions' cannot be discussed or justified in rational terms—since no common set of procedures for judging this rationality are acceptable, or even intelligible to both sides in the dispute. . . . Only after the victorious new paradigm is securely enthroned in acknowledged power can the rule of rationality be restored." *Human Understanding* (Princeton: Princeton University Press, 1972), 1: 102. Rorty has also been described as a relativist but I will argue against that interpretation in the next chapter.

13. I am thinking primarily of Putnam's "What is 'Realism'?," *Proceedings of the Aristotelian Society* (1975–76).

14. See Lukes' "Some Problems About Rationality," *Archives Européennes de Sociologie* 8 (1967), where he argues for both universal *and* context-dependent criteria of rationality.

15. Paul Feyerabend, *Against Method* (London: New Left Books, 1975), chap. 16.

16. See John Gardner, *Mickelsson's Ghosts* (New York: Vintage Books, 1982), p. 4.

17. Evans Fales, "Truth, Tradition, and Rationality," *Philosophy of Social Science* 6 (1976): 103.

18. Jay Rosenberg has responded to Richard Rorty's descriptive nihilism by remarking that one might allow a thousand vocabularies to bloom but the world will pick the bush every time. See the last chapter of *Linguistic Representation* (Dordrecht: D. Reidel, 1974).

19. Roger Trigg, *Reason and Commitment* (Cambridge: Cambridge University Press, 1973); and Sheldon Richmond, "On the Possibility of Rationality: Some Comments on Roger Trigg's 'Reason and Commitment'," *Philosophy of Social Science* 6 (1976): 163.

20. Peter Unger, *Ignorance: A Case for Universal Scepticism* (Oxford: Clarendon Press, 1975).

21. Keith Lehrer, *Knowledge* (Oxford: Clarendon Press, 1974).

22. Arthur Danto, "Historical Language and Historical Reality," *The Review of Metaphysics* 27 (1973): 257–58.

23. Donald Davison, "On the Very Idea of a Conceptual Scheme," *Proceedings and Addresses of the American Philosophical Association* 47 (1973–74).

24. Willard Van Orman Quine, "Two Dogmas of Empiricism," *From a Logical Point of View* (New York: Harper and Row, 1963), p. 43.

25. Willard Van Orman Quine, *Word and Object* (Cambridge: MIT Press, 1960) especially chaps. 2 and 6.

26. Thomas S. Kuhn, *The Structure of Scientific Revolutions* (Chicago: University of Chicago Press, 1962), p. 193.

27. Martin Heidegger, "The Age of the World Picture," *The Question Concerning Technology and Other Essays* (New York, Harper and Row, 1977), p. 128ff.

28. See especially Davidson, "Truth and Meaning," *Synthese* 7 (1967), and "Belief and the Basis of Meaning," *Synthèse* 27 (1974).

29. Donald Davidson, "Thought and Talk," in *Mind and Language,* ed. Samuel Guttenplan (Oxford: Clarendon Press, 1975), p. 149.

30. Ian Hacking, *Why does Language Matter to Philosophy?* (Cambridge: Cambridge University Press, 1975), p. 149.

31. Richard Rorty, "The World Well Lost," *Journal of Philosophy* 69 (1972).

32. See, for example, Israel Scheffler, *Science and Subjectivity* (Indianapolis: Bobbs-Merrill, 1967).

33. Thomas Kuhn, "Objectivity, Value Judgment, and Theory Choice," *The Essential Tension: Selected Studies in Scientific Tradition and Change* (Chicago: University of Chicago Press, 1977), p. 331.

34. See a related discussion in Richard Rorty, *Philosophy and the Mirror of Nature* (Princeton: Princeton University Press, 1979), pp. 333–42.

35. Max Deutscher, *Subjecting and Objecting: An Essay in Objectivity* (St. Lucia: University of Queensland Press, 1983).

36. Richard Bernstein argues that, without being aware of it, Kuhn has appealed to a conception of rationality very close to the tradition out of which Hans-Georg Gadamer is working. See Bernstein's *Beyond Objectivism and Relativism: Science, Hermeneutics, and Praxis,* pt. 2.

37. Charles Taylor, "Rationality," *Philosophical Papers, 2: Philosophy and the Human Sciences* (Cambridge: Cambridge University Press, 1985). Hubert Dreyfus has pointed out to me that, by not distinguishing the question of pluralistic conceptions of the meaning of life and society from a realist account of the rationality of science, my account of Taylor glosses his view that science has got it right about nature. Though Dreyfus's observation is right and the issue is important, it goes beyond my purpose in using Taylor's view here.

38. Peter Winch, "Understanding a Primitive Society," *American Philosophical Quarterly* 1 (1964). Reprinted in Brian R. Wilson's collection, *Rationality.*

Chapter Six

1. Richard Rorty, "The World Well Lost," *Journal of Philosophy* (1972): 665.

2. Richard Rorty, *Philosophy and the Mirror of Nature* (Princeton: Princeton University Press, 1979).

3. Richard Rorty, "Keeping Philosophy Pure," *Yale Review* (1965); Professionalized Philosophy and Transcendentalist Culture," *Georgia Review* (1976); "Overcoming the Tradition: Heidegger and Dewey," *The Review of Metaphysics* (1976); "Philosophy as a Kind of Writing: An Essay on Derrida," *New*

*Literary History* (1978–79); Introduction, *Consequences of Pragmatism,* (Minneapolis: University of Minnesota Press, 1982).

4. Rorty attempts to undermine epistemology-centered philosophy by reliving history, and one sort of criticism of him turns on the accuracy of his history. Ian Hacking, for example, has posed his objections to Rorty this way: "Rorty aims at undermining [epistemology]. This places him under two obligations. His history should be right in detail, and it should put in question what had formerly been taken for granted. The second obligation is by no means clear; for it is not that he wishes us to doubt some propositions, but rather to query the significance of a certain kind of activity. The very obscurity of the second obligation makes one insist quite vigorously on the obligation to tell the history right. Now I do not find Rorty's redescriptions altogether satisfactory." Hacking then discusses several historical issues—especially the one concerning the relation of Kant to the image of philosophy Rorty opposes—that show where he thinks Rorty's history is not quite right. Ian Hacking, "Is the End in Sight for Epistemology?" *Journal of Philosophy* (1980): 580–81.

5. Jaegwon Kim, for example, writes of Rorty's attempt to decry the idea of having a view without its becoming a view: "it is unclear how *any* cognitive activities can be carried out in a language in which no views can be expressed. Can any *questions* be framed in such a language? Can any *wishes* or *hopes* be expressed in it? Can any *exclamations* be conveyed? Don't all these presuppose the assertorial function of the language?" Jaegwon Kim, "Rorty on the Possibility of Philosophy," *Journal of Philosophy* (1980): 596.

6. In addition to Rorty's "Overcoming the Tradition: Heidegger and Dewey," see his "Wittgensteinian Philosophy and Empirical Psychology," *Philosophical Studies* (1977); and "Dewey's Metaphysics," in *New Studies of John Dewey,* ed. Steven M. Cahn (Hanover: The University Press of New England, 1977).

7. See, for example, Richard Bernstein, "Philosophy in the Conversation of Mankind," *The Review of Metaphysics* (1980); R. W. Sleeper, "Rorty's Pragmatism," *Transactions of the Charles S. Peirce Society* (1985); James Campbell, "Rorty's Use of Dewey," *The Southern Journal of Philosophy* (1984); Charles Guignon, "On Saving Heidegger from Rorty," *Philosophy and Phenomenological Research* (1986); John Caputo, "The Thought of Being and the Conversation of Mankind: The Case of Heidegger and Rorty," *The Review of Metaphysics* (1983).

8. Heidegger made the point about Nietzsche in numerous places, but a typical formulation of the claim is this: "The talk of overcoming metaphysics can also mean that 'metaphysics' is the name for the Platonism portrayed in the modern world by the interpretation of Schopenhauer and Nietzsche. The reversal of Platonism, according to which for Nietzsche the sensuous becomes the true world and the suprasensuous becomes the untrue world, is thoroughly caught in metaphysics. This kind of overcoming of metaphysics, which Nietzsche has in mind in the spirit of nineteenth century positivism, is only the final entanglement in metaphysics, although in a higher form." Martin

Heidegger, *The End of Philosophy,* trans. Joan Stambauch (New York: Harper and Row, 1973), p. 92.

9. Richard Rorty, "Deconstruction and Circumvention," *Critical Inquiry* (1984): 8.

10. See especially, Richard Rorty, "Against Belatedness," *London Review of Books* (1983); "Heidegger Wider Die Pragmatisten, *Neue Hefte für Philosophie* (1984); "Postmodernist Bourgeois Liberalism," *Journal of Philosophy* (1983); and "Le Cosmopolitisme Sans Emancipation," *Critique* (1985).

11. Charles Guignon, "Saving the Difference: Gadamer and Rorty," *Philosophy of Science Association 1982* 2 (1983): 361.

12. John Dunn, *Rethinking Modern Political Theory* (Cambridge: Cambridge University Press, 1985), p. 174.

13. Richard Eldridge, "Philosophy and the Achievement of Community: Rorty, Cavell and Criticism," *Metaphilosophy* (1983): 114.

14. See Rorty, "Method, Social Science and Social Hope," in *Consequences of Pragmatism,* and "Habermas and Lyotard on Postmodernity," *Praxis International* (1984).

15. Richard Rorty, "Postmodernist Bourgeois Liberalism," 585.

16. In a recent symposium on the philosophy of mind, he has made the same point in a more picturesque way by referring to the modern conception of mind as a blur. "The notion of 'mind' looks like a way of bringing these two notions—that of a knower and that of a moral agent or subject—together, of subsuming them under a single, clearer, concept. But it is not. The supposedly clearer concept is just a blur—the sort of thing you get when you lay tracings of two delicate and complicated designs down on top of each other." Richard Rorty, "Contemporary Philosophy of Mind," *Synthèse* (1982): 325.

17. He had offered the same sort of argument in "Mind-Body Identity, Privacy, and Categories," *The Review of Metaphysics* (1965); and "Incorrigibility as the Mark of the Mental," *Journal of Philosophy* (1970).

18. I have argued elsewhere that his disappearance theory is not really a materialist conception of the mind at all, but merely the result of a nihilism about descriptive vocabularies. See my "Is Eliminative Materialism Materialistic?" *Philosophy and Phenomenological Research* (1978); and "The Disappearance Theory and the Denotation Argument," *Philosophical Studies* (1980).

19. Thomas Nagel, "What Is It Like To Be A Bat?" *Philosophical Review* (1974): 441–42.

20. I have argued along compatible lines that Nagel has conflated two senses of subjectivity in his opposition to materialism. One notion is identical to the specifically Cartesian sense of epistemologically privileged inner episodes; the other has to do with a person's uniqueness. I claimed that the latter does not depend on the former, and since materialism is addressed to privileged and irreducible mental episodes, its truth is irrelevant to the uniqueness of the "I." See my "Materialism and the Inner Life," *The Southern Journal of Philosophy* (1978).

21. See Paul Feyerabend, *Against Method* (London: New Left Books, 1975).

22. Wilfrid Sellars, *Science and Metaphysics* (London: Routledge and Kegan Paul, 1968), chap. 6.

23. In the Introduction to his recent collection of essays, Richard Bernstein draws similar implications from the pragmatic defense of pluralism against the Western philosophical tradition: "They rejected all forms of totalizing schemes or totalizing critiques. They defended a robust pluralism that does justice to the tangled quality of our experience. But they did not think of pluralism as a type of relativism where we are imprisoned in our self-contained paradigms, frameworks, or forms of life. It is the openness of our limited horizons that they defended, not their closure." *Philosophical Profiles: Essays in a Pragmatic Mode* (Philadelphia: University of Pennsylvania Press, 1986), p. 18.

24. I owe this way of framing the ambiguity to Charles Guignon.

25. Michael J. Sandel, *Liberalism and the Limits of Justice* (Cambridge: Cambridge University Press, 1982).

26. Kenneth Gallagher, for example, has suggested such a criticism: "if 'personhood' is, as Rorty says, 'a matter of decision rather than knowledge, an acceptance of another being into fellowship, rather than a recognition of a common essence', the door is flung open to the intrusion of all sorts of unwelcome company into the conversation of mankind. Decision in the ordinary sense is often at the service of whim or pleasure, so why should it not be in this case? With the proper company, we might 'justify' any option that our pleasure dictates; Hitler's *pour-soi* found echoes in a satisfyingly large consensus of discussants. At this rate, the conversation would easily turn into a babble." "Rorty on Objectivity, Truth and Social Consensus," *International Philosophical Quarterly* (1984), pp. 122–23.

27. Translations from "Cosmopolitisme Sans Emancipation," are from Rorty's English typescript.

28. If I am right about this interpretation, it is all the more surprising that Rorty should have been accused of cultural imperialism at the Inter-American Congress of Philosophy at Guadalajara. For a copy of his talk and its hostile reception, see his "From Logic to Language to Play" and the special report in *Proceedings and Addresses of the American Philosophical Asosciation* 59 (June 1986).

29. Hannah Arendt, *The Human Condition* (Chicago: University of Chicago Press, 1958), p. 58.

30. Jean Starobinski, *Montaigne in Motion* (Chicago: University of Chicago Press, 1985), p. 253.

31. David Hume, *Enquiries Concerning Human Understanding and Concerning Principles of Morals,* ed. L. A. Selby-Bigge (Oxford: Clarendon Press, 1963), p. 161.

# Bibliography

Agassi, Joseph. "Rationality and the *Tu Quoque* Argument." *Inquiry* 16 (1973): 395–406.

Arendt, Hannah. *The Human Condition.* Chicago: University of Chicago Press, 1958.

———. *Lectures on Kant's Political Philosophy.* Edited by Ronald Biener. Chicago: University of Chicago Press, 1982.

Axinn, Sidney. "Rousseau *Versus* Kant on the Concept of Man." *The Philosophical Forum* 12 (1981): 348–55.

Bacon, Francis. *Essays and Historical Works of Lord Bacon.* London: George Bell and Sons, 1874.

———. *The Philosophy of Francis Bacon.* Translated by Benjamin Farrington. Chicago: University of Chicago Press, 1964.

———. *Francis Bacon: A Selection of His Works.* Edited by Sidney Warhaft. New York: Odyssey Press, 1965.

Baczko, Bronislaw. "Rousseau and Social Marginality." *Daedalus* 107 (1978): 27–40.

Baker, Keith Michael. *Condorcet: From Natural Philosophy to Social Mathematics.* Chicago: University of Chicago Press, 1975.

Barnes, Jonathan. "The Beliefs of a Pyrrhonist." *Elenchos* 4 (1983): 5–43.

Barnes, S. B. *Scientific Knowledge and Sociological Theory.* London: Routledge and Kegan Paul, 1974.

———. "Natural Rationality: A Neglected Concept." *Philosophy of Social Science* 6 (1976): 115–26.

Bartley, W. W. *The Retreat to Commitment.* London: Chatto and Windus, 1962.

Baudelaire, Charles. *Intimate Journals.* Translated by Charles Isherwood. Westport: Hyperion Press, 1957.

———. "The Painter of Modern Life." *My Heart Laid Bare and Other Prose Writings.* Translated by Norman Cameron. New York: Haskell House, 1975.

Beck, Lewis White. *Essays on Kant and Hume.* New Haven: Yale University Press, 1978.

Bernstein, Richard. "Philosophy in the Conversation of Mankind." *The Review of Metaphysics* 33 (1980): 745–75.

———. *Beyond Objectivism and Relativism: Science, Hermeneutics, and Praxis.* Philadelphia: University of Pennsylvania Press, 1983.

———. *Philosophical Profiles: Essays in a Pragmatic Mode.* Philadelphia: University of Pennsylvania Press, 1986.

Blumenberg, Hans. *The Legitimacy of the Modern Age.* Translated by Robert M. Wallace. Cambridge: MIT Press, 1983.

Brush, Craig B. *Montaigne and Bayle: Variations on the Theme of Scepticism.* The Hague: Martinus Nijhoff, 1966.

Burnyeat, Myles, ed. *The Skeptical Tradition.* Berkeley: University of California Press, 1984.

Bury, J. B. *The Idea of Progress: An Inquiry into Its Origins and Growth.* New York: Macmillan, 1932.

Campbell, James. "Rorty's Use of Dewey." *The Southern Journal of Philosophy* 22 (1984): 175–87.

Caputo, John. "The Thought of Being and the Conversation of Mankind: The Case of Heidegger and Rorty." *The Review of Metaphysics* 36 (1983): 661–85.

Cassirer, Ernst. *Rousseau, Kant and Goethe.* Princeton: Princeton University Press, 1945.

———. *The Question of Jean-Jacques Rousseau.* Translated by Peter Gay. Bloomington: Indiana University Press, 1963.

———. *Kant's Life and Thought.* Translated by James Haden. New Haven: Yale University Press, 1981.

Charron, Pierre. *Of Wisdom.* New York: Da Capo Press, 1971.

Charvet, John. "Rousseau and the Ideal of Community." *History of Political Thought* 1 (1980): 69–80.

Chisholm, Roderick. "Sextus Empiricus and Modern Epistemology." *Philosophy of Science* 8 (1941): 376–84.

Chisick, Harvey. *The Limits of Reform in the Enlightenment: Attitudes Toward Education of the Lower Classes in Eighteenth-Century France.* Princeton: Princeton University Press, 1981.

Cohen, Avner. "Sextus Empiricus: Skepticism as a Therapy." *The Philosophical Forum* 15 (1984): 405–24.

Condorcet, Antoine-Nicolas de. *Sketch for a Historical Picture of the Progress of the Human Mind.* Translated by June Barraclough. London: Weidenfeld and Nicolson, 1955.

Curley, E. M. *Descartes Against the Skeptics.* Cambridge: Harvard University Press, 1978.

Danto, Arthur. "Historical Language and Historical Reality." *The Review of Metaphysics* 27 (1973): 219–59.

Davidson, Donald. "Truth and Meaning." *Synthèse* 17 (1967): 304–23.

———. "On the Very Idea of a Conceptual Scheme." *Proceedings and Addresses of the American Philosophical Association* 47 (1973–74): 5–20.

———. "Belief and the Basis of Meaning." *Synthèse* 27 (1974): 309–23.

———. "Thought and Talk." In *Mind and Language.* Edited by Samuel Guttenplan. Oxford: Clarendon Press, 1975, pp. 7–23.

Derrida, Jacques. *Positions.* Translated by Alan Bass. Chicago: University of Chicago Press, 1981.

———. "Différance." *Margins of Philosophy.* Translated by Alan Bass. Chicago: University of Chicago Press, 1982: 3–27.

Descartes, René. *Philosophical Works of Descartes.* 2 vols. Translated by Elizabeth S. Haldane and G. R. T. Ross. Cambridge: Cambridge University Press, 1972.

Deutscher, Max. *Subjecting and Objecting: An Essay in Objectivity.* St. Lucia: University of Queensland Press, 1983.

Dreyfus, Hubert. "Holism and Hermeneutics." *The Review of Metaphysics* 34 (1980): 3–23.

———. "Why Current Studies of Human Capacities Can Never be Scientific." *Berkeley Cognitive Science Reports* (1983).

Dreyfus, Hubert L., and Paul Rabinow. *Michel Foucault: Beyond Structuralism and Hermeneutics.* 2d edition. Chicago: University of Chicago Press, 1983.

Dunn, John. *Rethinking Modern Political Theory.* Cambridge: Cambridge University Press, 1985.

Eisenstadt, S. N. "Intellectuals and Tradition." *Daedalus* 101 (1972): 1–19.

Eldridge, Richard, "Philosophy and the Achievement of Community: Rorty, Cavell and Criticism." *Metaphilosophy* 14 (1983): 107–25.

Fales, Evans. "Truth, Tradition, and Rationality." *Philosophy of Social Science* 6 (1976): 97–113.

Farrington, Benjamin. *Francis Bacon: Philosopher of Industrial Science.* London: Lawrence and Wishart, 1951.

Feyerabend, Paul. "How to be a Good Empiricist—A Plea for Toleration in Matters Epistemological." *Philosophy of Science, The Delaware Seminar,* vol. 2. New York: Interscience Publishers, 1963.

———. *Against Method.* London: New Left Books, 1975.

Foucault, Michel. *The Order of Things: An Archaeology of the Human Sciences.* New York: Pantheon Books, 1970.

———. *Birth of the Clinic: An Archaeology of Medical Perception.* Translated by Alan Sheridan. New York: Pantheon Books, 1973.

———. *Language, Counter-Memory, Practice.* Edited by Donald F. Bouchard. Ithaca: Cornell University Press, 1977.

———. *Discipline and Punish: The Birth of the Prison.* Translated by Alan Sheridan. New York: Vintage Books, 1979.

———. *Madness and Civilization.* Translated by Richard Howard. New York: Vintage Books, 1973.

———. *Power/Knowledge: Selected Interviews & Other Writings.* Edited by Colin Gordon. New York: Pantheon Books, 1980.

———. *The Archaeology of Knowledge.* Translated by A. M. Sheridan Smith. New York: Harper and Row, 1972.

———. *The History of Sexuality.* Vol. 1: *An Introduction.* Translated by Robert Hurley. New York: Vintage Books, 1980.

———. "The Subject and Power." In Dreyfus and Rabinow, *Michel Foucault: Beyond Structuralism and Hermeneutics.* 2d edition. Chicago: University of Chicago Press, 1983.

———. "What Is Enlightenment?" *The Foucault Reader.* Edited by Paul Rabinow. New York: Pantheon Books, 1984.

———. *The Use of Pleasure*. Vol. 2 of *The History of Sexuality*. Translated by Robert Hurley. New York: Pantheon Books, 1985.

Frankel, Charles. *The Faith of Reason: The Idea of Progress in the French Enlightenment*. New York: King's Crown Press, 1948.

Fraser, Nancy. "Foucault on Modern Power: Empirical Insights and Normative Confusions." *Praxis International* 1 (1981).

Frede, Michael. "Stoics and Skeptics on Clear and Distinct Impressions." In *The Skeptical Tradition*. Edited by Myles Burnyeat. Berkeley: University of California Press, 1984: 65–93.

Gadamer, Hans-Georg. *Truth and Method*. Translated by Garrett Barden and John Cumming. New York: Seabury Press, 1975.

Gallagher, Kenneth T. "Rorty on Objectivity, Truth and Social Consensus." *International Philosophical Quarterly* 24 (1984): 111–24.

Gillispie, Charles Coulston. *The Edge of Objectivity: An Essay in the History of Scientific Ideas*. Princeton: Princeton University Press, 1960.

Grimsley, Ronald. *The Philosophy of Rousseau*. Oxford: Oxford University Press, 1973.

Guignon, Charles. "Saving the Difference: Gadamer and Rorty." *Philosophy of Science Association 1982* 2 (1983): 360–67.

———. "On Saving Heidegger from Rorty." *Philosophy and Phenomenological Research* 46 (1986): 401–17.

Habermas, Jürgen. *Toward a Rational Society*. Translated by Jeremy J. Shapiro. Boston: Beacon Press, 1970.

———. *Knowledge and Human Interest*. Translated by Jeremy J. Shapiro. Boston: Beacon Press, 1971.

———. "Dogmatism, Reason and Decision: On Theory and Praxis in Our Scientific Civilization." In *Theory and Practice*. Translated by John Viertel. Boston: Beacon Press, 1974.

———. "Modernity versus Postmodernity." *New German Critique* 22 (1981): 3–14.

———. "The Entwinement of Myth and Enlightenment: Re-Reading *Dialectic of Enlightenment*." *New German Critique* 26 (1982): 13–30.

———. "Taking Aim at the Heart of the Present." *University Publishing* 13 (1984): 5–6.

Hacking, Ian. "Is the End in Sight for Epistemology?" *Journal of Philosophy* 77 (1980): 579–88.

———. *Why Does Language Matter to Philosophy?* Cambridge: Cambridge University Press, 1975.

Harrison, Geoffrey. "Relativism and Toleration." *Ethics* 89 (1976): 122–35.

Havens, George R. *Voltaire's Marginalia on the Pages of Rousseau*. Columbus: Ohio University Press, 1933.

Heidegger, Martin. *The End of Philosophy*. Translated by Joan Stambauch. New York: Harper and Row, 1973.

———. *Basic Writings*. Edited by David Krell. New York: Harper and Row, 1977.

———. *The Question Concerning Technology and Other Essays.* Translated by William Lovitt. New York: Harper and Row, 1977.

———. *Nietzsche.* Vol. 4, *Nihilism.* Translated by Frank A. Caprizzi. New York: Harper and Row, 1982.

Hesse, Mary, "Francis Bacon's Philosophy of Science." *Essential Articles for the Study of Francis Bacon.* Edited by Brian Vickers. Hamden: Archon Books, 1968.

———. *Revolution and Reconstruction in the Philosophy of Science.* Brighton: Harvester Press, 1980.

Hiley, David R. "Is Eliminative Materialism Materialistic?" *Philosophy and Phenomenological Research* 38 (1978): 325–27.

———. "Materialism and the Inner Life." *The Southern Journal of Philosophy* 17 (1978): 61–70.

———. "The Disappearance Theory and the Denotation Argument." *Philosophical Studies* 37 (1980): 307–20.

———. "Foucault's Analysis of Power: Political Engagement without Liberal Hope or Comfort." *Praxis International* 4 (1984): 192–207.

Horkheimer, Max. *Eclipse of Reason.* New York: Seabury Press, 1974.

Horkheimer, Max, and Theodor W. Adorno. *Dialectic of Enlightenment.* New York: Herder and Herder, 1972.

Horowitz, Maryanne Cline. "Pierre Charron's View of the Source of Wisdom." *The Journal of the History of Philosophy* 9 (1971): 443–57.

Hume, David. *A Treatise of Human Nature.* Edited by L. A. Selby-Bigge. Oxford: Clarendon Press, 1963.

———. *Enquiries Concerning Human Understanding and Concerning Principles of Morals.* Edited by L. A. Selby-Bigge. Oxford: Clarendon Press, 1963.

———. *The Letters of David Hume.* 2 vols. Edited by J. Y. T. Greig. Oxford: Clarendon Press, 1969.

Jarvie, I. C., and Joseph Agassi. "The Problem of the Rationality of Magic." *British Journal of Sociology* 18 (1967): 55–74.

Johnson, Oliver A. *Skepticism and Cognitivism.* Berkeley: University of California Press, 1978.

Kant, Immanuel. *The Educational Theory of Immanuel Kant.* Translated by Edward Franklin Buchner. Philadelphia: J. B. Lippincott, 1904.

———. *Critique of Pure Reason.* Translated by Norman Kemp Smith. London: Macmillan, 1956.

———. *Religion within The Limits of Reason Alone.* Translated by Theodore M. Greene and Hoyt H. Hudson. New York: Harper and Brothers, 1960.

———. *Groundwork of the Metaphysics of Morals.* Translated by H. J. Paton. New York: Harper and Row, 1964.

———. *Perpetual Peace and Other Essays.* Translated by Ted Humphrey. Indianapolis: Hackett Publishing Company, 1983.

Kekes, John. *A Justification of Rationality.* Albany: State University of New York Press, 1976.

Keohane, Nannerl O. "'The Masterpiece of Policy of Our Century': Rousseau on the Morality of the Enlightenment." *Political Theory* 6 (1978): 457–84.

Kim, Jaegwon. "Rorty on the Possibility of Philosophy." *Journal of Philosophy* 77 (1980): 588–97.

Kolakowski, Leszek. "Intellectuals Against Intellect." *Daedalus* 101 (1972): 1–15.

Kuhn, Thomas S. *The Structure of Scientific Revolutions.* Chicago: University of Chicago Press, 1962.

———. *The Essential Tension: Selected Studies in Scientific Tradition and Change.* Chicago: University of Chicago Press, 1977.

La Fontainerie, F. de. Translator and editor. *French Liberalism and Education in the Eighteenth Century.* 1932; reprint, New York: Burt Franklin, 1971.

Lange, Frederick. *The History of Materialism.* London: Routledge and Kegan Paul, 1957.

Lehrer, Keith. *Knowledge.* Oxford: Clarendon Press, 1974.

Lemert, Charles C., and Garth Gillan, *Michel Foucault: Social Theory and Transgression.* New York: Columbia University Press, 1982.

Livingston, Donald W. *Hume's Philosophy of Common Life.* Chicago: University of Chicago Press, 1984.

Livingston, Donald W., and James T. King, eds. *Hume: A Re-Evaluation.* New York: Fordham University Press, 1976.

Locke, John. *Essay Concerning Human Understanding.* 2 vols. Edited by Alexander Campbell Fraser. New York: Dover, 1959.

———. *The Educational Writings of John Locke.* Edited by James L. Axtell. Cambridge: Cambridge University Press, 1968.

Lukes, Steven. "Some Problems About Rationality." *Archives Européennes de Sociologie* 18 (1967): 247–64.

Lyotard, Jean-François. *The Postmodern Condition: A Report on Knowledge.* Translated by Geoff Bennington and Brian Massumi. Minneapolis: University of Minnesota Press, 1984.

MacIntyre, Alasdair. *After Virtue.* Notre Dame: University of Notre Dame Press, 1981.

Mates, Benson. "On Refuting the Skeptic." *Proceedings and Addresses of the American Philosophical Association* 58 (1984): 21–35.

Montaigne, Michel. "Apology for Raymond Sebond." *The Complete Essays of Montaigne.* Translated by Donald M. Frame. Stanford: Stanford University Press, 1965.

Naess, Arne. *Scepticism.* London: Routledge and Kegan Paul, 1968.

Nagel, Thomas. "What Is It Like To Be A Bat?" *Philosophical Review* 83 (1974): 435–50.

Nisbet, Robert. *History of the Idea of Progress.* New York: Basic Books, 1980.

Norton, David Fate, and Richard Popkin, eds. *David Hume: Philosophical Historian.* New York: Bobbs-Merrill, 1965.

Pascal, Blaise. *Pensées.* Translated by A. J. Krailsheimer. Baltimore: Penguin Books, 1966.

Patrick, Mary Mills. *The Greek Sceptics.* New York: Columbia University Press, 1929.

Perkins, Jean A. *The Concept of Self in the French Enlightenment.* Geneva: Libraire Droz, 1969.

Plato. *Republic. Collected Works of Plato.* Edited by Edith Hamilton and Huntington Cairns. Princeton: Princeton University Press, 1963.

Popkin, Richard. *The History of Scepticism from Erasmus to Spinoza.* Berkeley: University of California Press, 1979.

———. *The High Road to Pyrrhonism.* San Diego: Austin Hill Press, 1980.

Popper, Karl R. *The Open Society and Its Enemies.* London: Routledge and Kegan Paul, 1966.

———. *Conjectures and Refutations: The Growth of Scientific Knowledge.* London: Routledge and Kegan Paul, 1972.

Putnam, Hilary. "What Is 'Realism'?" *Proceedings of the Aristotelian Society* (1975–76): 177–94.

Quine, Willard Van Orman. *Word and Object.* Cambridge: MIT Press, 1960.

———. *From a Logical Point of View.* New York: Harper and Row, 1963.

Racevskis, Karlis. *Michel Foucault and the Subversion of Intellect.* Ithaca: Cornell University Press, 1983.

Richmond, Sheldon. "On the Possibility of Rationality: Some Comments on Roger Trigg's 'Reason and Commitment'." *Philosophy of Social Science* 6 (1976): 155–63.

Rorty, Richard. "Mind-Body Identity, Privacy, and Categories." *The Review of Metaphysics* 19 (1965): 24–54.

———. "Incorrigibility as the Mark of the Mental." *Journal of Philosophy* 67 (1970): 399–424.

———. "The World Well Lost." *Journal of Philosophy* 69 (1972): 649–65.

———. "Keeping Philosophy Pure." *Yale Review* 65 (1975): 336–56.

———. "Overcoming the Tradition: Heidegger and Dewey." *The Review of Metaphysics* 30 (1976): 280–305.

———. "Professionalized Philosophy and Transcendentalist Culture." *Georgia Review* 30 (1976): 757–69.

———. "Wittgensteinian Philosophy and Empirical Psychology." *Philosophical Studies* 31 (1977): 151–72.

———. "Dewey's Metaphysics." In *New Studies of John Dewey.* Edited by Steven M. Cahn. Hanover: University Press of New England, 1977: 45–74.

———. "Philosophy as a Kind of Writing: An Essay On Derrida." *New Literary History* 10 (1978–79): 141–60.

———. *Philosophy and the Mirror of Nature.* Princeton: Princeton University Press, 1979.

———. "Postmodernist Bourgeois Liberalism." *Journal of Philosophy* 60 (1983): 583–89.

———. *Consequences of Pragmatism.* Minneapolis: University of Minnesota Press, 1982.

———. "Contemporary Philosophy of Mind." *Synthèse* 53 (1982): 323–48.

———. "Against Belatedness." *London Review of Books* 5 (June 16–July 6, 1983): 3–5.

———. "Deconstruction and Circumvention." *Critical Inquiry* 11 (1984): 1–23.

———. "Habermas and Lyotard on Postmodernity." *Praxis International* 4 (1984): 32–44.

———. "Le Cosmopolitisme Sans Emancipation." *Critique* (1985): 569–80.

———. "From Logic to Language to Play." *Proceedings and Addresses of the American Philosophical Association* 59 (1986): 747–53.

Rosenberg, Jay. *Linguistic Representation.* Dordrecht: D. Reidel, 1974.

Rosenfield, Leonora Cohen, ed. *Condorcet Studies 1.* Atlantic Highlands: Humanities Press, 1984.

Rossi, Paolo. *Philosophy, Technology and the Arts in the Early Modern Era.* New York: Harper and Row, 1970.

Roth, Michael. "Foucault's 'History of the Present'." *History and Theory* 20 (1981): 32–46.

Rousseau, Jean-Jacques. *The Confessions.* Translated by J. M. Cohen. Baltimore: Penguin Books, 1954.

———. *The First and Second Discourses.* Translated by Roger D. Masters and Judith R. Masters. New York: St. Martin's Press, 1964.

———. "Letter to M. d'Alembert on the Theatre." *Politics and the Arts.* Translated by Allan Bloom. New York: Cornell University Press, 1968.

———. *On The Social Contract.* Translated by Judith R. Masters. New York: St. Martin's Press, 1978.

———. "A Preface to 'Narcisse: or the Lover of Himself'." Translated by Benjamin R. Barber and Janis Forman. *Political Theory* 6 (1978): 543–54.

———. *Emile, or On Education.* Translated by Allan Bloom. New York: Basic Books, 1979.

———. *The Reveries of the Solitary Walker.* Translated by Charles E. Butterworth. New York: Harper Colophon Books, 1982.

Sandel, Michael J. *Liberalism and the Limits of Justice.* Cambridge: Cambridge University Press, 1982.

Schapiro, J. Salwyn. *Condorcet and the Rise of Liberalism.* New York: Harcourt, Brace, 1934.

Scheffler, Israel. *Science and Subjectivity.* Indianapolis: Bobbs-Merrill, 1967.

Schofield, Malcolm, Myles Burnyeat, and Jonathan Barnes, eds. *Doubt and Dogmatism: Studies in Hellenistic Epistemology.* Oxford: Clarendon Press, 1980.

Sedley, David. "The Motivation of Greek Skepticism." In *The Skeptical Tradition.* Edited by Myles Burnyeat. Berkeley: University of California Press, 1984: 9–29.

Seidman, Steven. *Liberalism and the Origins of European Social Theory.* Berkeley: University of California Press, 1983.

Sellars, Wilfrid. *Science and Metaphysics.* London: Routledge and Kegan Paul, 1968.

Sextus Empiricus. *Outlines of Pyrrhonism.* Translated by R. G. Bury. Cambridge: Harvard University Press, 1933.

Sheridan, Alan. *Michel Foucault: The Will to Truth.* London: Tavistock Publications, 1980.

Sleeper, R. W. "Rorty's Pragmatism: Afloat in Neurath's Boat, But Why Adrift?" *Transactions of the Charles S. Pierce Society* 11 (1985): 9–20.

Starobinski, Jean. *Montaigne in Motion.* Translated by Arthur Goldhammer. Chicago: University of Chicago Press, 1985.

Steinkraus, Warren E. "Kant and Rousseau on Humanity." *The Southern Journal of Philosophy* 12 (1974): 265–70.

Stough, Charlotte L. *Greek Skepticism: A Study in Epistemology.* Berkeley: University of California Press, 1969.

Stroud, Barry. *Hume.* London: Routledge and Kegan Paul, 1977.

———. *The Significance of Philosophical Scepticism.* Oxford: Clarendon Press, 1984.

Sullivan, William M. *Reconstructing Public Philosophy.* Berkeley: University of California Press, 1982.

Taylor, Charles. "Interpretation and the Sciences of Man." *The Review of Metaphysics* 25 (1971): 3–51.

———. "Understanding in the Human Sciences." *The Review of Metaphysics* 34 (1980): 25–38.

———. "Foucault on Freedom and Truth. *Political Theory* 12 (1984): 152–83.

———. *Philosophical Papers, 2: Philosophy and the Human Sciences.* Cambridge: Cambridge University Press, 1985.

Toulmin, Stephen. *Human Understanding.* 2 vols. Princeton: Princeton University Press, 1972.

Trigg, Roger. *Reason and Commitment.* Cambridge: Cambridge University Press, 1973.

Unger, Peter. *Ignorance: A Case for Universal Scepticism.* Oxford: Clarendon Press, 1975.

Voltaire. *Voltaire: Selected Letters.* Translated and edited by Theodore Besterman. London: Thomas Nelson and Sons, 1963.

Wade, Ira O. *The Intellectual Origins of the French Enlightenment.* Princeton: Princeton University Press, 1971.

———. *The Structure and Form of the Enlightenment.* 2 vols. Princeton: Princeton University Press, 1977.

White, Morton. "Reflections on Anti-Intellectualism." *Daedalus* 91 (1962): 457–68.

Wilson, Bryan R. ed. *Rationality.* Oxford: Basil Blackwell, 1970.

Wilson, Margaret. *Descartes.* London: Routledge and Kegan Paul, 1978.

Winch, Peter. "Understanding a Primitive Society." *American Philosophical Quarterly* 1 (1964): 307–24.

Wokler, Robert. "'The Discours sur les sciences et les arts' and Its Offspring: Rousseau's Reply to His Critics." *Reappraisals of Rousseau.* Edited by Simon Harvey. New York: Barnes and Noble, 1980: 250–78.

Wolff, Robert Paul. *The Poverty of Liberalism.* Boston: Beacon Press, 1968.

Wolff, Robert Paul, Barrington Moore, Jr., and Herbert Marcuse. *A Critique of Pure Tolerance.* Boston: Beacon Press, 1965.

Wolin, Sheldon. "Hume and Conservatism." In *Hume: A Re-Evaluation,* ed. Donald W. Livingston and James T. King. New York: Fordham University Press, 1976.

Yolton, John W. *Locke: An Introduction.* Oxford: Basil Blackwell, 1985.

# Index